Andrea da Barberino and the Language of Chivalry

Andrea da Barberino
and the Language of Chivalry

Gloria Allaire

University Press of Florida

Gainesville Tallahassee Tampa Boca Raton
Pensacola Orlando Miami Jacksonville

02 01 00 99 98 97 6 5 4 3 2 1

Library of Congress Cataloging-in-Publication Data
Allaire, Gloria, 1954–
Andrea da Barberino and the language of chivalry / Gloria Allaire
p. cm.
Includes bibliographical references and index.
ISBN 0-8130-1528-6 (alk. paper)
1. Andrea da Barberino, b. ca. 1370—Style. 2. Romances, Italian—History and criticism.
3. Chivalry in literature. I. Title.
PQ4265.A6Z54 1997 97-8197
853'.2—dc21

The University Press of Florida is the scholarly publishing agency for the State
University System of Florida, comprised of Florida A & M University, Florida Atlantic
University, Florida International University, Florida State University, University of
Central Florida, University of Florida, University of North Florida, University of South
Florida, and University of West Florida.

University Press of Florida
15 Northwest 15th Street
Gainesville, FL 32611

To the memory of my grandmother, Elva (1895–1994)

CONTENTS

Preface ix

Abbreviations for Frequently Cited Works xii

Introduction. Andrea da Barberino and the Chivalric Tradition
   in Italy 1

1. Andrea da Barberino: Life and Works 5

2. Andrea's Narrative Style 14

3. The Case for *La Prima Spagna* 31

4. The Case for *Ansuigi* (*La Seconda Spagna*) 43

5. The Case for *Le Storie di Rinaldo da Monte Albano* in Prose 65

6. The Case against *Il Libro di Rambaldo* 93

Toward a New Perspective 123

Appendixes 125

Notes 133

Selected Bibliography 151

Index of Lexemes 171

Index of Manuscripts 175

General Index 177

Maps

1. Guerrino's travels 99

2. Rambaldo's travels 100

This book had its inception in 1984, my first year of graduate school, during a seminar on the Italian Renaissance epic taught by Robert Rodini. My interest as a budding literary scholar was drawn to chivalric material, and I at once determined to write my dissertation on Ariosto.

Additional course work and discussions with visiting Italianists prompted me to ponder the historico-literary background and sources of Ariosto's masterpiece. Pio Rajna had already explored the sources of the *Furioso*, among which were texts by a certain Andrea da Barberino. While doing additional readings in histories of Italian literature and in literary anthologies, I continually found fleeting references to this author and his texts. I modified my dissertation topic from the chivalric narratives of the northern courts to those of Florence under the oligarchy, from the sixteenth century to the fifteenth, and from verse to prose. Finally, on the strength of an anthologized passage from *Reali di Francia* that had charmed me, I decided on the notion of producing a comprehensive stylistic analysis of Andrea da Barberino's narrative cycle.

This seemed a workable project, and I began my bibliographical research with vigor. However, as the project progressed I realized that Andrea's most important text lacked a critical edition and that another, shorter text was unedited. The need for me to read all his works was apparent, in order to analyze properly his literary style and output. This need prompted me to study philology, paleography, and codicology as well as to make the ideological leap from Renaissance to medieval studies. I also became a book hunter and ferreted from handwritten library inventories and moldering published catalogs numerous forgotten manuscript exemplars by Andrea. Each codex discovered and the information it contained seemed to validate my intuitive selection of a topic.

Yet the firsthand examination of a large sampling of surviving manuscripts of prose chivalric texts raised new questions that needed to be solved before I could proceed. As I became aware of linguistic and stylistic differences and similarities between and among texts, I realized that before I could analyze Andrea's complex of narratives, I would have to establish definitively his corpus of works. This meant tackling the question of attributions. Close familiarity with the codicological and philological evidence contained in these manuscripts, including certain noteworthy textual variants, allowed a perspective comprehensive enough to argue for or against earlier attributions. Furthermore, to rule out objectively the apparent correspondences that may have been simply literary conventions or common linguistic usage, I had to compare those texts presumably by Andrea not only to one another but to a body of contemporaneous chivalric works from the same dialectal region. I have attempted to be as clear and rigorous as possible in the use of my data and in the presentation of my findings. It is hoped that this approach will be accessible to the general reader and may someday be utilized by specialists to study other problematic texts.

This book would not have been possible without the generous assistance of the Commission for Educational and Cultural Exchange between Italy and the United States, which sponsored a year of research in Italy under the auspices of the Fulbright program; the Wisconsin Alumni Research Fund, which sponsored the writing phase; and the Andrew W. Mellon Foundation, which funded additional research.

Similarly, many thanks are due the administrations and staffs of the following Italian libraries: the Biblioteca Apostolica Vaticana; the Biblioteca Palatina, Parma; the Biblioteca Marciana, Venice; the Biblioteca Estense, Modena; the Biblioteca Capitolare, Verona; and in Florence, the Biblioteca Berenson at Villa I Tatti, the Archivio di Stato di Firenze, the Biblioteca Marucelliana, the Museo Horne, and the Kunsthistorisches Institut. I am especially indebted to the *direzioni* of the Biblioteche Medicea Laurenziana, Nazionale, and Riccardiana, whose precious collections house the majority of the manuscripts consulted.

A collective word of thanks is also due many librarians of the following American libraries for their willing and knowledgeable assistance: the University of Wisconsin–Madison's Memorial Library and Special Collections Department, the Newberry and Regenstein Libraries in Chicago, and the Vatican Film Library of Saint Louis University.

Special thanks to colleagues Luisa Rappallino, Antonio Scuderi, Margaret Gallucci, and Veena Kumar for obtaining books and articles from Italy for me while I was still in the early phase of my research; to Juliann Vitullo for sharing with me parts of her dissertation, then in progress; to

Anke Gleber for help with the German texts cited in this study; and to Maureen Tilley for advice on liturgical passages. For codicological and paleographical advice, I am indebted to Giovanna Murano, Dennis and Consuelo Dutschke, Armando Petrucci, and Franca Nardelli. Warm thanks are also extended to Anna Maria Babbi, Aurelia Forni Marmocchi, Emanuela Scarpa, Franca Barricelli, Janis Bell, Jill Caskey, and Carol Lazzaro-Weis for their invaluable suggestions and *gentilezza*. Special appreciation is also due Outi Merisalo, who offered valuable advice on diplomatics during my Florentine sojourn; to Maureen Mazzaoui, Thomas D. Cravens, Robert J. Rodini, and Douglas Kelly, who read the typescript during its early phases; and to my former advisor, Christopher Kleinhenz, whose continuous encouragement and support made it a pleasure to carry this project to its completion.

Andrea's Works

A	*Aspramonte,* ed. Boni
B	*Guerrino,* Bodleian canon. ital. 27
C	*Guerrino,* BNCF Conventi Soppressi, C. 1, 720
E	*Ajolfo,* ed. Del Prete
F	*I Reali di Francia,* ed. Vandelli and Gambarin
G	*Guerrino,* Ricc. 2226
L	*Guerrino,* Laur. Gaddi reliqui 50
M	*Rinaldo* in prose, Laur. Med. Pal. CI, 4
N	*Nerbonesi,* ed. Isola
P	*Guerrino,* Paris B.N. fonds ital. 491 and 98
PS	*Prima Spagna* rubrics in Michelant, "Titoli"
R	*Rambaldo,* BNCF Pal. 578
R1	*Guerrino,* Ricc. 2266
R2	*Guerrino,* Ricc. 2432
R3	*Guerrino,* Ricc. 2267
R4	*Guerrino,* Ricc. 1921
R5	*Rinaldo* in prose, Ricc. 1904
RM1	*Rinaldo* in prose, Laur. Plut. XLII, 37
RM2	*Rinaldo* in prose, Laur. Plut. LXI, 40
S	*Ansuigi,* BNCF II.I.15
U	*Ugone,* BNCF II.II.58
Z	*Ugone,* ed. Zambrini and Bacchi della Lega

For *Ugone,* I have supplemented the Zambrini edition, which was based on a late version, with citations from BNCF II.II.58.

The bulk of citations from *Guerrino* are taken from Bodleian canon. ital. 27 (**B**); however, in damaged, illegibile, or problematic passages, I have included citations from Ricc. 2226 (**G**), as indicated.

Examples from the first five books of *Rinaldo* derive entirely from Laur. Plut. XLII, 37 (**RM1**). The last three books use Laur. Plut. LXI, 40 (**RM2**) as base text, supplemented by Laur. Med. Pal. CI, 4 (*M*) and Ricc. 1904 (**R5**) where portions of the text of **RM2** were lost.

Other Documents and Texts

Acquisto	La Seconda Spagna *e* l'Acquisto di Ponente *ai tempi di Carolomagno,* ed. Ceruti
Add.	*Romanzo cavalleresco inedito (British Library Add. MS 10808),* ed. Forni Marmocchi
Briquet	Briquet, *Les filigranes* (numbers refer to item number)
Canz.	Accademia della Crusca, *Concordanze del Canzoniere di Francesco Petrarca*
Crusca	*Vocabolario degli Accademici della Crusca,* 5th ed.
DC	*Concordanza della Commedia di Dante Alighieri,* ed. Lovera, with Bettarini and Mazzarello
Dec.	*Concordanza del* Decameron, ed. Barbina
Diario	*Alle Bocche della piazza,* ed. Molho and Sznura
ED	*Enciclopedia Dantesca*
Entrée	*L'Entrée d'Espagne,* ed. A. Thomas
Fassò	*Cantari d'Aspramonte inediti (Magl. VII 682),* ed. Fassò
Filoc.	Boccaccio, *Filocolo,* ed. Quaglio
Filos.	Boccaccio, *Filostrato,* ed. Branca
Fior.	*Fioravante,* ed. Rajna, appendix to *Ricerche*
FU	*Cantare di Fierabraccia e Uliuieri,* ed. Stengel
GDLI	*Grande Dizionario della lingua italiana,* ed. Battaglia
GSLI	*Giornale Storico della letteratura italiana*
Fatti	*Li Fatti de Spagna,* ed. Ruggieri
Melli	*I Cantari di Rinaldo da Monte Albano,* ed. Melli
OF	*Combattimento tra Orlando e Ferraù,* in *Spagna,* ed. Catalano, appendix
Orl.	"*Orlando:* Die Vorlage zu Pulci's *Morgante,*" ed. Hübscher
Ricerche	I Reali di Francia: *Ricerche intorno ai* Reali di Francia, ed. Rajna
Rotta	*La Rotta di Roncisvalle,* in *Spagna,* ed. Catalano, appendix
Sec. Sp.	La Seconda Spagna *e* l'Acquisto di Ponente, ed. Ceruti
Spagna	*La Spagna,* ed. Catalano
Tav. rit.	*La Tavola ritonda,* ed. Polidori
Tes.	Boccaccio, *Teseida,* ed. Limentani
Tris. ricc.	*Il Tristano riccardiano,* ed. Parodi
Zonghi	*Zonghi's Watermarks,* ed. Labarre

Libraries and Archives

ASF   Archivio di Stato, Florence
BNCF   Biblioteca Nazionale Centrale, Florence
Laur.   Biblioteca Medicea-Laurenziana
Ricc.   Biblioteca Riccardiana

In citations of manuscripts, all transcriptions are my own. These adhere as closely as possible to original forms and spellings, with accents, capitals, and minimal punctuation added to conform to modern usage.

Since many colophons lack precise dates or are of uncertain provenance, years are shown as found in the manuscripts and not converted to *stile fiorentino.*

Lexical Citations

References to *Rambaldo* folio numbers follow original numeration.
ger. = gerund
part. = participle
rel. = related form
var. = variant form

Multiple occurrences of a lexeme are shown in parentheses following the page, folio, or line where it is found.

In chapter 6, Rambaldo folio numbers follow the original numeration.

Andrea da Barberino and
the Chivalric Tradition in Italy

Resta insomma a spiegare, al riparo della letteratura umanistica,
nel campo proprio del più umile volgare, la preminenza a
Firenze fra il Tre e il Quattrocento di un uomo tutto intento alla
prosa come Andrea da Barberino.

DIONISOTTI, "APPUNTI SU ANTICHI TESTI"

In Italy, chivalric narrations based on Old French epics and Breton romances circulated from the twelfth century on, and the fusion of these disparate narrative materials took place quite early. Although records of the first written or oral transmission of this material have largely disappeared, the visual arts provide evidence of its former popularity: the mosaics with chivalric themes in the cathedrals of Brindisi and Otranto, or sculptures of Orlando and Oliviero on the doorways of the cathedrals of Verona and Modena. Nonliterary documents from the late twelfth and thirteenth centuries demonstrate the widespread use of heroes' names such as Orlando, Rinaldo, Rinieri, Guido, and Ugolino.[1] The popular characters and events were even absorbed into important literary texts of a nonchivalric nature: a Tuscan versification of Brunetto Latini's late thirteenth-century *Tesoro* contained a version of the *Rotta di Roncisvalle*,[2] and Dante included protagonists from both cycles in his *Commedia*.[3] Extant manuscripts, such as *L'Orlando* (Laur. Med. Pal. 78) and the *romanzo cavalleresco* (British Library Add. MS 10808), demonstrate the coexistence of *ottava rima* and prose versions by the late fourteenth century. Appalled Latin humanists decried the widespread recounting of the Paladins' adventures; despite their mocking observations, however, chivalric literature in Italy would thrive in its various guises well into the sixteenth century.[4] The genre's fullest flowering, which would produce the masterpieces of Boiardo and Ariosto, was still to come.

Situated between those writers who sought fame "tra gli ignoranti e vulgo"[5] and the illustrious authors whose audiences included the Medici inner circle and the Estense courts was the Florentine *prosatore* Andrea da Barberino, an author whose name is synonymous with chivalric literature in Italy. Although his art does not exhibit the polished elegance of High Renaissance poets, it should not be relegated to consideration alongside the anonymous *cantari,* many of which are the products of unskilled authors. Andrea wrote during the Florentine oligarchy just prior to the rise of the Medici, and his narratives reflect the ethos of a thriving European city whose bankers and international traders consciously projected the anachronistic norms of foreign aristocracies onto their own quasi-noble maneuverings.

Maestro Andrea's role was one of compiling, digesting, and reworking older literary models, endowing them with new resonance for his society. His nine works are closely based on French and Franco-Italian Carolingian cycle epics yet are not devoid of influence from Arthurian romances, Ovid, and Dante. His vast prose cycle includes the legends of Roland, Guillaume d'Orange, Renaut, Huon d'Auvergne, and Doon de Maïence. Terms, expressions, motifs, and characters derived from these reveal Andrea's *storie* to be closer to original French models than are those by other Tuscan authors of Carolingian cycle material. This close adherence implies a more "learned" approach to compilation than was apparently the practice of contemporary *cantatori;* that is, he did not introduce startling innovations, but he treated the tradition with respect, conserving its norms, plots, and characters. Yet far from slavishly imitating, or translating in the modern sense, Andrea selectively reworked the material, introducing elements of content, structure, style, and language from nonchivalric genres such as bestiaries, travel literature, and chronicles. Even when identifiable fictional sources survive, Andrea treated them with "una certa libertà . . . Andrea non traduce, di solito, ma rielabora, e a volte assai vastamente."[6] Though his debt to the earlier cycles is clear, Andrea retells these "histories" with a freshness and vividness that bring new life to the old forms. His verisimilar characters and depictions seem to emerge from the confining background of earlier narrative conventions in the way that a sculpture by his contemporary Donatello appears to free itself from its niche.

Andrea da Barberino exerted a long-lasting influence on later chivalric authors in Italy and abroad. His works were copied by hand as late as the mid-nineteenth century and enjoyed a publishing history that extended into the 1960s; despite their contemporary importance and their enduring popularity, however, they have suffered from critical misunderstanding.

Modern scholars have tended to follow the lead of the outraged Latin humanists in condemning Andrea's texts. This is likely because of "guilt by association" with chivalric texts of inferior quality or because Andrea chose to write in vernacular prose instead of the "proper" heroic verse form, the octave. Errors in dating and ill-informed attributions have persisted nearly to our own day, giving a false impression of his work. Furthermore, in the nineteenth and early twentieth centuries, Andrea's stories served as a principal source of inspiration for puppet theaters in southern Italy. The folklorist finds such a popular manifestation fascinating; literary scholars regard it as anathema. By witnessing the modern-day enthusiasm of the common—sometimes illiterate—folk for these tales, critics assumed a similarly unlearned medieval audience for Andrea's works. This phenomenon again resulted in their dismissing the original texts from serious consideration.

Still other critical misinterpretations may be attributed to dependence on unreliable popular versions, inadequate critical editions, or limited samplings of Andrea's texts. Repeated popular printings have so modernized Andrea's language, style, and content that the original texts are scarcely recognizable. Certain of his works are available only in late nineteenth-century critical editions that frequently do a disservice to the originals. Recent scholars who have attempted to analyze his style often rely on only one or two texts, usually *I Reali di Francia* or *Guerrino il Meschino*. Several recent studies that cite the unedited *Le Storie di Rinaldo* mention only two of the five known manuscripts, ignoring its later, more maturely written books. Various philological studies have examined single texts by Andrea with respect to their possible antecedents or within the larger textual traditions, but a thorough investigation of Andrea's entire corpus is lacking: in fact, some doubt has remained as to which works were actually his.

This study presents the first comprehensive examination of the life and works of the Florentine *prosatore*. It analyzes and reinterprets available material on Andrea, his texts, and their cultural and literary importance. The study identifies the principal elements of Andrea's style: although he worked from known models, certain narrative motifs, language, and structural devices appear to be his own and may be found consistently throughout his works. The remainder of the study is dedicated to establishing a definitive corpus of works for Andrea: it analyzes three

unedited anonymous texts and the surviving rubrics of a fourth to determine whether they may be his. A close examination of the content, characters, formal structures, and, especially, lexicon demonstrates that three
texts—*La Storia del re Ansuigi*, the lost *Prima Spagna*, and a prose
Rinaldo—were surely written by Andrea, and *Il Libro di Rambaldo* was
likely a mid-fifteenth-century imitation. In addition, the discovery of numerous unknown manuscript exemplars of Andrea's epic romances in-
creases our knowledge of his contemporary importance and also under-
scores the inadequacy of existing editions.

These new findings enhance our understanding of the position that
Andrea's work enjoyed in the book culture of late medieval and Renaissance Italy. His influence on later authors was greater than has been imag-
ined, his style and language are more learned than has been believed, and
his output is considerably more extensive. Such information demands a
reappraisal of this author and his works.

Andrea da Barberino

Life and Works

Although the authors of many medieval texts are doomed to anonymity, several documents offer clues to the identity of Andrea da Barberino. His name as author and "translator" survives in various manuscripts. In the colophons of others, copyists have added their own comments on his life. Tax documents furnish additional information. Andrea was born to Jacopo di Tieri de' Magnabotti or Magiabotti.[1] Because of the conflicting ages he reported in the *portate al catasto*, there is some question as to the exact year of his birth. In 1427, Andrea stated "ò passati anni 55";[2] and the document of 1431 declares "Maestro Andrea detto à anni 60 passati,"[3] so he was born at least by 1372.

His family originated in Barberino di Val d'Elsa, but it is not known whether Andrea was born there or in Florence proper.[4] A will drawn up by one "Jacopo di Tieri di Firenze" suggests that his family was already living in Florence near the time of his birth.[5] Given the rarity of the name "Tieri," this document in all probability pertains to Andrea's father. There is, however, no mention of a son. That Andrea later lived and worked in Florence is attested by a statement in the *Guerrino* of Laur. Gaddi rel. 50 indicating that it was "fatto e chompilato per 'l nobile huomo Maestro Andrea da fFirenze" (1r). Although the name Andrea was a common one and thus may seem inconclusive in proposing an attribution for his work, the two *portate* clearly prove the author's identity and furnish additional facts about his personal life.[6] The first lists his residence as "nel popolo [i.e., district] di Santo Filice in piazza, chonfalone della Ferza" (167r). He owned a house located in "via della Pergola" as well as two tracts of land, "nel popolo della pieve a sSettimo luogho detto Infarneta," which provided him with wine and grain. The second document shows that he purchased a third piece of land. He was twice widowed: his first wife was a certain Domenica; the second, Gostanza, was twenty-six years old in 1427. A third wife is listed in the *portata* of 1430: "Mona Riccha, sua donna, à anni 35" (90v). It appears that none of his marriages produced children. Andrea made his last will and testament on August 14, 1431, naming as heir his nephew Andrea di Giovanni di Franciescho, a mattress maker. The inheritance was reported on May 31, 1433. Andrea's death may therefore be fixed within the boundaries of these two dates.[7]

A rare reference to *uditore* (**F** 509) suggests that his works were read aloud *in piazza*. This seeming rhetorical flourish is borne out as factual by contemporary scribal testimony: the copyist of a *Guerrino* states that it was "conposto pel nobile homo Maestro Andrea che chantò in Sa' Martino" (**C** 1r). This location, the *piazzetta* of San Martino al Vescovo, was a favorite site for performances of *cantari*.[8] Such testimonies, combined with the tax records, demonstrate that Andrea was an established *cantatore*. While the term *cantatore* derives from *cantare*, which denoted poems in ottava rima, in medieval usage the title also applied to prose works. It could also be equated with "performer," as the Conventi Soppressi citation demonstrates. Various other documents refer to Andrea as "maestro." Discussing the fourteenth-century *Orlando*, Carlo Dionisotti defines the title *maestro* as "autore della storia, distinto da 'colui che la rimava'." This hypothesis is reinforced by the phrase "maestri delle storie," which occurs repeatedly in *La Tavola ritonda*.[9] According to contemporary usage, Andrea would thus have been considered the author or composer of the story, even though he also apparently recited the work in public.

For the late medieval Italian audience, a "story" recounted the life and adventures of its hero.[10] Earlier versions were often completed by later texts; thus, *L'Entrée d'Espagne* finds its sequel in *La Prise de Pampelune*, Luca and Luigi Pulci's *Il Ciriffo Calvaneo* in Bernardo Giambullari's continuation, and the *Orlando Innamorato* in the *Orlando Furioso*. Andrea participated in this drive for narrative completeness on an unprecedented scale. His several epic romances form a vast narrative cycle, the structural integrity of which has evoked critical praise: "La grandiosità dell'edificio che Andrea da Barberino ha saputo progettare ed innalzare, e la sapienza con cui ha saputo in esso congegnare le singole parti, distribuendole secondo un piano proporzionato ed armonico, rivelano in lui la perizia di un architetto sicuro."[11] The six books of *I Reali di Francia* find their logical continuation with *Aspramonte*, which nineteenth-century scholars erroneously believed was Book VII of *Reali*.[12] Next in order by subject matter follow the lost *Prima Spagna* and the *Seconda Spagna*, works attributed to Andrea.[13] The cycle continues with the seven-part *Storie Nerbonesi*, a free reworking of *chansons de geste* from the William of Orange cycle.

Similarly reworked from the French *Aiol* is *La Storia di Aiolfo del Barbicone*, securely attributable to Andrea by two citations in the text itself (**E** 2: 164, 295). Some manuscripts of *La Storia di Ugone d'Avernia* clearly ascribe this work to Andrea, as others do for *Guerrino il Meschino*.[14] Much internal evidence indicates Andrea as the author of the anonymous *Storie di Rinaldo da Montalbano* in prose. The unpublished *Rambaldo* has been attributed to Andrea because of its direct borrowings from *Guerrino* and *Ugone;* however, it is highly unlikely that Andrea composed this text.[15] The *volgarizzamento* of *Girone il Cortese* was also once attributed to Andrea by Francesco Tassi, an idea long since refuted by Fanfani.[16]

A word about titles is in order, since those chosen by modern editors do not always correspond to medieval *usus*. In the manuscripts these texts are most often referred to as "Books" or "Histories"—for example, "[Il] Libro de' Reali di Francia" (BNCF II.I.14) or "Le Storie d'Aspramonte" (Rome, Biblioteca Angelica 2263). *Aspramonte* is also referred to as "El libro delle nobile e gran battaglie d'Aspramonte" (Marc. ital. cl. 11, XXXVIII [6960], *incipit*) or, more succinctly, "Le Battaglie d'Aspramontte" (Ricc. 2308, 2410). The modern title *Le Storie Nerbonesi* for the Isola edition conforms closely to "Le Storie de' Nerbonesi" found in the *incipit* of BNCF II.IV.679 and the *explicit* of BNCF II.I.15.[17] This text is also termed "E' sette libri de' nerbonesi" in several codices.[18] The title *Guerrino il Meschino* for Andrea's best-known composition is actually a more recent development, the result of the work's proliferation in handwritten and printed forms. The original title, which appears in the *explicit* of several exemplars of *Aspramonte* and in various manuscripts of *Guerrino* itself, was "il libro chiamato el Meschino di Durazzo," sometimes abbreviated as "el libro chiamato meschino" (Marc. ital. cl. 11, XXXVIII; Bodleian Canon. ital. 27). Versions of the former title appear in the *incipits* of several manuscripts (Ricc. 2266, 2308, 2309, 2410; Paris B.N. fonds ital. 491; and Bodleian Canon. ital. 27). By 1470 the work was so well known that its hero's baptismal name "Guerrino" had crept into one copyist's title, even though for a large part of the story he is known only by the nickname "il meschino": "i[l] libro chiamato Meschino cioè Ghuerrino da Durazzo" (**C** 1r). The modern title may owe its origin, not to the manuscript tradition, but to incunabula such as *El Libro de Gverrino chiamato Meschino* (Venice: Christophorus de Pensis, 1493). The labels in the plates for extant engravings show that by the late fifteenth century "Guerrino" was supplanting "Meschino" as the name for this increasingly popular character.[19] Finally, the title chosen by Del Prete for his edition, *Storia di Ajolfo del Barbicone*, is partially accurate, since only the central portion treats that hero's adventures. Andrea's contemporaries would more likely have called the work "La storia del ducha Elia d'Orlino," a title found in the *incipits* of nearly all exemplars and in a mid-sixteenth-century library inventory.[20]

Although Andrea's chosen medium was prose, there are indications that he may have been a poet as well. The rubric of an unpublished *poemetto* discovered by Vittore Branca contains information that corresponds to our Andrea's life: "Qui chominc[i]a le stanze che fece *Maestro Andrea che chantò in pancha* d'una schermaglia che si fé in piaza de' Signiori 1423" (emphasis added).[21] The *congedo* of the work includes the words "Andrea me fecit" (84r). This discovery sheds new light on the question of whether Andrea composed the verse sections inserted in two of his prose narratives. It seems to bear out Ididio Ludovisi's earlier opinion on the *terza rima* sections of *Ugone:* "Per me quindi esso [il poemetto] non si può e non si deve attribuire ad altri che al Mangabotti [*sic*]."[22] Yet Andrea explicitly cited another poet in the rubric to *Ugone's* first rhymed section: "Ora qui comincia il libro quarto di Ugone, quando entrò nello 'nferno; e prima in versi trinari. Ed è composizione di Giovanni Vincenzio isterliano" (**Z** 2: 83; emphasis added). Perhaps the young author felt it necessary to invent this name as a claim of modesty. Yet the unedited *Storie di Rinaldo da Montalbano,* another probable early work by Andrea, contains the same insertion of an independent poem preceded by a clear reference to authorship: "Dice l'autor Maestro Michele che egli [il padiglione] era fatto in questa forma, propria chome segh[u]ita qui rrimando" (**M** 2v). In these cases, it seems justifiable to say that Andrea was citing external sources, now lost, or perhaps contemporary *cantastorie* of whom no written traces remain. Regarding the question of Andrea as poet, one may conclude that Andrea was sensitive to verse genres, including in his prose narratives appropriate passages by his contemporaries, and that although he preferred working in prose, he himself wrote occasional pieces in verse during the course of his long career.

Andrea's extensive production furnishes additional clues about his literary preparation and his life. Allusions to the Bible and its use as a subtext for plot events are frequent, and a long, otherworld journey in *Guerrino* clearly shows an acquaintance with Dante—not surprising, since in his day these two works were widely read.[23] He was conversant with numerous chansons de geste and Breton lays that would have been available either in the original French or in their Franco-Italian reworkings. In addition to those sources directly translated, compiled, or reworked, Osella suggests Andrea's awareness of many fictional works from the Trecento and earlier. Among the romances, Andrea knew Chrétien's *Cligès,* Marie de France's *Lai de Lanval,* the prose *Conte de la Charette,* and the *Tavola ritonda.*[24] Certain narrative affinities in *Guerrino* indicate Andrea's knowledge of the Rinaldo da Montalbano legends.[25] Some of Andrea's protagonists and events are modeled on classical or classical cycle works, such as the *Aeneid, I Fatti d'Enea* by Guido da Pisa, *I Fatti di Cesare,* the *Alexander Romance,* and Statius's *Thebaid.* He owned a manuscript that contained *volgarizzamenti* of Ovid's *Heroides,* Statius's *Achilleid,* and excerpts from Justinus's *Historiae Philippicae* (Laur. Gaddi rel. 40). For small-scale borrowings, one cannot always be sure whether Andrea knew a source in its original version, in vernacular translation, or through oral transmission. Andrea had a working knowledge of Latin, as shown by the geographical knowledge he gleaned from the new translation of Ptolemy's *Cosmographia* and by liturgical quotations sprinkled throughout his epic romances.[26] Andrea may have used actual Latin chronicles to furnish his narrations with verisimilar details. In *Nerbonesi,* for example, he cites "*la Cronaca Parigina* nel primo libro, chiamato *Franconestorum,* ne fa memoria" (1: 368n.6). Textual content and lexicon reveal Andrea's acquaintance with vernacular texts of the preceding centuries such as *Il Libro di novelle e di bel parlar gentile,* the Villanis' *Cronica,* Mandeville's *Travels,* and Boccaccio's *Teseida* and *Filocolo. Guerrino* and, to a lesser extent, *Ugone* also demonstrate clear debts to the spurious *Letter of Prester John.*

Frequent citations of place names offer further clues about Andrea. The high frequency of geographical references in his texts are from written sources like Ptolemy but also reflect the lively contemporary interest in travel for commercial or religious purposes. Rajna notes Andrea's seemingly intimate knowledge of places off the beaten path, such as "il nome di un quartiere di Sutri, . . . quello altresì di una povera osteria di Roma e di alcune località di quei intorni, la Suvereta e la Pignea."[27] In addition, an apparent eyewitness description of the Pantheon occurs in *Guerrino,* Book III: Andrea states that a mosque "è minore che Santa Maria Ritonda la quale Io vidi nella ciptà di Roma" (**B** 38v). Since the protagonist has not yet visited Christendom, this "io" can only refer to the author himself. Other evidence suggests firsthand knowledge of foreign locations. Suchier points out a reference in *Nerbonesi* (1: 61) to the Parisian "chiesa di Santa Maria Fiordalisi" near a small bridge, which corresponds to Sainte-Chapelle at the Palais de Justice. Andrea represents the Rhone region of France with the same uncanny accuracy.[28]

The phenomenon of Andrea's works' longevity has attracted critical attention. Critics have repeatedly noted that *Reali* and *Guerrino* were still being read and performed in the twentieth century, but they have not determined the transmission of his works closer to his own day. A consid-erable body of manuscript evidence reveals the lasting popularity Andrea's works enjoyed (see Appendix A). An unedited *Aiolfo* bears the earliest date of any extant manuscript of Andrea's work—1433. Only one un-dated manuscript (Bodleian Canon. ital. 27, *Guerrino*) is done in a hand that may be earlier than 1433.[29] Of some seventy manuscripts and frag-ments, none can be dated with certainty from Andrea's lifetime, indicat-ing that Andrea may not have allowed his works to circulate in written form while he was alive. This, combined with the fact that no autograph has yet been discovered, might suggest that Andrea followed the old prac-tice of dictating his works. However, one colophon refutes such a hypoth-esis: "Questo libro ène una chopia d'uno libro ch'è di mano d'Andrea di T[i]eri de' Magna botti da Barberino di Valdelsa, maestro di chanto" (BNCF, Magl. Cl. XXIV, 146*bis*, 150r). This copyist is only one of two who in-cluded Andrea's surname; he must have been in some way connected to Andrea's family or knew his fortunes well. His statement about the manu-script being the first descendant of an autograph may be authoritative. Furthermore, a small unedited Tuscan book inventory dated August 4, 1424, lists—alongside saints' lives, prophecies, cantari, and other prose romances—a book that contains the legend of "boxolino filiuolo del dugo ugolino" (BNCF, Nuovi Acquisti 509, rear flyleaf). Bosolino, son of Ugolino di Gualfreda, was an important protagonist in Andrea's *Aiolfo*. The brief description of this inventory offers tantalizing evidence that portions of Andrea's texts may have circulated during his lifetime.

While *Reali* and *Guerrino* were printed in the fifteenth century, re-ceiving at least three and fifteen incunabular editions, respectively, other works by Andrea continued to circulate in manuscript form until well into the sixteenth century. The latest dated *Aspramonte* was copied in 1493, and the latest dated *Ugone* in 1511, but dated exemplars of *Nerbonesi* survive from 1504 through 1534.[30] A modern manuscript copy of *Reali* was made in 1736: once belonging to Luigi Celotti (MS 137), and then to Sir Thomas Phillipps (MS 929), it is now in a private collection. Even after the works of Pulci, Boiardo, and Ariosto circulated and through the boom years of romance publishing, interest in the older prose narratives by Andrea never abated.

Just as Andrea drew from a variety of medieval predecessors, his own works became in turn the sources for chivalric texts of the later Quattro- and Cinquecento. This is true of several anonymous Tuscan prose texts that were probably composed in the decades after Andrea's death. One finds identifiable allusions to *Reali* and *Aspramonte* in the prose *Spagna*

(Laur. Med. Pal. CI, 3).[31] In the mid-Quattrocento, *Nerbonesi* exercised an even greater influence. Entire passages were copied verbatim from *Nerbonesi* into the two short prose narratives found in the Biblioteca Ambrosiana manuscript C 35 Sup.[32] Similarly, the unedited prose *Il Povero Aveduto* (Laur. Plut. XLIV, 30) explicitly mentions *Nerbonesi* as its source four times, and certain plot elements as well as the name of its principal character derive from that text.[33] There are plot similarities between *Guerrino* and the unedited *Fortunato*.[34] *Rambaldo* (BNCF Pal. 578) contains passages copied directly from Andrea's *Guerrino* and *Ugone*. Another anonymous Tuscan narrative, *Storia di Rinaldino da Montalbano* (ed. Minutoli), contains characters and situations present in or inspired by *Aspramonte, Nerbonesi, Le Storie di Rinaldo,* and *Guerrino.*

Andrea's reworkings directly occasioned several ottava rima reworkings. The anonymous epic poem of British Library, Add. MS 22821, is a freely adapted northern Italian setting of *Reali,* Book I.[35] Michele Catalano believed that the *Spagna magliabechiana* (BNCF II.I.47) was modeled on Andrea's *Aspramonte,* an assertion contested by Boni, who concluded that Andrea was not its only source. Nevertheless, this text recalls *Nerbonesi* explicitly (388r).[36] Certain details in an anonymous fifteenth-century verse *Aspramonte* demonstrate that its poet knew Andrea's *Reali.*[37] The soldier-poet Michelangelo Cristoforo da Volterra, *trombetto* (b. 1466), has left two *poemetti* based on Andrea's works. The first part of his unedited *Storia del conte Ugo d'Avernia* in octaves (Laur. Med. Pal. 82) corresponds to the genealogical chapter of *Reali.*[38] A second *poemetto—La incoronazione del re Aloysi*—was printed in the early Cinquecento and explicitly cites *Nerbonesi* as a source more than once.[39] In the same period Cristoforo Fiorentino, called L'Altissimo, did a versification of *Reali,* Books I and II, which was printed at Venice in 1534.[40]

Nerbonesi inspired various characters and plot elements of Luca and Luigi Pulci's *Il Ciriffo Calvaneo,* which cites it several times.[41] Although Franca Ageno identified allusions to Andrea's *Reali* and *Aspramonte* in Luigi Pulci's *Morgante,* the influence of two other texts by Andrea— *Guerrino* and *Rinaldo*—on *Morgante* has thus far gone unnoticed.

Boiardo may have been aware of Andrea's texts, though the degree of influence is debatable. Giulio Razzoli alludes to certain similarities of *Orlando Innamorato* to *Reali* and *Aiolfo.* Ferdinand Castets notes that the prose *Rinaldo* that we propose is Andrea's "est une des sources où Boiardo a puisé le plus volontiers." On the other hand, Antonio Franceschetti has argued against Boiardo's complete reliance on Andrea's *Aspramonte,* and for a conflation of sources.[42]

Andrea's works served as sources for an array of major and minor Renaissance texts. Rajna's study of the sources for the *Orlando Furioso* views Andrea's texts as only part of the humus from which Ariosto's poem emerged; however, Ariosto may have had in mind three episodes from *Guerrino:* the description of Prester John's kingdom, the Earthly Paradise, and the transformation of the Sibyl of Norcia and her attendants into serpents.[43] According to Neri, the same text may have inspired the "seduzioni voluttuose" in *Italia liberata da' Goti* by Trissino.[44] More evidence of the migration of Andrea's works to the Este court in Ferrara is found in the classicizing poems of Tito Vespasiano Strozzi.[45] The protagonist of Teofilo Folengo's *Baldus* searches the world, in clear emulation of Guerrino, to learn the identity of his father, encountering pirates, enchantments, monsters, and even traveling to the Inferno. Among the titles of chivalric romances Baldus had read are "Realia Franzae," "Asperamontem," and "Meschinique provas."[46] The half-man, half-dog character Falchetto in *Baldus* is a descendant of Andrea's Pulicane in *Reali.*[47] Folengo's *Orlandino* is a satirical verse setting of *Reali,* Book VI. Similarly, the first four *canti* of Ludovico Dolce's *Orlando* owe an obvious debt to *Reali,* Book VI, and, to a lesser degree, to *Aspramonte.*[48] Dolce's *Palmerino* may have been derived from the Castilian translation of *Guerrino.*[49] The birth and marvelous infancy of Machiavelli's Castruccio Castracane were modeled not on classical sources but on the young Orlando of *Reali,* Book VI, chap. 58.[50]

Andrea's texts experienced a certain notoriety throughout the peninsula and outside Italy as well. A French translation of *Guerrino* done by Jean de Rochemeure was printed at Lyons by Oliuier Arnoullet for Romain Morin, in 1530, under the pseudonym "J. de Cuchermoys." The translator's autograph manuscript survives.[51] The French *Guerin mesquin* was reprinted several times in different cities: three times in Paris, by Alain Lotrian et Denis Janot, by Jehan Bonfons, and by Nicolas Chrestien, all undated; and twice in Troyes, by an unknown publisher in 1620 and by Oudot in 1628.[52]

During the late fifteenth-century Spanish vogue for *romanzi,* Andrea's works enjoyed renewed interest. The *Noches de Invierno* is but a poor reworking of *Reali.*[53] *Guerrino* was translated into Castilian by a certain Alonso Hernández Alemán and printed in Seville in 1512.[54] Its account of the Sibyl of Norcia informed the central theme of the *Auto de la sibila Casandra* by Gil Vicente.[55] Ironically, the translated *Guerrino* was then reimported into Italy in the guise of a "Spanish" romance. Tullia d'Aragona states in the preface to her *Il Meschino altramente detto il Guerino* (composed ca. 1543–46) that she worked from a Spanish text.[56] Bernardo Tasso's *Amadigi di Gaula* (1560) may have been indirectly influenced by Andrea, since the author of his Spanish model probably derived many characters and events from the *Guerrino* translation.[57] Still later, Guarino Mezquino had won a place in Cervantes' pantheon of "caualleros auentureros" where its protagonist was mocked alongside heroes with older pedigrees such as Fierabas, Carlo Magno, Rey Artus de Ingalaterra, Tristan, and Lançarote.[58]

Guerrino's appeal endured through the centuries.[59] It influenced certain elements of minor works such as *Tito Vespasiano ovver Gerusalemme desolata* by G. B. Lalli and the dramatic epic poem *Sibilla* by Sartorio.[60] A condensed version of *Guerrino* in octaves was printed at Venice (1689) and later at Rome (1815). This *poemetto* was reprinted at Naples (Avallone, 1849) and anthologized in our day.[61] Another anonymous text that shows the continuing interest fueled by *Guerrino* is found copied in two apparently unedited manuscripts (XIX-25 and XX-91) at the Biblioteca Nazionale in Naples. This lengthy, original ottava rima poem continues Andrea's adventure romance, as its first folio announces: "Libro di arme e di amore dove si narra le gloriose geste dei Figli del Guerino Meschino, dei Figli del ferocissimo Artibano, dei Figli del valente Alessandro." (Artibano and Alessandro were Guerrino's companions in the final chapters of Andrea's text.) While the paper bears a nineteenth- or twentieth-century watermark, someone has written "1500" (a false date?) on the first folio of each tome.

Reali, Aspramonte, and *Guerrino* also entered Neapolitan and Sicilian folklore, furnishing subject matter for *cantastorie* and puppet theaters. Rajna observed that one of these street performers had recited a version of *Guerrino* at least two hundred times during his career. This text was the most cherished in the popular repertoire and was normally reserved for Sunday evening performances. These entertainments were not directed only at children; they generally had adult male audiences. One scholar has claimed that portions of the chivalric ethos that survived in these retellings inspired the special brand of Sicilian machismo, which, in part, led to the development of the Mafia.[62] The tendency of modern cultural appropriation of Andrea's *Il meschino* was not confined to the Mezzogiorno: a satirical periodical published in Milan from 1882 to 1950 bore the title *Il Guerino;*[63] and a Bolognese sports magazine, founded in 1912, is entitled *Guerin Sportivo.* A drama by Domenico Tumiati, *Guerrin Meschino,* was performed in Argentina around 1912.[64] Italian cultural fascination with Guerrino continues: a novelistic homage to this hero's later incarnation as *pupo* has appeared as recently as 1993.[65]

Andrea's Narrative Style

Andrea's propensity for a historiographic style was first noted by Rajna and reiterated by numerous other critics, although without thorough analysis.[1] This trait was dealt with most convincingly by Paul Grendler. His revisionist discussion presents Andrea as an author possessed of "a humanistic mentality" who infused his epic romances—more properly, *istorie*—with "some of the techniques of early Renaissance humanistic historiography." Grendler reexamines Andrea from the standpoint of the developing nonfictional genre rather than with respect to medieval chivalric narratives, thereby shedding new light on earlier criticisms that Andrea's texts lack the nationalist and religious fervor of his French models.[2] The "lay, secular tone," which sharply contrasts with that of the chanson de geste tradition, is completely in line with the style of Italian Renaissance historiography.[3]

Many elements in Andrea's acknowledged texts demonstrate his striving for verisimilitude in his epic romances. Although his characters and subject matter would be termed "fictional" by the modern reader, Andrea attempts to endow them with a historical patina. To give his texts the appearance of chronicles, he cites "real" or fictive historiographic sources. These include not only the traditional Turpin (**A** 30) but French "historical writings," "chronicles," and "books":

> in molte scritture non fu menzionato Gostantino, e tutte *le scritture istoriche di Francia* lo chiamano il re Agnolo . . . (**F** 287)
> La nostra *cronica* di Urmano di Parigi dice che . . . (**F** 63)
> secondo questa *cronachetta* . . . (**F** 109)
> Alcuno *libro,* ch'io honne trovato, dice ch'una fonte apparí nella prigione; . . . *molti* [libri] non ne fanno menzione, che sono *franciosi.* (**F** 177)

La Cronaca Parigina nel primo libro, chiamato *Franconestorum*, ne fa memoria . . . (**N** 1: 368n.6; emphasis added above)

From these and other explicit remarks, it appears that Andrea followed actual texts and did not just formulaically cite fabulous authorities or repeat situations learned from orally transmitted stories.

Most Italian authors of Carolingian cycle material employed ottava rima as the desired register for their works' heroic content, but Andrea's deliberate choice of prose imitates "true" historical genres more successfully than verse could.[4] By moving a step away from poetry (that is, "art"), he makes the events recounted seem more naturalistic. Andrea's structure and style, notably in *Reali* and *Ugone*, parallel those of Giovanni Villani's chronicle. His language is more akin to political dispatches or real chronicles, especially Matteo Villani's, than to contemporary chivalric literature. His texts demonstrate other specific resemblances to a private Florentine diary (BNCF Panciat. 158). This journal spans the years 1382–1401, the period of Andrea's young adulthood, and he would surely have been aware of many of the events it describes. The two Florentines may have had the same educational background, since the language and texture of Andrea's fictional narrations directly parallel the anonymous diarist's various reports of historical battles, processions, and political maneuverings.

Andrea's concern for verisimilitude motivated his choice of models and textual variants as he compiled his important cycle. In the proem to *Guerrino*, Andrea tells us how he rediscovered old material that a new audience may now enjoy: "mi sono dilettato di cierchare molte storie novelle. Et avendo piaciere di molte storie, trovai questa leggienda che molto mi piacque" (**B** 1r). Although this declaration may seem a mere literary topos, other passages in his epic romances display the author's conscious search for all variants of a source with an eye to the most realistic:

Alcuno libro dice ch'ella fu una radice, ovvero barba d'erba, ch'aveva questa vertù; ma *a me pare più verisimile* una prieta preziosa, o corno di lioncorno, perché dice ch'era buona contro al veleno; o corno di dragone, ch'è contrario a veleni e a loppio. (**F** 154)
Alcuni hanno detto che v'andò il re, *ma i più dicono che* non è vero. (**F** 336; emphasis added)

This careful research work, or at least the fiction of scholarly comparison of source materials, is unusual among contemporary writers of *cantari* and seems more sincere than the stock appeals to Turpin.

Other characteristics of Andrea's prose that lend it the texture of a chronicle are its regular form and careful ordering, the use of precise dates, and the enumeration of captains and troops preparing for battle. Dates often include month, day, and year as well as references to feast days:

> e questo fu negli anni del nostro signore Gesù Cristo ottocento XXXVII a dì 29 del mese di Giugno . . . (**N** 1: 241)
> e trovoronsi in Oringa sessantamila cavalieri cristiani, sanza i pedoni, e a dì 15 d'Agosto, il dì di Nostra Donna, si partirono . . . (**N** 2: 4)
> giunsono . . . a dì 15 d'Aprile, negli anni di Cristo 861 . . . (**N** 2: 412)

One frequently has a sense of time passing, since Andrea indicates through various chapters the days or months between events.

Statistical passages often serve as a prelude to battle: commanders and their battalions are enumerated along with the knights and/or infantry. This type of passage frequently fills an entire chapter.

> La prima schiera furono quattromila: questa condusse Ugone, Gilfroi e Aguentin le Normando, re Salamone, e 'l conte Galerano. . . . Le [*sic*] seconda furono settemila cavalieri: questa condusse Mellon d'Angrante e Guido di Guascongna e 'l marchese Berlingieri. La terza furono quindicimila cavalieri: questa condusse il re Disidero di Pavia, el dux Namo di Baviera, e con loro in compangnia Riccieri vassallo. La quarta furono ventimila cavalieri: questa condusse il re Ottone e Guido d'Estivers. (**A** 118)

In addition, parallel catalogs within these chapters often give the composition of both the Christian and "Saracen" armies.[5] Such passages have provoked modern criticism of Andrea's style as "monotonous,"[6] but they were a commonplace in medieval literature. Functionally, they are crucial for laying a foundation for the narration of the battle: captains and their battalions operate as units and at times carry out intricate maneuvers, especially in *Nerbonesi*. Rhythmically, enumerative chapters provide a natural pause in the narrative which allows suspense to build as the reader anticipates the impending action. When the battle actually begins in the next chapter, the anticipatory tension is released, lending greater momentum to the events narrated.

A wealth of place names and detailed itineraries contributes to the chronicle-like texture of Andrea's works. In comparison to Trecento romances that relied mostly on an abbreviated voyage motif ("and they rode so much, they arrived"),[7] Andrea frequently enumerates the various points along a character's journey. Passages describing trade routes, pilgrimage routes, or territories conquered during military campaigns appear in *Reali* and *Aspramonte*, two presumably early works.[8] In one scene from *Aspramonte*, an African spy recounts a completed mission: "'Singnore, io sono stato in Talia e a Roma, e vidi papa Lione . . . e passai Toscana e Lombardia, e andai in Ungheria e in Buemia, e nella Mangna alta e nella bassa; e vidi Baviera e Braibante, e Nizimbors, e Brandibors, e Fiandra, e Colongna, e l'isola d'Inghilterra, e Frigia bassa, Brettangna, Cibilcalia, Maganza, Borgongna, Savoia, e Provenza, e poi n'andai in Franza'" (**A** 9).[9] No such passage is found in the *Chanson d'Aspremonte*, but Andrea's is much amplified with respect to the same episode in *Cantari d'Aspramonte*, a possible source:

> "I' vo' che ttu m'intenda.
> Di Cristianità cercat'ò [ben tutto] . . . :
> i' fui in Francia, a Parigi e a Molione
> e ad Agia nella Magna e a Vignone."
> (Fassò, IX, 5, 4–5, 7–8)

A passage from *Aiolfo* describes the adventures of Guido di Bagotte during his exile from France:

> Andossene in Affrica, e cominciò al monte Atalante ad andare alla ventura per provare sua persona. . . . E andò a una città ch'è sotto al monte Atalante, che si chiama Gades. . . . E poi n'andò per le terre de' Dragondi. . . . Poi n'andò in Maritania a Ciesaria. . . . E poi passò in Barberia a Trapoli, Acasia, Ventere, Latismagna, Advoes, Balsadin: tutte queste città cercò . . . e poi n'andò a Pentapoli e a Tervine e ad Arsinea a Polimonte e a Venne. . . . E poi n'andò a una città che si chiamava Cirenesi, capo della provincia di Cinerei. . . . Poi n'andò in Alessandria e in Babillonia al Soldano. (**E** 1: 25–26)

The unabridged passage achieves a nice formal balance between listing the knight's itinerary and his adventures in each location.

Andrea's cartographical erudition reaches its apex in *Guerrino*, certain episodes of which reveal the tone of an actual *relazione di viaggio*. Geography serves as an ordering principle in *Guerrino* (see Map 1), a fact explicitly stated in the opening rubric: "Qui chomincia il primo libro chiamato il meschino di Durazo . . . *e tracta tutte e' tre le parti del mondo, cioè Asia, Africa e Uropia*" (**B** 1r; emphasis added). The hero's quest for his lineage takes him on a contiguous exploration of the known world. Part of his route follows that of the heroes of antiquity, especially Alexander the Great, as is noted several times in the text:

"Et viddi la grande ciptà detta Allessandria Vittiaria la quale fecie fare Allessandro di Maciedonia per difendere quello reame da' Tartari che sono da indi i·llà." (**B** 24r)

"Questa Allessandria Earada [i.e., Herat] fecie fare el grande Allessandro mangno, Re di Maciedonia, per dimostrare d'essere stato in questi paesi." (**B** 27v)

"Queste grandissime alpi che ttu vedi sono le montangnie che fanno tre gironi dove Allessandro fecie serrare la bocha di questi tre giri di montangnie." (**B** 28r)

To some scholars, Andrea's geography seemed fantastic,[10] but comparison with medieval maps and portolan charts indicates its authenticity.[11] Some problems of identification are the result of differences between medieval and modern usages, or even changes in topographical features (new routes for rivers, silted-in ports, etc.). Other difficulties arise from copying errors, a frequent phenomenon when unfamiliar proper names occur. The majority of toponyms in the following excerpt describing a military campaign correspond to actual locations on medieval maps and portolans.[12]

Et partito da Chomopoli, passò il grande fiume Tegris. Ed entrò con l'oste nella religione di Mes[o]pontania, e prese la città detta Nilibis e Nacieforia, e prese Edessa. Et passò el fiume Ierapolis, e prese una ciptà che n'è insul lago detto Lago Asco. . . . Et passato il lago, prese a una città ch'à nome Samoscha. . . . Et partito Guerrino dalla città di Samoscha, n'andò insino al mare di Setalia et prese una ciptà ch'è insul mare chiamata Allessandretta. E poi si volse inverso Damascho et prese un'altra città detta Antioccia, e [prese] Torosa et Solin, e ppoi giunse a tTeripoli [**G**: Tripoli] in Soria . . . e venne a Baruti. Et chom'ebbe preso Baruti, n'andò a Damascho, e' quali gli renderono le chiavi prima ch'egli giungniesse, e gridarono: "Viva el soldano di Persia," e non vollono altra battaglia. Et partito da Damascho, prese Siar e Arciea [**G**: Anchrea], et giunsono a Ciesaria e Bettelin [**G**: Bettalem], et Gierusalem. (**B** 48v–49r and **G** 75v)

It is difficult to identify accurately place-names in medieval accounts, given obsolete forms and corruptions of spelling that occur due to the copying process. Nonetheless, most of these places can be identified as follows: Tigris, Mesopotamia, Nisibis (= Nusaybin), Nicephorium (= Raqqa), Edessa, Hierapolis, Samosata (?), Setalia, Alexandretta, Antioch, Tortosa (= Tartus), Solem (?), Tripoli "in Syria" (= Tarabulus), Beirut, Damascus, Sur, Acre, Caesarea, Bethlehem, and Jerusalem.

Another element of medieval travel literature is an "anthropological" concern for describing exotic peoples, their lives and customs, a trait belonging to both real and fictionalized travel accounts. Andrea may have heard about foreign lands from returned Florentine pilgrims such as Lionardo Frescobaldi, Giorgio di Guccio, or Simone Sigoli. Sources for the exotic were readily available to Andrea in the form of widely circulated texts like the *Letter of Prester John,* Alexander's *Letter to Aristotle,* and *Mandeville's Travels.* An early indication of Andrea's interest in the exotic is found in *Reali.* In this passage, he sketches various attributes of a people who had conquered England: their origin, appearance, religious practice, and unconventional way of doing battle.

> Questa gente avevano sottoposta l'Inghilterra alla loro signoria. . . . Adoravano le stelle e 'l sole e la luna. Questa gente sono chiamati di loro patria Cimbrei e Liombros, e alcuni gli chiamano Alzimenii, e sono molto grandi di statura. Questi avevano presa tutta l'isola, e lo nome dell'Ingloys si diedono eglino, perché la lingua loro voleva dire Inghilesi. . . . [V]enivono sanza schiere, ma tenevano di larghezza dugento braccia e non più. (**F** 272)

The majority of such descriptions occur in the central books of *Guerrino,* wherein numerous exotic races are described during the course of the hero's travels. Such details enhance the feeling of verisimilitude in an otherwise fictional account. In an episode set in Prester John's kingdom, Andrea describes the city, its economy, and the appearance of its citizens who are mobilizing against an attack by their warlike neighbors:

> Et giungniemo a una città molto grande nella quale noi entramo dentro, e vidi grandissimo popolo; ed è questa città inn uno bello piano nel mezo d'una montagnia detta Giabasta e 'l fiume del Nillo. . . . Questa giente sono tutti neri, e vestono panno di lino molto sottile. Et alchuno vidi vestito di panno di lana di colore biacco, cioè d'aria, e alchuni di seta allessandrina. Molti fondachi vidi d'ongni ragione mercantia: parvemi molto piena di mercatanti. Vidi molte femmine vestite di panni lini tanto sottili che 'l sole faceia vedere le loro menbra . . . et i loro capelli ànno corti, innanellati chome [gli] agnielli quando nascono. Et giunti [noi] in piazza di questa città detta Drachonda, vidi molta giente armata [chon ma]zze ferrate e archi assai; e po[che spade] ànno, poche arme di dosso e qu[elle sono] di coiame cotto. . . . Ed io adoma[ndai]: "Che giente sono e' cienamoni?" Risp[osonmi]: "Sono huomeni grandi, molto fer[oci, pastori di b]estiame e domano li alifanti.

Et [per la gra]nde abondanzia de' beni terreni, [mon]tano in superbia."
(**B** 42v and **G** 81v)

Fights with lions and serpents or dragons were a commonplace in the
Old French epic. In *Guerrino*, Andrea expands his zoological repertoire
beyond the conventional to various wild beasts and monsters described
by Saint Isidore, Brunetto Latini, and compilers of bestiaries. He includes
them as matter-of-fact, naturalistic occurrences stripped of any moralizing allegories. After dispatching an unlucky beast, the hero frequently
comments upon its dimensions and appearance. Compare, for example,
this passage from an unedited Florentine bestiary of the mid-fifteenth
century to a passage from *Guerrino:*

> Manticora è una bestia che sta inn India, e à tre gienerazioni di denti
> nella boccha e faccia d'uomo e gli ochi guerci e a colore sanguignio, e
> chollo di leone, choda di scharpione, voce come zufolo; e mangia
> volentieri charne d'uomo, e à grande vigore, e piedi a modo di leone
> ... (BNCF, Magl. Strozzi XXI, 135, 34v)
>
> In [questo] modo vidi questa bestia: el chorpo suo era atto lionino,
> molto fiero aspetto, vel[trato atto a chorrere. La sua testa era ritra]tta
> a huomo, e pelosa; avea tre ordini di denti in boccha; le ganbe e lle
> zampe a[vea] leonine con grande presa d'unghioni. La sua bocie era
> bocie d'uomo, ma non [è ch'ella] s'intendesse. Et molto forte zufolava
> e fischiare come fanno i serpenti. E lla sua pelle era di colore di lupo
> bigierongnola, e el pelo corto e folto; lunga presa di bo[cha, coda] lunga
> e pannochiuta, ed è chiamata questa bestia "Armatichore." (**B** 30v and
> **G** 48v)

Many particulars found in the Strozzi bestiary also appear in Andrea's
description: the human head, three rows of teeth, leonine paws, and the
whistling or hissing sound. Both the bestiary and Andrea locate the
manticore's habitat in "India." The detail of swift running ability appears
in another Tuscan bestiary copied perhaps in the second quarter of the
fifteenth century (Ricc. 2183, 5v).[13]
Just as geography informs the structure of *Guerrino*, genealogy per-
forms a similar function in the whole of Andrea's cycle. His consistent
treatment of genealogy reveals his skill as a compiler in a way no other
element does.[14] Andrea not only preserves certain relationships inherited
from Old French epics (Milon d'Anglant as father of Roland, Rainier as
father of Olivier and Aude, etc.), but he seems to have absorbed French
historiographers' use of genealogy as "conceptual metaphor" or "percep-

tual grid."[15] Where discrepancies occur because of variants in textual traditions, he chooses the version that seems most logical or authoritative and adheres to it throughout his cycle. For example, he considers Clarice to be the mother of Rinaldo and not his wife (as she is in Add. 10808). Besides preserving the lineages of major heroes, Andrea seeks to incorporate those of minor personages as well, at times inventing relatives to fill existing gaps. Not only does he furnish detailed lineages for characters, but he links them to antiquity, thereby conforming to a prevalent medieval discourse.[16] Thus the "reali di Francia" are given a pedigree reaching back to Emperor Constantine himself (**F** 564); Aiolfo and his father, Elia, the count of Campagna, are descendants of the Scipioni of Rome (**E** 1: 1). Although Andrea did not invent the notion of including the family trees of fictional characters in narratives (there is a genealogical chapter at the end of *Fioravante*, clearly a source for *Reali*), no other Italian chivalric author of his day displayed such an extensive interest in genealogy.

Andrea's language is a clear, pure Tuscan. Despite the fact that he was frequently translating from French or Franco-Italian, it is remarkably free of Gallicisms.[17] Modigliani observed that Andrea's prose was "abbastanza agile, spesso efficace ed il periodo . . . discretamente elaborato con una sufficiente coordinazione delle sue parti." In general, Andrea's language was richer and more varied than that used in other Tuscan chivalric narratives of the day. Boni has asserted that Andrea possessed "l'intenzione di levarsi un poco al di sopra della prosa popolaresca, e una certa ambizione d'arte." Maurizio Vitale has noted that certain "pretensioni di cultura che, pur sul fondo dimesso di quella prosa d'andamento spontaneo e popolare e di carattere idiomatico . . . animano il cantastorie letterato con *una ricerca lessicale più varia.*"[18] This subject itself is worthy of study; however, to date no one has undertaken a systematic description of Andrea's language.

Andrea achieved a certain stylistic "decorum" through a varied use of registers, shaped according to the particular narrative needs of a passage.[19] Although a few critics have found Andrea's prose somewhat monotonous, most consider it economical, expressive, and fluid.[20] The following description of a combat is illustrative of Andrea's ability to keep the action moving. This is achieved by the number and variety of verbs in conjunction with the breathless onrush of subordinate clauses:

> Preso del campo, e' due franchi singnori si dierono delle lance sì gran colpi che passarono gli scudi e parte dell'arme, e ruppono le lance, e aurtoronsi, e caddono per terra e' cavalli e ' singnori. Ritto, Almonte trasse Durindarda, e Carlo trasse Gioiosa, e cominciarono tanto terribile

battaglia che era una maraviglia, e gran pezo durò, sì che amendue
trassudavano, sì che l'arme tutte sudavano di sudore, e l'uno non
vantaggiava l'altro, e molto si travagliavano l'uno l'altro, e si rom-
pevano gli scudi in braccio e tagliavansi l'arme, e in molte parte si
ferivano, per modo che ongnuno sanguinava aspramente. (**A** 146)

Andrea's prose is richer in realistic elements than that of his chivalric
models.[21] The sense of the quotidian, complex intrigues, and psychological realism of certain non-epic episodes have been compared to Boccaccio's
novelle.[22] This tendency may be found in earlier prose romances, such as
the fourteenth-century *Fioravante*, and therefore cannot be considered
unique to Andrea. For example, the episode in which the young Fioravante
cuts off the beard of his fencing teacher who snored too loudly during a
riposo is found in both *Reali* (146–47) and *Fioravante* (367). This infu-
sion of realism from the *novella* and a shift in tone, which the Old French
epic underwent in Italy, allowed a greater degree of psychological validity
in chivalric literature, a trend in which Andrea fully participated. His penchant for historical, geographical, and genealogical verisimilitude extended
to his psychological portrayals as well. This trait alone demands from scholars a better appreciation of Andrea's work.[23] Perhaps nowhere do Charlemagne's youthful adventures find better expression than in his prose.[24]
The following examples illustrate the range of psychological verisimilitude in Andrea's narratives. In the first example, the young king Aluigi
touchingly comforts his regent Guglielmo, who has just received word of
an impending war:

E mentre che leggevano il breve giunse Aluigi, e videgli molto turbati.
Disse Aluigi: "O conte Guglielmo, perché siete voi così turbati?"
Rispuose Guglielmo: "O figliuolo mio delle fortune, la paura, ch'io
òne, che la tua persona non riceva impedimento, è quello che mi fa
turbare, pensando a quanto pericolo tu se'." Disse Aluigi: "O Guglielmo,
non vi isgomentate; se Iddio mi dona grazia ch'io venga sì grande
ch'io pigli la signoria, ancora ve lo meriterò." Guglielmo lagrimò per
tenerezza, e abbracciollo, e baciollo, e benedisselo. (**N** 1: 288)

In another scene, Ugo's vassal registers various emotional responses, ranging from shock and fear to joy and relief, upon discovering his lord's mi-
raculous return from Hell:

Gualtieri riguardò all'uscio, e quello vidde aprire, e vide uscire Ugo in
sull'uscio; il che di subito stimò che fusse spirito che avesse presa quella
forma per ingannarlo e mettergli paura; e spaventato, segnossi il viso,

e volea fuggire; ma Ugo lo chiamò, dicendo: "Gualtieri, non temere, che io sono Ugo tuo signore." Gualtieri pure si fuggiva, e Ugo seguitandolo lo prese, e confortatolo lo rassicurò; e quando Gualtieri fue certificato ch'egli era Ugone, non ebbe mai la maggiore allegrezza: e abbracciatolo, lo teneva stretto; no·llo potea per tenerezza lasciare, baciandolo, versando infinite lagrime; e non poteva per tenerezza parlare. (**Z** 2: 188–89)

A third example, remarkably modern in its content, articulates a son's love for his mother as well as the repressed filial desire to kill the primal father, which Freud theorized.[25] Namieri, who has been cursed by his father, Amerigo, and exiled, receives a message from his mother. He now wishes he had slain his father in an earlier duel when he had the chance:

Disse Aliscardo: "O Namieri, la tua madre Almingarda mi disse, ch'io te la raccomandassi, ch'ella non fu cagione di cacciarti di Nerbona, e ch'ella ti portò nove mesi nel suo ventre; e mandatisi raccomandando per l'amore di Dio, e per l'amore madernale, e pel latte, che del suo petto cavasti." Queste parole feceno tanto intenerire Namieri, ch'egli gittò grosse lagrime, non per l'amore paternale, ma per l'amore della madre. Nondimeno tanto potè l'odio del padre, che vinse l'amore maternale, e disse: "O Aliscardo, quanta pena m'à dato il traditore Amerigo colla sua maladizione, che sono sei anni ch'io non ò dormito in terra murata, . . . volesse Iddio quando mi provai con lui ch'io l'avessi ferito col ferro con tutta mia possa, che questo non mi sarebbe intervenuto!" (**N** 1: 168–69)

One also finds evidence that Andrea's literary interests extended beyond his chivalric sources. Episodes in which a departing hero forsakes his beloved recall Vergil's Aeneas. The suicide of Fegra Albana (**F** 127) clearly echoes that of Dido. Classical allusions and similes abound in Andrea's cycle:[26]

Non fu già mai tale nè simile battaglia al tempo de' Troiani, quando e' Greci disfeciono Troia la grande. (**A** 197)
è più forte che Achille, o Ettorre, o Trojolo, o Paris . . . (**Z** 1: 268)
Quale Achille dice Omero, quale Ettor dice Dares, quale Orlando dice Turpino . . . arebbe potuto vantaggiare Mirabello? (**E** 2: 115)

Andrea's classicism is especially evident in *Ugone* when the hero, guided through Hell by Aeneas and William of Orange, encounters numerous mythological and legendary figures of antiquity: "Giunse su per la riva uno dimonio, che pareva mezzo uomo et mezzo cavallo, et aveva uno arco in mano; . . . e vidde Enea, onde gli tirò l'arco gridando: 'O traditore figliuolo d'Anchise, io t'ho pur giunto! et poi terrotti in Corcido [Cocito], dov'è Antenore, che fue tuo compagno a tradire lo Re Priamo!'" (**Z** 2: 98–99). A similar use of verse dense with classical names may be found in the *cantare* signed "Maestro Andrea."[27] Although the *Aeneid* and other classical texts had long since been translated into the vernacular and circulated in the fourteenth century, extended displays of material from antiquity are rare in contemporary *cantari*. This remarkable similarity may signal that Andrea was the author of both the verse sections in *Ugone* and of the unedited *cantare*.

Unlike other contemporary Tuscan authors who dealt with Carolingian cycle material, Andrea includes numerous quotations from Latin liturgical and devotional discourse in *Ugone* and *Guerrino*. Although these texts (the Sanctus of the Mass, the Seven Penitential Psalms, hymns, and prayers) would have been well known to any Catholic layman of Andrea's day, it is unusual to find these pious phrases included in an otherwise secular literary form. This tendency, begun in *Ugone*, reappears with more flourishes in *Guerrino*: "Te Deum laudamus" (**Z** 1: 315, 2: 217; **B** 98r); "Nunc dimittis servum tuum, Domine" (**Z** 1: 333); "Gloria in excelsis Deo" (**Z** 1: 333); "Ecce quam bonum et quam jucundum fratres in unum" (**Z** 2: 32). The hero repeats the formula "Gesu nazareno Cristo, nel tuo nome *salvum me fach*" on numerous occasions to protect himself from his demonic guides during his trip through Purgatory and Hell (**B** 89v–98r). The more beneficent spirits of Purgatory and Paradise sing various praises:

"Miserere nobis domine secondo mangnia(m) misericordia(m) tuam."
(**B** 91r)
"Salve regina [mater] misericordia vita." (**B** 91v)
"Osanna inn excielsis deo." (**B** 91v)
"Padre del cielo et dio, miserere nobis." (**B** 92r)
"Domine sante pater onnipotens etterne deus." (**B** 93v)
"Domine ne in furore tuo arguas me." (**B** 98r)
"Santus, santus, santus, dominus deo sabaoch plenin sun cieli e terra. Osanna in excielsis. Benedictus qui venit in nomine domini." (**B** 100r)
"Consumatum este." (**B** 100r)
"Eccie ancilla domini." (**B** 100r)

Not only do Andrea's literary models and linguistic choices reflect his wide interests, but the numerous orations in his texts reveal a quasi-humanistic appreciation of the arts of rhetoric.[28] Andrea may have derived such passages from Boccaccio's *Teseida*[29] or directly from Statius. Alongside other attributes of military leaders and ambassadors he praises their elegant speaking: "molto bello parlatore" (**A** 60), "savio e nobile parlatore" (**A** 179), "serenissimo oratore" (**N** 2: 112). In the tradition of the good Saladin, Saracens as well as Christians are endowed with this ability.[30] An example of this ethnic balance is found in *Nerbonesi*, Book V, where two formal addresses by Guglielmo encouraging his forces to rally and fight are directly paralleled by a Saracen lord urging his own people to withstand the invasion by the Christian army.[31] The following example is typical of the elevated passages often found in the mature works of Andrea:

> "O traditori, non tanto contro a' Nerbonesi, quanto contro al vostro sangue medesimo! Ch'avia fatto a voi la gestra [gesta] di Nerbona? Non vi rammentate che la spada de' Nerbonesi rimise Carlo in sedia? E non vi rammenta ch'Amerigo fu figliuolo di Bernardo da Mongrana, fratello di Gherardo da Fratta? Il quale Bernardo perdè tutta la sua signoria per servire a Carlo, e siamo privati della signoria di Borgogna, e di Provenza, e di Savoia, e di tanto reame, e quanto pericolo abbiamo portato per mantenere questo reame! E se a voi increscieva d'Aloigi, perché non pigliavate la signoria quando Carlo Magno la dava a qualunque la voleva? Ma voi, usurpatori, per superbia, e per ruberia, e per la invidia giudicasti contro alla ragione, e così comandiamo che, per amore del vostro lignaggio, voi in su la piazza di Parigi, per rimembranza, siate impiccati tutti voi quindici, e tutti quanti gli altri sieno dicollati." (**N** 1: 329)

It has been pointed out that Andrea at times employs complex Latinate periods "nei luoghi più solenni, come nelle orazioni e nelle epistole."[32] An example is "'Santissima corona, e ispada di giustizia, a cui conviene ricorrere ogni uno che à fede cristiana, io ricorro a te, come a mio signore, che mi aiuti nella mia avversità, e questa ispero che sarà il fine delle nostre guerre'" (**N** 2: 494). Normally, however, Andrea's syntax is simpler, resembling the freshness and directness of a storyteller: "Lo 'mperadore rispose che non farebbe niente sanza il suo consiglio" (**B** 11r). Elsewhere, Andrea crafts more formal speeches for his protagonists:

> "O charissimo fratello, se ll'animo mio fusse dato a cchupidità di singnioria, chrede la tua mente che ll'animo mio avesse pensiero del mio padre? Cierto no; ma, dimi, Allessandro, la singnioria di questo rengno, come mi potrebbe rendere il mio padre il quale io voglio ciercare [per essere certo] di che sangue io sono. E sse io per questo sto pensoso perché non so quale si sia d'esso, quanto maggiormente debbo pensare

che tu m'ài honorato e affrancato di suggiettitudine, e amo più la tua persona che me medesimo! Come torre' io lo 'mperio a tte, nato di così gientile sangue, etd io non so ch'io mi sia?" (**B** 15r and **G** 23r)

In another passage, an imprisoned hero apostrophizes his absent family members: "'Oimè, padre mio, io t'andava cercando per lo mondo! O nobile sventurato padre Ajolfo, tu non sai e non credi che sieno vivi e' tuoi figliuoli. . . . Oimè, Mirabello, fratello mio, tu se' in Francia co' nostri parenti, ed io . . . sono in Trebusonda in prigione, e miseramente morrò! O dolce madre mia Lionida, con quanti dolori ci partoristi nella torre di Losanna; e nella torre di Trebusonda finirò la mia giovane vita!'" (**E** 2: 53–54). These shifts in register provide a stylistic variety that is nonexistent in *cantare* literature.

Another trait that sets Andrea apart from "popular" authors of his day is an elemental courtliness in the presentation of his material.[33] The inclusion of romance was not an innovation on Andrea's part: the amorous component of the Matter of Britain had long since found its way into the more warlike narrations of the Matter of France. However, the sensitive and humane manner in which Andrea treats these love stories charm the reader.[34] Having eradicated *luxuria* from most of these relationships, or condemning it when it occurs, Andrea creates romantic encounters between women and men (of various ages, races, and creeds) that are truly ideal. In the tradition of the ancient Greek romances, these contain moments of great tenderness, enacted by couples of genteel lineage and delicate sensibilities who comport themselves nobly despite many obstacles. Here follows the endearing portrait of Alda and Orlando's first meeting, which takes place during a magnificent feast at Gherardo's palace in "Vienna":

E quando ebbono presso che desinato giunse in sala una sorella [Alda] di quello giovinetto [Ulivieri], sonando dolcemente una arpa. . . . Ed era allora Alda d'età di dodici anni. E giunta dinanzi a Carlo, gli fece tanta gentile riverenza che Carlo rise e dielle la sua benedizione, e baciolle la fronte. . . . Orlando, vedendo Alda tanto bella, infiammò del suo amore, e non le poteva levare occhio da dosso, ma tanto si temeva che Carlo non se ne avedesse, che spesso abassava gli ochi in terra, e tanto l'accese l'amore d'Alda ch'egli stava come uomo fuori di sé. E non fu persona che se ne avedesse se non la fanciulla medesima. (**A** 254–55)

A similar scene had appeared in the fourteenth-century prose *Aspramonte*, but Andrea handles it more skillfully.[35] Here, the lovely music and the beautiful appearance of the young girl, the emperor's delighted reaction, the timidity of the young Orlando—previously shown in a fierce fight for Carlo's life—and the understated final comment on Alda's recognition of his love have a cumulatively pleasing effect upon the reader.

Andrea was cognizant of contemporary street singers who treated the same battles and adventures of the Paladins. Although his language at times echoes the conventional formulae in ottava rima versions of these tales, in some cases Andrea has expanded them to create his own phraseology. Maria Cabani, in her compendium of *cantare* formulae, has identified certain "formule di tipo esclamativo" ("Oh quanto," for example, "Deh quante" and "Ahi quanti"):

> *Oh quanto* fu quel drapel <crudo e> fello
>   (Fassò, XXIII, 40, 5)
> *Deh quante* spade vediesi menare
>   (*Spagna*, XXXII, 22, 1)
> *Ahi quanti* traean guai ad alta voce
>   (*Spagna*, XXXIV, 26, 6)[36]

It appears that Andrea developed these interjections into more detailed, emotional ones of his own. The fact that he was writing in prose and therefore not bound by line length or rhyme scheme facilitated these innovations. One such recurrent phrase expresses the author's empathy with the mothers and wives of men who were being cruelly butchered in battle:

> O quante povere madre perdevano i loro figliuoli! Oh quante donne rimanevano vedove! (**F** 97)
> O quante madre perdevano e' loro figliuoli, e vedove rimanevano! (**A** 199)
> Oh quante misere madre perdevano e' loro allattati figliuoli! Oh quante donne rimanevano vedove! Oh quanti rimanevano popilli del loro padre! (**A** 123)
> O quante misere madri perdevano i loro figliuoli, e quante i loro fratelli, e loro mariti, e padri! (**N** 1: 507–8).[37]

The particular inclusion of the mothers' lamentations may be derived from a similar passage in Boccaccio (*Tes.*, VIII, 100).

Another expression that occurs frequently in Andrea is a clause introduced with *cioè* to gloss an unusual word or concept or simply to reinforce the word's presence in the narration. Such glosses—actually a type of authorial interjection—reflect Andrea's concern for precise descriptions and further enhance the verisimilar tone of his prose:

> scudi d'oro . . . cioè monete chiamate scudi . . . (**A** 287; cf. **N** 1: 263)
> questo gonfalone, cioè una bandiera de l'arme sua . . . (**N** 2: 254)
> nell'ultime parte d'Italia, cioè nella Chalavria . . . (**U** 67r)
> impiccare su per le rovere, cioè su per le quercie . . . (**E** 1: 137)
> del formento, cioè del grano . . . (**E** 1: 145)
> sonò lo squillone, cioè la campana del dì . . . (**E** 1: 303)[38]

Although this sort of "formula" may seem unremarkable, among contemporary *cantari* and *romanzi* examined for this study analogous glosses using *cioè* appear only twice (*Fior.*, 337, 356). Of these two occurrences, the second may well be a self-correction by the copyist.[39]

A final example to illustrate Andrea's adaptation of *cantastorie* phraseology is the interlace formula *Torna la storia*.[40] One finds only two similar phrases in other Tuscan Carolingian material prior to or contemporary with Andrea: "Torna a seguitare di" and "Alla mia storia torna seguitando" (*Orl.*, XLVI, 2, 8, LI, 2, 8).[41] Once again, this expression may not seem individualistic enough to be considered representative of a single author; however, despite a function identical to formulae in other Italian chivalric texts, *Torna la storia* appears to be used only by Andrea.

Vandelli has noted Andrea's normal clarity in ordering his material: "Si pensi ora allo studio costante di Andrea da Barberino di concatenare strettamente e logicamente le varie parti della narrazione."[42] The division of texts into books and chapters according to their content is consistent throughout Andrea's work. The formal balance he achieves by tailoring content to chapter divisions is comparable to that of the Ariostan octave. In addition, chapters may at times be united by their related contents to form dyads or small groups within a book. Often an expository chapter (an embassy, a declaration of war, the mobilization of an army, a conspiracy, political negotiations, or a parliamentary debate) prepares for the more action-filled events narrated in the next chapter or chapters. For example, *Reali*, Book IV, chapter 67, describes a rally of troops prior to battle while the encounter itself takes place entirely in chapter 68. Conspirators plot against the young Carlo's life in *Reali*, Book VI, chapter 37, and put their plan into action in chapter 38. In this manner, the chapters' pacing and complementary content create internal rhythms within the work itself. Often the slower tempo of one chapter filled with meticulous description erupts into a burst of energy at the beginning of the next, and the latter's quickened tempo will then be continued throughout. The *temps morts* in Andrea (such as enumerating battalions) must be viewed as pauses necessary to sustain the excitement and suspense of a lengthy narration. The modern reader must learn to understand the clues encoded within a narrative to better appreciate its structuring. The sudden appearance of several new knights, for example, signals the reader that a battle of some consequence is in the making and creates a certain suspense. If we approach the text the way medieval readers might have, many modern critical objections to Andrea's art collapse.

Just as chapters are divided based on content, larger formal divisions follow the exigencies of the ongoing narrative logic. Many chapters that comprise single battles conclude quite naturally as the champions return to their domiciles, exhausted troops eat, tend their wounds, and relax. A longer campaign concludes logically with the description of its aftermath. Thus, a series of chapters or an entire book may end with the retreat of the conquered, the realistic details of burying or burning the dead, and celebration by the victors. These celebrations are often emotionally heightened by a marriage or a coronation. Episodes of peace and domestic tranquility are not unknown. In these narrative pauses, new spouses often conceive the next generation of heroes, knights and ladies participate in various courtly *divertissements*, and the traitorous few plot some new mischief against the heroes. Such tranquil moments between wars or adventures are generally brief, perhaps because idleness was viewed as dangerous: "Ma la contastante fortuna e gl'invidiosi fatti delle cose del mondo, apparecchiati di dare mutamento alle cose, subito turbarono el felicie piacere d'Ajolfo" (**E** 2: 94).[43]

It is also possible to identify internal rhythms within the prose itself. Frequently chapters open with a past participle or a gerund that summarizes an action just completed or under way. This provides both a sense of closure, insofar as the first action mentioned may be connected to events in the preceding chapter, and an engaging introduction to the material of the chapter that follows. Yet, even while looking back to previous events, such an opening acts as a "mainspring" that not only propels the first period of the new chapter but unleashes the narrative energy necessary to sustain the momentum of the whole chapter:

> Essendo apparita la mattina, Amerigo comandò ch'eglino andassino a uno suo giardino . . . (**N** 1: 51)
> Cercando l'abate con questi sei l'ostiere, 'l cattivo Namieri era molto adirato . . . (**N** 1: 61)
> Partito Ugieri Danese dalla corte, poco istante i sei figliuoli d'Amerigo si mossono dal palagio d'Orlando . . . (**N** 1: 72)

In these passages a subordinate action is briefly alluded to before a second, predominant one supersedes it, creating a sense of urgency and tension in the succession of competing verbs.

Although verbs function admirably to keep the story moving, polysyndeton in Andrea's periodic construction may have the opposite effect for the reader unfamiliar with this common medieval practice: "'Carissimi fratelli, per la grazia di Maometto voi m'avete eletto per vostro imperadore e fatto singnore d'Asia e d'Africa; e sono passati sette anni che noi abbiamo con ongni studio racolta e bandita questa oste, e abbiamo tutta questa vernata tenuto campo fermo a quest città, la quale ancora si difende; e non veggio modo che per forza d'arme noi la possiamo avere'" (**A** 34). It is difficult to attribute polysyndeton to a particular author's style, since conjunctions can be quite easily inserted in the copying process.

Many of these stylistic components (classical allusions, formulae, rhetorical and Latinate constructions) exist in other late medieval texts, and their incorporation or application differs from author to author. Thus, determining "style" becomes a matter of identifying to what degree standard narrative or linguistic traits were incorporated or omitted in a given author's works. Two hallmarks of Andrea's style are verisimilitude and detail, with the second supporting though not depending on the first. The use of a "precise" time span, of a genealogical framework, of a global geography, and of naturalistic physical and psychological details creates a vast canvas on which conventional characters and events are painted. The magnitude of Andrea's accomplishment is enhanced by his variety of tone and lexicon. Popular elements are harmoniously juxtaposed with semierudite ones. Episodes of fierce battle are interspersed with examples of genteel courtliness. The reader familiar with his complete cycle cannot help being impressed by the depth and scope of the fictional world presented and the care with which it is drawn.

The Case for *La Prima Spagna*

When the known works of Andrea are viewed as a whole, one senses his authorial intent to create a huge cycle formed as seamlessly as possible from numerous individual French and Italian models.[1] However, when only those works with sure attributions are considered, a sizable narrative gulf stands between *Aspramonte* and *Nerbonesi*. This gap would logically be filled by narrations of the first and second wars of Charlemagne in Spain. There is some indication that Andrea did compose both a "Prima Spagna" and a "Seconda Spagna." Rajna included a *Spagna* in prose in his tentative ordering of Andrea's output.[2] Unfortunately, extant evidence has not been thoroughly studied, and past attributions of such texts to Andrea are philologically untenable.

Modern awareness of the two texts begins with the historian Leopold von Ranke's early nineteenth-century discovery of a manuscript in the Albani library in Rome that contained three prose epics, an *Aspramonte*, a *Prima Spagna*, and a *Seconda Spagna*, copied contiguously.[3] Upon the dispersal of the Albani collection, this manuscript was regrettably lost at sea while being transferred to Germany.[4] However, sets of rubrics for the first two texts had luckily been copied in 1849 and were published by Michelant ("Titoli"). By comparing the first set with surviving exemplars of Andrea's *Aspramonte*, Boni ascertained that the initial text in the Albani manuscript was without doubt Andrea's (*Aspramonte*, ed. Boni, xxiv–xxv). For the other two texts the lost manuscript contained, the task of identifying their contents is more difficult. All that remains of the *Prima Spagna* is the transcribed rubrics; the *Seconda Spagna*'s rubrics and text have been lost.

Andrea was cognizant of the pivotal Spagna story. Internal evidence suggests that he was already well acquainted with it by the time he wrote *Nerbonesi*. In this text, a description of festive tapestries includes among the subjects depicted the entire Carolingian cycle up to that point in the story (**N** 1: 351–53). A long section referring to *Reali* pertains only to that text's sixth book, the so-called Mainetto. This particular content directly recalls the opening rubric of the lost Albani codex: "Inchominciasi la honorata storia ch'è chiamata l'Aspramonte che fue dopo el libro chiamato el Mainetto che fue el sezo libro de' Reali di Francia."[5] Like Andrea, the writer of the Albani rubrics conceived of the Spagna cycle as beginning not with the obvious first war in Spain and defeat at Roncisvalle, but with young Carlo's years of exile in Spain, a time in which "lo re di Spagna, chiamato Galaffo, era servito da Carlo Magno alla tavola; cioè *quando Carlo era piccolo*" (**N** 1: 351; emphasis added).

Careful scrutiny of scant secondary testimonies yields evidence that the lost *Prima Spagna* could have been composed by Andrea. From Ranke's comment that the entire Albani manuscript numbered "nearly" 400 folios ("Zur Geschichte," 163), we can estimate the length of the lost *Prima Spagna*. Subtracting the average length of *Aspramonte* (147 fols.) and the length of the *Seconda Spagna* found in BNCF II.I.15 (26 fols.) from a generous 400-folio total, one attains 227 folios as the maximum length possible. Although variables (Ranke's imprecise estimate, variation in scribal hands, blank folios or lacunae, and so on) prohibit a definite conclusion, it is probable that the lost *Prima Spagna* numbered at least 100 folios. Given that there were 188 chapters, the total length could easily have reached 150 folios. This would have been considerably longer than *Ugone* and either shorter than, or approximately equal in length to, *Aspramonte*. The higher number (227 fols.) is also conceivable, given that several exemplars of *Guerrino* range from 190 to 209 folios with one imperfect manuscript (Ricc. 1921) containing 227 extant folios. Thus, the length of the lost text was well within the norms set by Andrea's other narratives.

Surviving data for the Albani manuscript support the hypothesis that Andrea was the author of these texts. This was not an isolated instance of chivalric works by one author existing side by side in a single codex: the two prose romances edited by Ceruti from Ambros. C 35 Sup. present a similar case. Their stylistic, linguistic, and narrative elements, as well as a reference to *Acquisto* in the fourth chapter of *Seconda Spagna*, suggest that they are by the same anonymous author.[6] Similarly, several codices of Andrea's texts contain multiple exemplars: BNCF II.I.14 preserves *Reali* and *Aspramonte; Nerbonesi* and *Ugone* are copied in sequence in Vatican, Barb. lat. 4140; Laur. Redi 177; and Parma, Pal. 32.[7] In each of these cases, the works paired are known to be by Andrea.

Next, one must consider the date of the lost Albani manuscript. At first glance, a date of 1508 (or 1509, a possible transcription error) may seem too late to be authoritative. Yet dated manuscripts of Andrea's known epic romances were copied as late as 1493 for *Aspramonte*, 1511 for *Ugone*, and 1534 for *Nerbonesi* (see Appendix A). Thus, the date of copying for the lost Albani texts is also within an acceptable range of probabilities.

Colophon evidence is still more striking. A Laurentian exemplar of *Nerbonesi* (Plut. XLIII, 18) was copied by "bartolomeo di franc(esc)o di bartolomeo cimatore" (122r). The lost Albani manuscript was copied by one "Francesco di Bartolommeo Cimatore," according to Ranke ("Zur Geschichte," 163). The nineteenth-century transcription of the rubrics states that it was "chopiato per me Bartolomeo di Franco Cimatore."[8] The form "Franco" was no doubt a careless transcription of the common contemporary abbreviation for "Francesco" as used in the Laurentian manuscript. This suggests that Cimatore was an admirer of Andrea, probably assembling a collection of his epic romances as time permitted. This is not the only case of multiple copies of Andrea's works being owned by the same person. For instance, a certain Giordano di Michele Giordani copied an *Ugone* (BNCF II.II.59) and a complete *Rinaldo* in prose (Laur. Plut. XLII, 37 and Ricc. 1904).[9] Like the Albani manuscript's scribe, the copyist of Plut. XLIII, 18 showed a concern for precise dating, including even the hour in his colophon: "chominciato a scrivere di mia propia mano a dì 20 di giugnio a ore dua di notte, e 'l detto libro fue finito a dì 20 di ottobre 1504 a ore 23 e 1/2,e chominciossi chome è detto di sopra nel 1504" (122r).

With regard to the provenance of the manuscript and the citizenship of its copyist, available data from Plut. XLIII, 18 are inconclusive. The single watermark found throughout (Briquet, 4411) dates after 1460 but has several identical varieties ranging from Rome (1460–65) to Florence (1496). Although it seems likely from the language and style of production that Cimatore was Florentine or, at any rate, Tuscan, he may have had personal or commercial connections with the other Italian cities indicated by the paper (Macerata, Volterra, Naples, Udine). He probably belonged to a family of tradesmen as his name suggests. Via dei Cimatori, which still exists, was constructed in the historic center of Florence in 1301, and by 1381, there were two Cimatori inscribed in the Arte della Lana.[10]

Finally, one must consider the explicit attribution of authorship within codices. Many surviving exemplars give Andrea's name as translator or author, but this is not always the case. Complete, undamaged manuscripts of the widely circulated *Guerrino* that do not name Andrea include Ricc. 2266 and 2432; Paris, B.N. fonds ital. 491 and 98 (the two parts of one complete *Guerrino*); and Bodleian canon. ital. 27. Copies of *Aspramonte* in which Andrea is not identified within the original text or colophon include Biblioteca Angelica 2263; Ricc. 2308, 2309, and 2410; Biblioteca Moreniana, Frullani 12; BNCF II.II.56; and BNCF Pal. 583 and 677. The question of a text's authorship should not be avoided merely because its exemplar has not been conveniently labeled in a near-contemporary hand. Even when contemporary attributions within manuscripts do occur, they must be viewed with caution, as in the case of the *Credo* and the *Sette salmi penitenziali,* once erroneously attributed to Dante.[11] To formulate an attribution, one must examine internal evidence furnished by the text itself.

How might the content of a *Prima Spagna* have fit into Andrea's cycle of works? In the *Nerbonesi* tapestry description, the summary of events from *Reali,* Book VI, is followed by that of *Aspramonte.* The description of the battle against Troiano leads directly into an abbreviated account of Carlo's first war in Spain. Although the *explicit* of *Aspramonte* announces "el libro chiamato il Meschino di Durazzo," its final two chapters—both extremely short—could have been later additions. In fact, the end of chapter 157 (ed. Boni) acts as a sort of "first conclusion" and prepares a sequel that would have treated the first war in Spain: "E alla Penticosta tutti e' baroni giurarono d'essere con Orlando a 'cquistare la corona di Spangna." It may be that the *Prima Spagna* did not enjoy a great reception and that Andrea or later scribes appended the more successful *Guerrino* as the new continuation of *Aspramonte.*

The résumé of the war in Spain found in *Nerbonesi* proves Andrea's awareness of that cycle and matches the content of the lost *Prima Spagna* rubrics, but the information provided is so general that any connection to Andrea's oeuvre is hardly conclusive (**N** 1: 352). Furthermore, *La Spagna* existed in several Italian versions in verse and prose: *L'Entrée d'Espagne, La Prise de Pampelune, Li Fatti de Spagna,* and the verse *Spagna.* Catalano assumed that the lost Albani *Spagna* must have been identical with the unedited Laur. Med. Pal. CI, 3 because the rubrics of the former paralleled the content of the latter.[12] Yet mere similarity of content is not enough to establish identity of a text. For example, *Fioravante* was a direct model for Andrea's *Reali,* but differences occur even within the "same" story. Furthermore, detailed studies of allusions contained in Med. Pal. CI, 3 have shown that its author was directly inspired by both *Reali* and *Aspramonte* and was therefore someone writing after Andrea.[13] More important, the style and language of Med. Pal. CI, 3 do not resemble Andrea's.[14] This example demonstrates the pedestrian and almost comic tone in dialogue given to the arch-traitor Gano: "'Io non sono però sì forte da me che io pottesi chonttradire a la pottençia dello re Charlo, e perrò mi chonviene chiudere gli ochi e inghiottire di questi bochoni'."[15] The Gano of Andrea— and indeed of most fifteenth-century Italian narrators—never quails before Carlo.

More significant is the presence in *Prima Spagna* rubrics of unusual names and minor characters that display direct links to other works by Andrea. Affumato is the nickname of the youthful hero Aiolfo (**E** 1: 8, 13, 16). In each instance, the term is used as a proper name.[16] Among other chivalric texts examined the word occurs only once (in Add. 10808, 89v) and clearly as an adjective. The appearance of the appellation l'Affumato in *Prima Spagna* is therefore of primary importance in establishing a link to Andrea: "E' Saracini erono tutti sbigottiti per lla forza dello *assumato*" (chap. 95). The misspelling of unusual proper names on first occurrence is a well-known phenomenon in the medieval scribal process. In this case, the similarity of the *s/f* lettering in late medieval cursive hands may also have accounted for the error. In the rubric to chapter 100, the copyist or transcriber spells the name correctly: "ragionoro[no] di torre *l'Affumato* al loro soldo." In both rubrics the use of this adjective as a proper name parallels its usage in *Aiolfo*.

The second remarkable correspondence concerns a son of King Salamone of Brettagna. In *Reali*, this character's name appears in a punning etymology: "di Salamone nacque Liones, ma per l'uso dell'arco fu chiamato *Achiron*" (567). However, no such son of Salamone exists, according to the chanson de geste tradition. The nickname Achiron (Chiron) is found only in Andrea, thus furnishing another important clue to the authorship of the lost *Prima Spagna*. The rubric for chapter 144 had read "*Chironn* figliuolo di Salamone." This character is further identified as "*Chiron* che Charllo lascio luoggotenente di Parigi" (chap. 138). He also serves as ambassador to Marsilio (**PS**, chaps. 144–47). These functions correspond to the tripartite role of Ghione in the verse *Spagna*: he is son of Salamone, lieutenant at Paris, and ambassador to Marsilio.[17] Although the author of *Prima Spagna* and Andrea were both familiar with the same source text, the name change Ghione > Chiron occurs only in Andrea. This could have resulted either from a misreading of the model or from the deliberate importation of the classical name by a learned author.

Classical and medieval sources for the name Chirone were readily available to Andrea. The notion that Chiron raised Achilles appears throughout the *Achilleid* by Statius, a copy of which Andrea owned; in Dante's *Commedia* (*Inf.*, XII, 71); and in Boccaccio's *Teseida* (VIII, 56, 1–2). Any of these may have inspired Andrea's portrayal of this character (**E** 2: 101–2).

Both Chiron and Achilles are mentioned in the *cantare* attributed to Andrea.[18] The insertion of the classical name Chiron into the Carolingian cycle and its specific application to identify the son of Salamone are persuasive evidence that Andrea was author of the lost *Prima Spagna*.

Other genealogical relationships peculiar to Andrea's conception of the cycle are reflected in the *Prima Spagna* rubrics. The identification of Liones/Chiron with the "gesta de' Reali di Brettagna," a minor house in Andrea's vast construction, provides a blood tie between this son of Salamone and the Ansuigi who becomes king of Spain (discussed in the next chapter). According to the genealogy given at the end of *Reali*, Chiron and Ansuigi are first cousins. Regarding Ansuigi's link to the Breton dynasty, the rubric for chapter 183 states that the newly elected king of Spain was "Ansuigi di ripess di Brettagnia." Thus, even in its smallest detail, the *Prima Spagna* apparently matched information found in *Reali, Nerbonesi,* and the attributed *Ansuigi*. No other Italian author preserved this lineage for Ansuigi.

In addition to similarities of plot and characters, the lost *Prima Spagna* shares specific narrative motifs with the known works of Andrea. Heraldry was a conventional feature in medieval texts long before Andrea. Various devices, especially for the more famous knights, were dictated by tradition. Like Andrea, the *Prima Spagna* author knew and included the standard emblems such as "Oro e fiamma," the sacred banner of Christendom carried by Carlo's armies against the Saracens, and the "quartieri d'Orllando" (rubric, chap. 106).[19] When treating this material, the author of *Prima Spagna* acknowledges his debt to tradition, but a keen sense of detail provokes him to add a qualifier: "Ansuigi si messe in sulla torre una bandiera a quartieri, *ma non chome quella d'Orllando*" (chap. 113, emphasis added). This type of statement is also characteristic of Andrea, who often adjusted his models for verisimilitude and was ever concerned with "accuracy" in his narration. Like Andrea, the author of the lost *Prima Spagna* may have felt compelled to maintain the notion of a *bandiera a quartieri* from his model, but his strong sense of "factuality" nevertheless demanded a gloss.

The same desire for verisimilitude is reflected in pragmatic references to burials and cremations of the dead after tremendous battles; these are used regularly by Andrea and are also found in *Prima Spagna*. The funerary topos exists in contemporary chivalric texts, but in less detail. One text even suggests the inevitable fate of corpses left on the battlefield:

Avendogli e' Cristiani messi in rotta,
facien per corvi e per avoltoi pasto.
    (*Spagna*, XXXIII, 22, 4–5)

The treatment in other texts mainly addresses the burial of Christian bodies
and does not treat Saracen dead.[20] By contrast, Andrea, concerned with
quotidian details, frequently describes how the dead are cared for "perché
non corrompessino l'aria."[21] Such passages may have been inspired by
Boccaccio's *Teseida* (II, 51, 1–2, X, 3) or by Statius's *Thebaid* (XII, 712):
"comandorono che 'l paese fusse *netto* de' corpi morti" (**F** 141). Obse-
quies chosen are appropriate to the rank of the deceased. At times Andrea
makes a further differentiation according to faith: "Guglielmo ordinò ch'e'
corpi morti de' cristiani fussono onorati di sepoltura, e i saraini fussono
consumati per fuoco" (**N** 2: 298 n. 2).[22] Remarkably, the *Prima Spagna*
rubrics include two generic references to cleaning the battlefields after
major encounters and one specific mention of cremating Saracens:

> fece nettare la chanpagnia di morti ... (chap. 101)
> fue sgombetta di morti la pianura ... (chap. 109)
> e' Sarracini per fuocho consumati ... (chap. 177)

The first of these includes the verb *nettare*, related to the adjective found
in the citation from *Reali;* the third closely resembles the language of the
Nerbonesi passage. Therefore, with regard to language and narrative details, it again appears that the lost *Prima Spagna* could have been composed by Andrea.

Another motif that the *Prima Spagna* rubrics share with Andrea's works
is the idea that everyone will become rich from the booty taken from
defeated opponents. Andrea uses this motif to signify a resounding Christian victory after a Saracen rout. It often accompanies the burial topos to
provide a sense of closure to important internal episodes: "Tutti i Cristiani
furono ricchi della roba de' Saracini" (**Z** 1: 166; cf. **Z** 1: 300). The division
of winnings is dependent upon the largesse of the war captain, as this
passage, the only occurrence of this motif among texts examined, illus-
trates: "E così rimase tutto il campo a Fiovo e tutto il guadagno, e donollo
a' suoi cavalieri" (*Fior.*, 349). Andrea echoes this sentiment in various passages, in the last explicitly insisting on the importance of fairly dividing
the spoils:

> dividendo il guadagno fatto fra la gente dell'arme. (**F** 204)
> fece tutto il guadangno partire tra la sua gente ... (**A** 220)

tutta la robba partirono tra lla giente . . . (**B** 70v)
lla preda fue giustamente divisa tra lla giente dell'arme. (**B** 113v)

No less than four examples of this motif are found in the *Prima Spagna* rubrics. The first states the notion of winning possessions from the defeated opponents, but not of distributing spoils among participants: "Chome Orllando . . . ordi[nò] partirsi e venire inverso Panpalona chon molta roba e sua dagniata e vettovaglia" (chap. 61). Here the meaningless "sua dagniata" is surely a transcription error. The adjective "guadagnato/a" in conjunction with various nouns is common in Andrea: "tesoro fue guadagnato" (**F** 125); "la guadangnata preda" (**A** 103); "la roba guadagnata" (**N** 2: 618). The other *Prima Spagna* examples stress the division of spoils by wise captains and explicitly describe the net effect of this action:

> Chome [Orllando] . . . chontentò tutti chol tesoro . . . (chap. 56)
> Orllando . . . divise tutto el tesoro che ogniuno avesse la sua parte. (chap. 101)
> Chome Lionagi, spartito ch'ebe el tesoro, tutti gli uomini gli volevano bene . . . (chap. 102)

The vocabulary of these citations ("roba," "tesoro," "dividere," "spartire") also bears a strong lexical resemblance to that of Andrea's recognized texts, but reveals a dissimilarity when compared to *Fioravante* ("il guadagno," "donare").

In a study of *Reali*, Forni Marmocchi has pointed out that the reference to an imperial bodyguard was peculiar to Andrea:[23] "Aveva Carlo molti nimici, ed era molto odiato, in tanto che sempre erano alla sua guardia cinquecento uomini armati" (**F** 563). His successor, even less secure, had a larger personal guard: "Lo re d'Ungheria ordinò a suo soldo diecimila cavalieri a guardia d'Aluigi. . . . El conte Guglielmo soldò quarantamila cavalieri, e tenevagli per le circustanze a vicino . . . e a Parigi teneva quegli Ungheri, e sempre continovo ventimila cavalieri alla sua guardia, e d'Aluigi" (**N** 1: 273–74). While special detachments of bodyguards for rulers do not appear in similar chivalric texts, this rare motif does occur in the *Prima Spagna* rubrics: "Chome Charllo sentì che Orllando tornava da Nobile e voleva farlo morire e armossi lui e la sua gguardia" (chap. 62).

One final narrative motif in *Prima Spagna* and in Andrea's texts demands consideration. This involves administering a curative bath to a champion after a long day of individual combat. Baths mentioned by other authors often occur under different circumstances: as prelude to *adoubement* ceremonies or for simple cleansing purposes.[24] Herbs for a bath are mentioned in the *Tris. ricc.* (125), and healing baths after tournaments in *Tris. ricc.* (60) and *Tav. rit.* (83); however, in Andrea's texts, the bath motif is bracketed by a series of other components. Two champions locked in mortal combat spend an entire day trying unsuccessfully to defeat each other. At dusk they agree to postpone the fighting until the next morning. Each hero returns to his respective camp, where he is greeted and given a healing bath. Following this, he dines and goes to bed:[25]

> Ulivieri tornò la sera nella città tutto rotto e afranto per la fatica della battaglia, . . . onde Gherardo ordinò che gli fusse fatto uno odorifero bangno, e poi che Ulivieri fu andato a dormire . . . (**A** 292)
> combatterono insino alla sera . . . e lasciarono la sera, e feciono saramento di tornare l'altra mattina. . . . E la sera fu molto onorato Rinovardo da Guglielmo, e fattogli un bagno molto confortativo, e cenato, andò a dormire. (**N** 2: 599–600)

Andrea's fully developed bath motif is included in one rubric of the lost *Prima Spagna:* "Chome Orllando fece patto chon Ferraù di ritornare l'altra mattina alla battaglia, e d'achordo si partirono; e Orllando si tornò nel champo chon grande festa ed entrò in uno bagno e poi s'andò a posare" (chap. 26).

Beyond the presence of similar narrative motifs, an important criterion for determining a text's authorship is its lexical similarity to other works. In order to demonstrate this relationship, I compared significant lexical elements in the *Prima Spagna* rubrics to those of Andrea's recognized works. Words and phrases were considered because of their stylistic uniqueness, frequency, or rarity. Having isolated these key words, I checked the sampling against a control group of non-Andrean, Tuscan texts that treat, for the most part, the same Carolingian material and that date from the Trecento or early Quattrocento. These included the anonymous chivalric romance of British Library, Add. 10808 (ed. Forni Marmocchi), *Cantari d'Aspramonte* (ed. Fassò), *I Cantari di Rinaldo* (ed. Melli), *Orlando* (ed. Hübscher), *La Rotta di Roncisvalle* and *La Spagna* (ed. Catalano), *Fioravante* (ed. Rajna), *La Tavola ritonda* (ed. Polidori), and *Il Tristano riccardiano* (ed. Parodi). Terms used regularly by other authors or that appeared in passages borrowed from Andrea were eliminated from consideration. The resultant group also contains particular words and expressions that are unusual enough to have resisted polygenetic scribal origination (see Index of Lexemes). They therefore seem to indicate conscious authorial insertion. It is important to recall that in general the lexicon of rubrics is not exceptional; hence the presence of any noteworthy items is remarkable.

Several rare words and expressions identified as belonging to Andrea's vocabulary do appear in the *Prima Spagna* rubrics. *Alloggiarsi* and *colazione* are not employed in any of the chivalric control texts, nor in the *Commedia* or the *Decameron*. The earliest documented usage of *alloggiarsi* is by Vespasiano da Bisticci, writing after Andrea (*GDLI*, 1: 332).[26] However, Andrea's known epic romances are saturated with this word. Both Andrea and the chronicler Matteo Villani used the spelling *colazione* (*GDLI*, 3: 274), and this noun is used in several of Andrea's texts.[27] The *Prima Spagna* includes both words in its rubrics ("s'alloggiò," chap. 139; "collazione," chap. 160).

Real-world terminology demonstrates an author's interest in verisimilitude and protocol. *Chapitoli*, referring to the terms of a treaty, is common in documents of the period; however, it does not appear in the chivalric texts examined.[28] The noun is in works by Andrea (**A** 253; **E** 2: 68, 69) and in the *Prima Spagna* rubric for chapter 164. Similarly, the verb "notificare," not used in control texts, the *Commedia*, the *Decameron*, or Petrarch's *Canzoniere*, appears occasionally in Andrea's works, as well as once in *Prima Spagna* ("notifichò," chap. 109).[29]

In chapter 2, we pointed out Andrea's stylistic appreciation of public speaking ability on the part of his commanders, and the many orations in his narrations. The phrase "una bella diceria" is not unique to Andrea, but its frequency in *Prima Spagna* suggests an author who, like Andrea, included many such passages to lend variety to a narrative genre in which battles predominate.[30] The inclusion of speeches proves a shared concern for historical verisimilitude (cf. *Diario*, 81). Its frequent use in this portion of Andrea's narrative cycle suggests that the lost *Prima Spagna* was designed to appear in the cycle between *Aspramonte* and *Nerbonesi*. Lexical connections of this nature could also be useful in establishing an order of composition for Andrea's works.

The *Prima Spagna* rubrics and Andrea's historically realistic texts share several terms pertaining to arms and warfare. "Metter(si) in punto" is extremely common in Andrea's battle narrations, but is not found in other chivalric texts.[31] It is used in the *Prima Spagna* rubric for chapter 88. The military title "capitano generale" or its inversion "generale capitano" is found several times in Andrea's works, but only twice in control texts and never in Dante, Petrarch, or Boccaccio.[32] The first form occurs in the *Prima Spagna* rubrics (chap. 67). A related form is found in the anonymous Florentine *Diario:* "chapitano di ghuerra generale" (97).

Gioielli, used to refer to the decorations on knights' helmets, developed from the older form "gioie." While *gioielli* is never found in Dante or Petrarch, it is used in the *Decameron,* and multiple times in most of Andrea's epic romances.[33] "Giojegli" occurs in the *Prima Spagna* rubric for chapter 121.

The noun *fibbia,* which appears in *Prima Spagna* (rubric, chap. 149), is never used in chivalric control texts nor in the works of the *Tre Corone.*[34] The employment of this homey term recalls Andrea's love of details, especially with regard to knights' apparel and the armorial accoutrements. A notable appearance of the term *fibbia* is in the dramatic conclusion of Andrea's *Aspramonte,* Book I (39).

Several expressions from the *Prima Spagna* rubrics demonstrate a similarly close connection to Andrea's lexicon. The phrase "tutte le bocche disutole" in the *Prima Spagna* (chap. 103) is related to other expressions used to describe maladroit troops in *Reali, Nerbonesi,* and *Guerrino.*[35] Although this usage does not appear in the *cantari* examined, it does belong to the lexicon of actual chronicles: the adjective with the same meaning occurs in Malispini's *Storie fiorentine* and Matteo Villani's *Cronica* (*GDLI,* 4: 836).

The expression *disfare . . . infino a' fondamenti* is a favorite of Andrea's and occurs in most of his works. It is found only once among control texts (*Fior.,* 403) and not at all in Dante, Petrarch, or Boccaccio, nor is it cited by the *GDLI.*[36] Its inclusion in the *Prima Spagna* rubrics (chap. 182) provides additional evidence to suggest Andrea was the author of that text. Similarly, *tagliare a pezzi* (used to describe furious acts of war or revenge) occurs regularly in all Andrea's works, but only four times among control texts and again in the anonymous *Diario* (30, 99, 159, 217).[37] It appears once in the *Prima Spagna* rubrics (chap. 44).

Come la cosa stava and its permutations occur throughout Andrea's proven epic romances.[38] This phrase occurs only once in the chivalric literature surveyed and once in a similar form in the *Decameron.* A variant found in *Reali, Nerbonesi,* and *Aiolfo* appears in the *Prima Spagna* rubrics: "tutta la chosa chome stava" (chap. 176).[39]

The *Prima Spagna* rubric for chapter 183 indicates a lively debate within Carlo's council of barons: "Chome lo rre Charllo fece diceria a' suoi baroni del partire o ssì o no; e poi feccion parlamento chi aveva a rimanere re di Spagnia. Chi diceva uno e chi un'altro." The phrase "Chi diceva uno e chi un'altro" certainly owes much to the conventional "intervento commentativo" found in other *cantari,*[40] but "o ssì o no" is telling, since it rarely occurs in any of the texts examined. However, the same notion of characters on the horns of a dilemma is expressed in nearly the same language elsewhere in Andrea:

Rinovardo intese le parole del padre, e *dal sì e dal no* combattia l'animo. (**N** 2: 523)
Fuvvi grande contrasto *dal sì al no.* (**N** 2: 537; used here also in a parliamentary debate)
Tutto el dì combattè *tra 'l sì e 'l no.* (**E** 1: 260; emphasis added here and above)

Finally, we recall the interlace formula apparently unique to Andrea's works, *Torna la storia.* Given that this formula appears more often within chapters than in rubrics, it is remarkable to find ample evidence of its usage in the *Prima Spagna:* seven occurrences among the rubrics.[41] Perhaps no other single piece of lexical evidence points more strongly to Andrea's being the text's author.

The Case for *Ansuigi* (*La Seconda Spagna*)

The final text in the Albani manuscript Ranke discovered was a *Seconda Spagna*. Although it has been lost and no part of it was ever recorded, a wealth of evidence suggests that this text probably corresponded to an extant *Storia di Ansuigi, re di Spagna* found in BNCF II.I.15.[1] This manuscript was copied in the second half of the fifteenth century, and before 1504. The fact that the text precedes an exemplar of *Nerbonesi* immediately calls to mind a connection to Andrea. This Tuscan prose reworking of *Anseïs de Carthage* was known to a handful of nineteenth-century scholars, but it was never published, and its attribution to Andrea has never been proven.

It is generally assumed that Andrea wrote an account of Charlemagne's second war in Spain, but the title "Seconda Spagna" has been used rather loosely to refer to any of various extant versions of the legend, in rhyme or prose. There is, for example, the prose text from Ambros. C 35 Sup. published by Ceruti under the title *La Seconda Spagna*. Although this version borrows passages verbatim from Andrea's texts, it is clearly not by him and differs considerably in content and style from *Ansuigi*.[2]

A word about titles is in order. Rajna and Brettschneider referred to the first text in BNCF II.I.15 as "l'*Ansuigi*," a name derived from the designation "Storia di Ansoigi Re di Spagna" written on the manuscript by a librarian or by someone compiling an inventory. Catalano rightly takes issue with this denomination, protesting that "*Storia del re Ansuigi* è titolo arbitrario, assegnatole da chi redasse l'indice del manoscritto."[3] However, to avoid confusion I reserve "Seconda Spagna" for the Ceruti edition; the redaction in the third part of the manuscript found by Ranke is the "Albani" or the "lost *Seconda Spagna*"; and the somewhat arbitrary title *Ansuigi* refers to the text found in II.I.15.

Before we present evidence that *Ansuigi* is by Andrea and that it probably corresponded to the lost *Seconda Spagna*, we must consider modern critical opinion and clarify some persistent misunderstandings. There was once some confusion as to the text's autonomy because a well-known manuscript, BNCF II.I.14, contains *Reali* and *Aspramonte* copied contiguously. The opening rubric of the lost Albani manuscript had also pointed out this cyclical connection: "Inchominciasi la honorata storia ch'è chiamata l'Aspramonte che fue dopo el libro chiamato el Mainetto che fue el sezo [*sic*] libro de' Reali di Francia."[4] Thus, some nineteenth-century critics considered *Aspramonte* to be Book VII of *Reali*, with the *Prima Spagna* and *Seconda Spagna* being called Books VIII and IX, respectively. This accounts for the somewhat misleading title of Michelant's article: "Titoli dei Capitoli della Storia Reali di Francia."

Gaston Paris apparently had only secondhand knowledge of the Albani manuscript, since he drew his evidence from the studies by Ranke and Michelant. Referring to Ranke's remarks on its content, Paris proposed that the *Seconda Spagna* must have corresponded to the French epic poem *Anseïs*. Next he cited Michelant's rubrics to hypothesize that the ending chapters of the *Prima Spagna* must have prepared for a Tuscan version of *Anseïs*. He noted the related content of the texts and suggested that they were originally conceived as a large cycle by a single author. In a later essay, Paris put forth a new attribution, which somewhat marred his earlier, more perceptive assessment. He rather belatedly took up Ceruti's publication of *La Seconda Spagna*, accepting it at face value as the one supposedly written by Andrea on the basis of title and similar subject matter alone.[5] This distorted view has persisted.[6] By contrast, Rajna corrected the confusion regarding the autonomy of *Reali* and *Aspramonte*. Although he accepted Paris's judgment that all three texts of the Albani codex were probably by Andrea, he proposed his own purely conjectural order of composition.[7]

Léon Gautier was familiar with II.I.15 and cited its first text as "la Storia del re Ansuigi"; however, in discussing it, he assigned the BNCF manuscript (former Magl. Cl. VI, 7) an incorrect shelfmark ("manuscrit 8"), thereby implying the existence of extant exemplars of this text. Gautier did not at first concern himself with proposing an attribution: throughout his discussion of *Nerbonesi* exemplars—many of which bear Andrea's name—he did not see fit to mention the Florentine *rédacteur*. In the subsequent volume of his work, Gautier was on firmer ground, naming Andrea as author of *Reali* and *Nerbonesi*, though still not voicing an explicit attribution for *Ansuigi*. Unfortunately, Gautier's earlier misrepresentation of the *Ansuigi-Nerbonesi* manuscript tradition was repeated by Ruggero Ruggieri: "Sta di fatto che in vari manoscritti le *Storie Nerbonesi* seguono immediatamente alla ScSp [*Seconda Spagna*]."[8] In fact, there are no other surviving cases in which the two texts are copied together.

A few other scholars have alluded to the *Ansuigi* manuscript or to a hypothetical *Seconda Spagna* by Andrea without making significant contributions toward solving the puzzle. Albertazzi, Nyrop, and Croce—following the lead of Rajna and Paris—unhesitatingly included *La Spagna* and *La Seconda Spagna* among Andrea's output. Catalano thoroughly studied all extant versions of the *Spagna* in verse and in prose, but when referring to II.I.15 calls it simply "[la] *Seconda Spagna* di Andrea da Barberino" without offering further proof of authorship.[9] In *Anseïs de Cartage*, Brettschneider examined all versions of that legend, but barely mentioned II.I.15.

Must the question of Andrea's authorship of a "Second Spain" be left to subjective speculation, often influenced by the ethnocentric viewpoints of earlier critics, or can we rigorously apply what data have come down to us to reach a philologically valid conclusion? This chapter interrogates textual and lexical evidence furnished by the extant *Ansuigi* in order to determine its possible authorship and to examine its possible rapport with the known texts of the lost Albani manuscript. Ranke's study preserves some important remarks on the content of the lost *Seconda Spagna*.[10] The lost text presented the struggle of the king whom Carlo left to defend Christian territory in Spain against Marsilio. According to Ranke, it contained "risqué spots" and "adventure"—presumably of the amorous sort—which the text later denounced as the ruin of great empires. King Agolante, who had played a large role and was killed in *Aspramonte* (218–19), reappears alive. Furthermore, in this version Marsilio does not die, but flees to Egypt. Significantly, the end of the Albani text had announced a continuation under the title "Nervonesi," an as yet unedited text that Ranke was at a loss to identify.

All these conditions of the lost text's content are met by the *Ansuigi* of II.I.15. In it, the lustful daughter of Iseres is blamed as the cause of the second war in Spain: "Per lla rabbia e falsità e tradimento d'una femina eran morti tanti singniori" (9r); "dissegli che questa era figliuola d'Iseres e ch'ell'era istata chagione di tanto male quant'era stato" (26r). Agolante's reappearance and his second death in a combat are included (3v–4v) as is a reference to the text's sequel *Nerbonesi* (26v). For the unusual event of Marsilio's flight to Egypt, return to Spain, and subsequent defeat, the *Prima Spagna* rubrics, *Ansuigi*, and *Nerbonesi* present identical versions. This occurs at the end of the Albani *Prima Spagna*, thus enabling the character's return in the *Seconda Spagna*. The description of a pavilion in *Nerbonesi* reiterates the notion of Marsilio's return and death: "e come [Marsilio] tornò [ad] assediare Ansuigi, e come Carlo gli fè tagliare la testa" (**N** 1: 352–53). This passage proves that Andrea was already acquainted with some version of *Anseïs* by the time he composed *Nerbonesi*, Book III, one that tallied with the version in the *Prima Spagna* and *Ansuigi*. Finally, the end of *Ansuigi* (II.I.15) explicitly refers to its sequel *Nerbonesi* just as the lost Albani manuscript had: "Non sse ne tratta più qui perché si chonta nel chominchiamento de' Nerbonesi che seguita dopo questo" (**S** 26v).

The probable identical versions of the second war in Spain as found in the lost *Seconda Spagna* and in *Ansuigi* argue for a possible relationship of *Ansuigi* to the *Prima Spagna*. Narrative events found in the rubrics for chapters 179–81 involve Carlo's offensive against Marsilio's realm and the latter's subsequent flight to Egypt. It is clear that the authors of both the *Prima Spagna* and *Ansuigi* rejected the version of Marsilio's death as described in the verse *Spagna* (XXXIX, 17). Similarly, both held that Marsilio fled to Egypt, only to return for the second war. The reappearance of Marsilio in *Ansuigi*, as in the lost *Seconda Spagna*, is therefore prepared.

A comparison of rubrics from the end of the lost *Prima Spagna* with the opening of *Ansuigi* shows distinct plot similarities. Both accounts state that, after the tragic defeat at Roncisvalle, Carlo learned of Gano's role in the betrayal and had him executed:

> Cap.° 178. Chome Charllo sep[p]e da lLanbarigi tutto el tradimento e chome Ghano fue poi squartato. (Michelant, "Titoli," 404)
> Dopo la rotta di Roncisval[le] e lla morte de' xij paladini di Franza al tenpo di Charlo Mangno per 'l tradimento di Ghano di Maghanza, il quale e' sopradetto Charlo fecie isquartare . . . (**S** 1r)

Carlo's reacquisition of Spain is celebrated in both the Albani rubrics and in *Ansuigi*:

> Cap.° 182. Chome Charllo rispose agli anbasciadori ed ebe la terra [di Siraggosa] . . . e poi cholla gente ch'aveva in picholo tenpo si chonquistò tutta la Spagnia ch'era sotto la signoria che teneva Marsilio. (Michelant, "Titoli," 405)
> Charlo, seguitando la vettoria de' saraini e avendo presa la Spangnia, si andò a Sanfaghonia [*sic?*], essendo in gran festa e g[i]ubillo per l'aquistato rengnio. (**S** 1r)

Another point of correspondence between the *Prima Spagna* rubrics and *Ansuigi* concerns a lesson in good government that Carlo gives

Ansuigi. The rubric to chapter 184 begins "Chome Charllo inchoronò Ansuigi della Spagnia e molto l'am[a]estrò." Although the text for the *Prima Spagna* is lost, just such a scene is portrayed in detail in *Ansuigi:* "Allora Charlo si lo fecie levar [r]itto, e fecielo singniore, e puoselo a ssedere a llato a ssé; e poi gli disse: 'Idio t'achrescha in singnioria e in baronia . . .'; e poi disse che mantenessi singnioria e giustizia a ongniuno" (**S** 1r). Later, this instruction continues more explicitly: "Charlo . . . chiamò a ssé Ansoigi e feciegli giurare di mantenere sing[n]ioria e fedeltà a ongniuno, e preghòllo che gli fossino rachomandati e' poveri popilli e vedove e fanciulli" (**S** 1v). The topos itself is an old one, already registered in the model *Anseïs,* but the linguistic similarities of this lesson in *Ansuigi* to the speech in *Nerbonesi* are too striking to be dismissed. Here, the elderly Carlo wants first to find a trustworthy regent to guide the young Aluigi until he comes of age: "'Io vi prego che tra voi tutti sia eletto uno barone gentile, il quale sia sofficiente che mantenga ragione e giustizia a poveri e a ricchi, a uomini e femmine, a grandi e a piccoli, a vedove e a popilli'" (**N** 1: 245–46). The *Prima Spagna* concluded with Ansuigi's coronation as king of Spain and Carlo's return to Paris, events recounted at the beginning of *Ansuigi:*

> Cap.º 185. Chome lo re Charllo tornò in Parigi chon tutta la baronia . . . (Michelant, "Titoli," 405)
> E l'altra mattina chome fu dì, e Charlo fè mandare la grida ch'ongnuno metersi in punto e' chariagi, che voleva partire; e charicharonsi le some, e montò Charlo a chavallo cholla baronia . . . e partissi, e tornoronsi in Franza Charlo chon tutta la sua baronia. (**S** 1v)

Having examined the relationship of the conclusion of the *Prima Spagna* and the beginning of *Ansuigi,* we must now compare the conclusion of *Ansuigi* to the beginning of *Nerbonesi.* This will facilitate positioning the text among Andrea's works. For two earlier works in Andrea's cycle, Rajna observed that "le ultime narrazioni del libro sesto [di *Reali*] sono ordinate a preparare l'*Aspramonte,* come le prime di questo romanzo si rappiccano e perfettissimamente combinano con quanto è detto nei R[eali]."[11] In like manner, one finds not only the clear reference at the end of *Ansuigi* to *Nerbonesi* but also a summation of the former's closing content at the beginning of the latter. The first chapter of the original version of *Nerbonesi* (most likely designed to follow *Ansuigi*) began with immediate reference to Carlo's return from the second war in Spain. Isola's edition of *Nerbonesi* seems to have followed a later, second branch of the text, one that features a long genealogy of the characters as a proem to its first chapter. When this passage is skipped, the connection between *Ansuigi* and *Nerbonesi* is readily apparent. Such a connection seems even more likely, considering that a single scribe had copied both the Albani manuscript and an unedited *Nerbonesi* that begins thus:

> [T]ornato Charllo dalla sechonda ghuerra che fece in Ispagnia nella quale sochorse Ansuigi. Questo Ansuigi aveva Charllo inchoronate d'Ispagnia nella prima guerra, ed era di gentile sanghue. E' rre Marsilio gli avea tolta la signioria, e Charllo gliele rende e fece tagliare la testa a Marsilione. Quando ebbe renduta la signioria allo re Ansuigi, si partì d'Ispagnia e andonne a Nerbona. (Laur. Plut. XLIII, 18, 1r)

The *incipit* of this exemplar corresponds (with the exception of one word) to that of II.I.15, thereby suggesting that the extant Cimatore copy of *Nerbonesi* was intended to follow a *Seconda Spagna* whose text must have been virtually identical to our only extant exemplar. In fact, Carlo's visit to Narbonne, his vehicle, Guglielmo's lifting Carlo from the cart, and Carlo's blessing on Guglielmo described at the end of *Ansuigi* are all present at the beginning of *Nerbonesi:*

> [A Carlo] era stato fatto a Panpalona un char[r]o, e 'nsul char[r]o entrò in Panpalona in sengnio di trionfo, e 'nsu quel charro si partì. E chaminando di giorno in giorno tanto che chapitò a Nerbona, e giugniendo al palazo, Guglielmo, figliuolo d'Amerigho, cho[n] una bella riverenza e chon un bello modo prese Charlo e levòllo molto soave di sul charro, e Charlo el benedisse. (**S** 26v)
>
> Quando [Carlo] ebbe renduta la signoria a re Ansuigi si partì di Spagna, e andonne a Nerbona . . . ed era in questo tempo Guglielmo d'anni sedici. . . . Essendo giunto Carlo al palagio d'onde vedeva Amerigo, ed era in su una carretta, che quasi per vecchiezza non poteva cavalcare, e volendo Carlo ismontare della carretta, Guglielmo l'abbracciò, e portòllo infino in su la porta del palagio; e quando lo puose in terra Carlo si maravigliò che uno fanciullo di sì poca età l'avesse potuto portare. . . . Allora Carlo prese Guglielmo per lo ciuffetto de' capegli, e disse: Se tu vai per vita, sarai ancora prod'uomo. E benedisselo. (**N** 1: 5–6)

Despite the overall similarities of the above passages, the triumphal car of *Ansuigi* has become something of a wheelchair for the geriatric Carlo of *Nerbonesi.* It seems that, in expanding the episode at the time of writing *Nerbonesi,* Andrea chose to emphasize the ages of the protagonists, facts completely lacking at the end of the economical *Ansuigi.* However,

Ansuigi does stress Carlo's poor health: "Buoso disse chome Charlo era malato" (**S** 14r); "Charlo . . . giacieva in una chamera malato, ed era stato malato vij anni" (**S** 20v). His long-term illness is further aggravated by the journey to aid the besieged Ansuigi: "Torna la storia a Charlo che, sendo la notte nel letto, era molto pegiorato o per lla faticha del chaminare o che dovessi essere" (**S** 22v). The identical thematics of old age and the war appear in *Nerbonesi*: "Essendo Carlo nella sua vecchiezza, poi che della seconda guerra di Spagna era tornato" (**N** 1: 6).

More specific recollections of *Ansuigi* are embedded throughout *Nerbonesi*, especially with regard to characters and genealogy. The author of *Ansuigi*, like Andrea, affirms the primogeniture of Ansuigi's son Guidone, based on Guion or Guis from the French model:

> giunsse . . . chol figliuolo magiore d'Ansoigi chiamato Guidone. (**S** 26v)
> e maladisse . . . Tibaldo d'Arabia ch'avia morti tutti i figliuoli d'Ansuigi. Ver'è che si diciea che 'l maggiore, ciò fu Guidone, era in prigione. (**N** 1: 254–55 and n.)[12]

Another passage from *Nerbonesi* recalls characters from *Ansuigi* and names a younger son of Ansuigi as well:

> "Io sono lo sventurato Guidone, figliuolo del re Ansuigi di Spagna, il quale Ansuigi incoronò Carlo Magno. . . . Dopo la sua morte, io e 'l mio fratello Joans pigliammo la paterna signoria. E il terzo anno che noi savamo fatti signori, passò lo re Tibaldo in Spagna, e noi combattemmo con lui, e nella battaglia fu morto Joans, mio fratello, e io fu' messo in prigione. E morto Ramondo di Navarra e Guido di Borgogna." (**N** 1: 384–85)

The last two characters provide another solid link to the content of *Ansuigi*. Ramondo di Navarra, called "il Pro," and Guido di Borgogna, were among those Carlo left as councilors to Ansuigi: "Charlo . . . chiamò di nuovo Iseres e Guido di Borghongnia e Ivesi di Brach e Ramondo il Pro, e rachomandò loro Ansoigi" (**S** 1v). Later in Andrea's narrative cycle, the role of "Guido di Borgognia, el quale morì nella Spagnia con Ansuigi di Bretagna" is remembered (**E** 1: 200). Many of these characters originated in the French *Anseïs*: Jehan, Tieri, Ysoré, Gui de Borgoigne, Yves de Bascle, and Raimons de Navare. Thus Andrea clearly knew a version of *Anseïs* by the time he wrote *Nerbonesi* and *Aiolfo*, and he could have incorporated the same information in his hypothesized earlier work, *Ansuigi*.

Although the figure of Guidone as Ansuigi's firstborn son does appear in other Italian reworkings of the *Seconda Spagna* material,[13] references to Joans, the second son, and Teris, a bastard, occur only rarely in French models.[14] The parentage of these characters in *Ansuigi* matches genea-logical accounts in Andrea's other works: "Ansoigi ... fu re di Spagna; di questo Ansoigi nacque Joans e Guidone, ed uno bastardo ch'ebbe nome Terigi" (**F** 567); "questi due frategli figliuoli del re Ansuigi ... Guidone e Ioransi [var.: Ioans] suo fratello" (**N** 1: 23); "uno figliuolo del re Ansuigi, ma era bastardo, e avia nome Terigi" (**N** 1: 24). The author of *Ansuigi* not only subscribes to Andrea's version but demonstrates the same close aware-ness of written French sources:

> La figliuola d'Iseres ... aveva auto uno figliuolo maschio d'Anssoigi che la ingravidò la notte ch'ella dormì cho·llui, ed era già grande; e v'avendo sentito chome Iseres [s]uo padre era istato morto, un dì ella chiamò el figliuolo e disse: "Figliuol mio, io voglio dare questo chastello ad Ansoigi. Vattene a llui, che ttu se' suo figliuolo ..." (**S** 25v)
> El sopradetto ghar[z]onetto, figliuolo d'Ansoigi, s'inginochiò dinanzi a Charlo chiedendo battesimo ... e spogliato, lo battezò e puosegli nome Teris. E re Charlo lo fecie chavaliere e donògli Chobeles ... (**S** 26r)

One minor figure in *Ansuigi* without French or Italian precedent may have been invented by Andrea. This character, who appears again only in *Nerbonesi* and *Acquisto*, is the son of Morando di Riviera: Morandino. The single passage in Isola's edition of *Nerbonesi* that mentions this fig-ure seems poorly copied or transcribed: "Morandino figliuolo di Riviera" (1: 24). It may be correct in other exemplars. Morant de Rivier, son of Doon de Maïence, had appeared regularly in chansons de geste.[15] His Ital-ian incarnation Morando di Riviera serves as Carlo's *balio* in *Reali* (468), defender (509–11), and councilor (531), and dies at Aspramonte (**A** 193). However, his son Morandino is unique to Andrea. The diminutive fre-quently indicates not so much youth or inexperience as a more recent pedigree: in keeping with narrative praxis, one finds a Bosolino and an Ugolino in *Reali* (566), and an Aiolfino, grandson of the eponymous hero, in *Aiolfo*.

We have seen how Andrea preserved the notion of Ansuigi's three sons in *Ansuigi* and in other works. How does Ansuigi's own parentage com-pare among texts? According to *Entrée* (2: 309), the Anseïs who became king of Jerusalem and later king of Spain was the brother of Hugues (Hue, Hues, Huon) de Blois. This notion of brotherhood is conserved in later Italian texts based on the Franco-Italian model.[16] The name of Hugues's

fief (Blois) seems to have become confused with that of Roland's (*Blaye,
Blavie* > It. *Blava* > *Brava*), leading to the prevalent notion in Italian texts
that Hugues and Anseïs were cousins of Roland.[17] One passage in the
verse *Spagna* differs from the traditional account: "Ugon rispose:—
Borgognon son io/della gentile gesta di Chiarmonte" (XVIII, 45, 1–2).
According to the *Prima Spagna* rubrics, there seem to be two different
Ugoni: the first "tornò in sua terra" (chap. 110), but the second—"l'altro
fratello Uggone"—traveled eastward searching for Orlando and en route
"trovò Ansuigi suo fratello" (chap. 111). In II.I.15, Ansuigi is frequently
accompanied by an unidentified Ugone who seems to conform to the
brother of literary tradition. The authors of *Prima Spagna* and *Ansuigi*
clearly subscribed to the same notion.

The Italian texts that treat the war in Spain concur in making Ansuigi
Ugo's brother and Orlando's cousin. Only Andrea's texts provide a
more detailed genealogy for Ansuigi: remarkably, nowhere in Andrea's
works is he called Orlando's cousin. Unlike other Italian authors, Andrea
followed the French tradition that Ansuigi was related to the famous
Salamone di Brettagna and to Carlo Magno himself:

> nies fu au roi Karlon;
> Par son baptesme Anseïs ot a non;
> Fiex fu Rispeu et cousins Salemon.
>   (*Anseïs*, ed. Alton, ll. 82–84)

Within Andrea's cycle, however, are two versions of Ansuigi's genealogy,
both of which include his relation to the house of Brettagna. In the shorter
family tree (**F** 436; **A** 172), Anseigi lo Brettone or di Brettagna is the father of Angelett le Bretton and the Ansuigi who later becomes king of
Spain. Angelett is killed at Aspramonte (**A** 252), but the Ansuigi mentioned, a frequent companion-at-arms of Orlando, appears to be alive at
its conclusion. Eripes di Brettagna, a veteran knight of Carlo's generation,
is active in *Reali* (Book III, 259–69) and in *Aspramonte* (193, 206), but he
is not specifically identified as Ansuigi's father.

It is the second version of Ansuigi's lineage that is more pertinent to
this investigation. The extensive genealogical listing at the end of *Reali*
traces the "schiatta di Brettagna" back to King Arthur: "Dopo la morte del
re Artú, regnarono in Brettagna Bretonante e lo re Cordonas. Di Cordonas
nacque Angelier, d'Angelier nacque Salamier, di Salamier nacque Codonas,
di Codonas nacque Salardo, di Salardo nacque Eripes, e d'Eripes nacque
Anseigi, d'Anseigi nacque el re Salamone ed Eripes, di Salamone nacque
Liones . . . d'Eripes nacque Ansoigi, che fu re di Spagna" (**F** 567). Anseigi

is the father of Salamone in both versions, but in the longer version Eripes intervenes between Anseigi and the Ansoigi "who was king of Spain." Of Italian texts surveyed, only Andrea's conserve the father-son relationship found in *Anseïs*; in fact, other Italian authors surveyed never mention Ansuigi's father. The longer version also tallies with two passages from *Nerbonesi:* "Ansuigi, figliuolo di Ripes di Bretagna" (1: 221); "'l re Ansuigi figliuolo d'Eripes di Bretagna, el quale fu nipote di Carlo, e Carlo l'avia lasciato re di Spagna quando l'acquistò" (1: 254 and n.). In II.I.15, the protagonist is described precisely as "figliuolo d'Eripes di Brettangnia e qugino di Salamone di Brettangnia e nipote di Charlo mangnio" (1r), a striking parallel to the account Andrea preferred.

An examination of *Ansuigi* from the standpoint of its content reveals several narrative motifs in common with proven works of Andrea. Because of the brevity as well as the economical style of *Ansuigi*, any such evidence is extremely significant. One hallmark of Andrea's style is his detailed portrayals of monstrous races and beasts. His concern for verisimilitude extends to descriptions of giants:

> Viddono insul ponte uno huomo molto grande—uno gioghante—e nero chome charbone, gli ochi rossi che parieno di fuocho e grandi chome dua grandi spechi e aveva la testa molto grande, e' denti suoi parevano di cing[h]iari, e grosse l'altre menbra. (**U** 37v–38r)
> è di grandezza x gomiti . . . (**E** 1: 73)

A brief passage in *Ansuigi* features the statistical measurement of height and the same eye color that Andrea employs elsewhere: "Ed eravi uno singniore chiamato Chanamons . . . che avevo chon secho una sua madre gioghantessa ch'era grande xv piè, e aveva gli ochi rossi chome fuocho" (14v).

One also finds the motif that "to the victor belong the spoils" scattered throughout *Reali, Aspramonte, Nerbonesi, Aiolfo,* and *Guerrino.*[18] This may seem a topos common to battle narrations, but there are only two such references in other texts examined, one in *Fioravante* (349), a work known to have directly influenced Andrea,[19] and one in *Seconda Spagna* (ed. Ceruti, 101), of which much was derived from Andrea. The motif's inclusion in *Ansuigi* therefore seems significant: "E giugnendo e' cristiani a' padiglion di Marssilio, non v'era nessuno sì povero che non diventassi richo della roba de' saraini" (24v).

Andrea includes texts of women's love letters, often filling entire chapters in the process. In this he may have been influenced by the *Heroides,* a copy of which he owned in translation, or by similar passages in other chivalric narratives.[20] There is clear evidence of one such passage in *Ansuigi*, but the letter's text has been truncated by the less learned copyist who evidently preferred action-filled battles to rhetorical niceties. He began copying the content of the letter, but terminated it with a brusque "ecietera." This word is never used in like manner in any of the manuscripts or printed editions of Andrea's texts examined:[21] "E dettegli il picholo brieve, Ramondo laprers [*l'aperse*], el quale dicieva chosì: 'Amicho charissimo, la tua Brandamonte ti si rachomanda e màndati mi[lle] salute, avisandoti che per tuo amore non posso <non posso> nè dì nè notte posare; siché letta la presente, ti priegho che mi vengha a vedere al mio padiglione sichura mente; e non ssi farà per Marsilio questo fatto' *ecietera*" (**S** 12v).

In addition, *Ansuigi* shares various lesser motifs with certain of Andrea's works. The first, an enumeration of clerical figures present at solemn occasions or in propitiatory processions, reflects the events and language of actual historical accounts such as the anonymous Florentine diary:

> tutto il cherichato. . . e cho' molti riligiosi . . . (*Diario* 133; cf. 163)
> fece venire molti religiosi, preti e frati . . . (**F** 384)
> e fèssi loro inchontro molta giente e preti e frati e di molti religiosi chon molte reli[q]ue sancta [*sic*] . . . e 'ntorno alle tavole erano molti preti e vescovi. (**S** 26v)

The phrase *molti religiosi* from *Reali* is directly mirrored in *Ansuigi*.[22] It occurs elsewhere in Andrea, although not always in the context of a procession or ceremony (**F** 421; **Z** 2: 133, 162).

Another linguistic similarity between *Reali* and *Ansuigi* is found in a scene of amorous coupling:

> E cominciaronsi molto ad amare, e tanto adoperavono gli atti dell'amore . . . (**F** 536)
> E chominciando insieme gl'atti d'amore, ferono più volte l'amorosa danza. (**S** 2v)

Dress is a narrative element that Andrea uses to denote royalty, solemnity, or proper morality: its inclusion reflects his culture's obsession with appearances and sumptuous clothing. In *Reali,* the young Carlo learns from the queen of Spain what is expected of one who serves at court: "La reina mandò per Mainetto e dissegli: 'Tu servirai dinanzi alla mia figliuola; fa' che tu sia onesto, e sopra tutto di vestimenti,' perché Mainetto vestiva corto. Ed ella gli donò uno ricco vestimento di scarlatto, lungo insino a' piedi" (477). In *Nerbonesi*, a messenger's distinguished status is known first because of his attire: "Egli era vestito lungo, e realmente" (2: 587). In

Aiolfo, the hero is honored with the gift of a garment from his beloved. Andrea has by now found a special French(?) term for a long, rich garment: "Donò a Lionida uno de' vestimenti che Ajolfo gli avea donati, ch'era molto lungo, chiamato trainas" (**E** 1: 58).[23] A simpler version of this rare motif of long, regal dress is found near the end of *Ansuigi* in a description of priestly garb: "E dimandòllo che giente quell'era ch'era chosì onorata e avevano chosì lunghi e' panni" (26v). In all cases, the long garments are associated with elevated status, solemnity, and honor, and reflect the historical reality of magnificent Florentine ceremonies held in Andrea's time.[24]

Although biblical allusions occur frequently in *cantari*, especially in their religious invocations, references to the *Vendetta di Gesù Cristo* are rather rare. This anti-Semitic legend circulated in written form by Andrea's day. One vernacular exemplar is found in a near-contemporary miscellany, BNCF Magl. Cl. XXXV, 169, copied prior to 1444. Carolingian cycle texts of the period contain only one such reference (Fassò, XI, 51, 7), but Andrea alludes to this event more than once:

> E predicògli, e disse chi fu Cristo, . . . e come Vespasiano fece la vendetta. (**F** 6)
> Disse Ugho: "Benedetto sia Tito e Vespesiano che tanti ne fecie morire per vendetta di Giesù Cristo . . ." (**U** 64r)
> Maggiore strazio faremo de' Cristiani che non fè Vespasiano de' Giudei . . . (**A** 51)
> No[i] ne faremo magiore istrazio che non [f]è Tito e Vesp[a]siano de' Giudei. (**S** 20r)

One recalls that Andrea's *Aspramonte* was the first text in the lost Albani codex. The linguistic affinity of *Ansuigi* and *Aspramonte* suggests that *Ansuigi* may have been the text that followed it.

A final rare motif, found in only one control text, appears in *Reali*, *Ugone*, *Aiolfo*, and *Ansuigi*. Here, a "Saracen" converts to Christianity and receives baptism, but does not change his or her name:

> "Ed io no gli muteroe già nome." (*Tris. ricc.*, 9)
> non gli mutò nome. (**F** 22)
> non mutò loro nome. (**Z** 1: 231)
> non le mutò nome . . . (**Z** 1: 302)
> avea vaghezza di non mutare nome . . . (**E** 1: 140)
> non volle mutar nome . . . (**S** 17v)

The most complex of these citations, that in *Aiolfo*, may indicate a later work, since the apparently unique motif has in the hands of the more mature author been somewhat expanded.

Turning next to an examination of idiomatic expressions, we recall Andrea's adaptation of various conventional *cantare* formulae to suit his stylistic needs. Several of his favorite expressions appear in the *Ansuigi* manuscript. There are the *cioè* type glosses Andrea employed frequently:

gli diede el sengno della sing[n]ioria, cioè lo 'nchorono (**S** 1v)
Chasto Fiorito, cioè un chastello di Spangnia che chosì si chiamava . . . (**S** 20v)

The formulaic outcry "O quanto" upon witnessing the carnage of battle was a commonplace of *cantare* literature, but the citations in *Ansuigi* conform closely to Andrea's extended form and language:

O quante madre perdevano e' lor mariti e figliuoli! (7r)
O quante madre perdevano e' lor figliuoli! (12r)
O quante madre perderono e' loro figliuoli, e quante vedove e popilli rimase! (17r)

The interlace formula *Torna la storia* was a trademark of Andrea's style. Despite related formulae found in other texts, the unadorned version he preferred appears no less than nine times in the brief *Ansuigi*.[25]

In the narration of individual combats, Andrea at times uses the phrase *e poco vantaggio vi fu*.[26] This appears in modified form in *Ansuigi* as "niuno vantaggio vi fu" (12r), a phrase identical to one in *Nerbonesi* (1: 363). Another expression without parallel in other texts of its genre, *giungere ira a ira e forza a forza*, appears with variants in *Reali*, *Nerbonesi*, *Ugone*, and *Aiolfo*, and twice in *Ansuigi*: "agiunto ira a ira e forza a forza" (18v) and "giugniendo forze alla forza e ira all'ira" (22r).[27] The ubiquitous *tagliare a pezzi* is used in *Aspramonte*, *Nerbonesi*, *Ugone*, *Aiolfo*, and *Guerrino*, but only rarely in control texts (see chapter 3). It occurs three times in *Ansuigi* in various forms.[28]

The author of *Ansuigi* and Andrea share the tendency to employ inventive similes. One example compares the noise and fury of full battle to the destruction of the world:

pareva che il mondo si dovesse disfare. (**A** 105–6, 166; **U** 29v, 83v–84r; cf. **N** 2: 281)
pare(v)a che 'l mondo si dovessi disfare. (**S** 8r, 23r)

The only similar occurrence among our chivalric control texts features an alternate verb: "pareva che 'l mondo se sfacesse" (*Spagna*, XXVIII, 33, 2). In another case, *Nerbonesi* and *Ansuigi* equate cowardly behavior in battle with that of chickens:

andavano inverso i nimici uccidendoli come se fussino polli (**N** 2: 73)
"Traditore che tu sse,' e chodardo, che stai rinchiuso chome e' polli
nella stia . . ." (**S** 17v)

Manuscript evidence, textual similarities, specific thematic ties, and idiomatic expressions indicate a direct relationship of *Ansuigi* to works by
Andrea. Perhaps the most rigorous test is to examine the lexicon of *Ansuigi*
with respect to Andrea's. Upon carefully dissecting *Ansuigi*, one finds a
plethora of distinctive words and expressions that, apart from more general stylistic symmetries, indicate that Andrea was probably its author.

The first lexical group consists of single words or short phrases that
appear in several epic romances by Andrea and in *Ansuigi* as well. Of
these items, only four (*asprissimo, dibattersi, maninconoso, petrone*) occur in other chivalric texts of the period; two (*alloggiamento, colezione*)
are in late Trecento chronicles, but not in chivalric texts; and four (*notificare,
alloggiarsi, riediguardo, gioielli dell'elmo*) appear in no control text. Several (*a buon'ora, allattare, carissimo, deretano, balestrata, licenziare*) suggest influence from the *Decameron*, and one (*dibattersi*) is used in Dante's
Commedia. There is hardly a trace of Petrarchan language in this lexicon.

Asprissimo, dibattersi, maninconoso, and *petrone* appear infrequently
in anonymous Carolingian cycle texts. While the superlative *asprissimo*
may not seem extraordinary to a modern reader, in reality it scarcely en-
ters the vocabulary of chivalric literature of the period, appearing only in
the fragmentary *Rotta* (VI, 20, 5), the *Decameron* (II, 8), and *I Cantari di
Rinaldo* (Melli, XXXIX, 32, 5, XLII, 13, 6). Despite its rarity in other texts,
it appears frequently in all known texts by Andrea and once in *Ansuigi*
(8r).[29] *Dibattersi* appears once in the refined prose of *Fioravante,* a known
model for part of *Reali;* however, it is not in other chivalric texts. The
GDLI registers both Dante (*Inferno*) and Andrea under the same meaning, "muovere in qua e in là."[30] The verb appears in *Reali, Aspramonte,*
and *Aiolfo,* and once in *Ansuigi* (22r). The third example, *maninconoso,*
may be found in four of Andrea's known texts and in *Ansuigi.*[31] A word
that appears rarely in chivalric texts is *petrone,* a place for royalty to dis-
mount in front of a palace. It occurs in Fassò only once with this meaning
(X, 14, 1), yet appears regularly in works by Andrea. It is therefore significant to find the noun used in the same context three times in *Ansuigi.*[32]

Alloggiar(si) was used by Andrea more often than the older form
albergare found in the *Purgatorio* and the *Decameron* (GDLI, 1: 287).
Considering this verb's absence from chivalric literature, its frequent uti-
lization in texts by Andrea as well as in the brief *Ansuigi* is remarkable.[33]
The later Trecento substantive form *alloggiamento* appears in all Andrea's

epic romances and in *Ansuigi*.[34] Even more striking is the modified *alloggiamenti di frasche*, which indicates field lodgings during military campaigns. This idiosyncratic term may be found in both *Reali* (351) and in *Ansuigi* (7v). Two other rare nouns from the *Prima Spagna* rubrics are found in *Ansuigi* as well: *cholezione* (13r) and *notifichando* (10v).

The military term *antiguardo* and its variants are common in chivalric control texts; however, its unusual opposite, the Gallic *riediguardo*, appears in Andrea's *Aspramonte* and in *Ansuigi*. The variant *retrighuardo* is also in *Ansuigi*, with still other variants in *Aspramonte, Reali,* and *Nerbonesi*. This word's use suggests reliance on actual French sources, perhaps *La Chanson de Roland* itself.[35]

Another rare term is the modified *gioielli dell'elmo*. As noted in the preceding chapter, *gioielli* is found in the *Decameron* and throughout Andrea's cycle. The modified form holds more interest for this investigation. Earlier authors had described the practice of ornamenting helmets with jewels, but their terminology differed from Andrea's.[36] However, the similarity of language between *Nerbonesi* and *Ansuigi* is noteworthy:

Diegli uno grande colpo in su l'elmo . . . e tutti i gioielli mandò per terra. (**N** 1: 511)

Dettegli un cholpo che ttutti e' gioelli del elmo mandò a tterra. (**S** 17r)

Tutti e' gioeg[l]i del'elmo mandò per terra. (**S** 18v)

Diede un grande cholpo insul'elmo a Charlo per modo che tutti i gioelli che v'eron su mandò per terra. (**S** 24v)[37]

The occurrence of identical terminology in *Ansuigi* and in *Nerbonesi* is another strong indication that these works have the same author.

A buon'ora, allattare, carissimo, deretano, balestrata, licenziare, rarely used by writers of chivalric *cantari*, were employed by Dante, Boccaccio, Andrea, and the author of *Ansuigi*. The adverbial expression *a (di) buon'ora* is found in the *Decameron* as well as in *Reali, Aspramonte, Ugone, Aiolfo,* and *Guerrino*.[38] The concern for establishing precise times for activities such as the commencement of battles is in keeping with Andrea's pseudo-chronicle style. Both variants occur in *Ansuigi*—*a* (26r) and *di* (14v, 25v). *Allattare*, another unusual term found in the *Commedia*, the *Decameron*, and the *Tavola ritonda*, is in nearly all Andrea's epic romances, and in *Ansuigi* as well.[39] *Carissimo* is used frequently in all Andrea's texts, but only twice in our chivalric controls. Andrea's including it in the salutation of speeches or letters followed by its head noun (*fratello, signore, figliuoli*) directly mirrors usage by Boccaccio.[40] *Deretano, balestrata,* and *licenziare* again suggest the *Decameron*'s influence. The first makes scattered appearances in the *Commedia*, the *Decameron*, the *Tristano riccardiano*, and the *Tavola ritonda*; the second occurs only twice in the *Decameron*; but the last is found nineteen times in Boccaccio's *novelle*.[41] *Diretano* and *licenziare* are used by Matteo Villani.[42] These terms are found in Andrea's works and in *Ansuigi*.[43]

Ansuigi shares several rare, short expressions with Andrea's proven epic romances. These may be divided into three categories: those occurring in nonchivalric texts, those found infrequently (one to three times) in other chivalric texts, and those unique to Andrea's lexicon. Phrases outside the chivalric canon that are found in *Ansuigi* and in texts by Andrea are *bella diceria*, *ben fare*, *giusta mia (sua) possa*, and *come il fatto stava*. The first, used to portray a military leader's speech to troops, is used frequently by Andrea and occurs once in *Ansuigi* (11r). *Ben fare* appears in the literature of the great fourteenth-century triumvirate Dante, Petrarch, and Boccaccio, but only once in control texts.[44] Its moral connotation suggests that the author who included this term possessed a nobler purpose for his writing than the *cantastorie* who frequently strove for action-packed narratives. The curious expression *giusta mia (sua) possa* appears in nearly every text by Andrea and in *Ansuigi*, yet has no parallel among control texts.[45] The *Enciclopedia Dantesca* defines *possa* as "'potenza,' 'forza,' variamente intese. Talora si tratta di 'forza fisica'" (4: 616). The *GDLI* cites Giamboni's *giusta la possa mia* as the closest to Andrea's preferred version (6: 905). Another expression found in *Ansuigi* as well as in Andrea's texts is *come il fatto stava*. Once again, this phrase is not part of the linguistic stock of the average *cantastorie*, but does occur twice verbatim in the *Decameron*, and once, in a variant form, in *I Cantari di Rinaldo*.[46] The related *come la cosa (si) stava* is also found in *Ansuigi* (S 11v, 12v).

Andare a vicitare, *fare piazza*, and *mortale nimico (nimico mortale)* appear infrequently in other chivalric texts, but occur regularly in Andrea and in *Ansuigi*. *Andare a vicitare* is used in all works by Andrea and in *Ansuigi*.[47] The expression *fare piazza* is used quite often in Andrea's works when a knight slashes his way through a *mêlée*. It is found four times in *Ansuigi*.[48] The *GDLI* shows no chivalric author earlier than Pulci for this usage (13: 328). *Mortale nimico* occurs in the feminine in the *Decameron* (V, 8) and only once—inverted—in Petrarch's *Canzoniere* (129, 6). Among control texts, it is in Fassò (XI, 58, 5, XVIII, 43, 5), Melli (VIII, 38, 4), *Tris. ricc.* (160, 186), and *Tav. rit.* (I, 302, 351, 356, 410; [plur.] 78, 352). Not unknown to other authors, it seems to be a favorite of Andrea and appears repeatedly in his epic romances, including once in *Ansuigi*.[49]

None of the unusual expressions *Come di sopra è detto*, *lamentarsi della fortuna, (e) nota che,* and *sotto brevità* are found in the chivalric control texts; however, they occur in the majority of Andrea's epic romances and in *Ansuigi* as well. The authorial reminder to readers *come di sopra è detto* and its variants are common in the works of Andrea, and two versions occur in *Ansuigi*.[50] Only dissimilar forms are in texts by other authors.[51]

Although the topos of Fortuna was widespread in medieval literature, in control texts it is not coupled to the verb *lamentarsi*. Outside the Carolingian cycle, the expression *lamentarsi della Fortuna* appears once in the courtly romance *Paris e Vienna:* "E cusì duramente se lamentava Viena de la fortuna che li andava tanto contraria" (ed. Babbi, 199). It is indicative of an author whose narrative distance from his characters is short: not only do they suffer the inevitable turns of fate, but their reactions are psychologically realistic. The elegiac expression is found in all Andrea's narratives except *Ugone*, and four times in *Ansuigi*.[52] Once again, the inclusion of such nuances in the Carolingian cycle marks an author with those "pretensioni di cultura" indicated by Vitale.

In her analysis of *cantare* literature formulae, Cabani discusses "il passaggio dal 'voi' al 'tu,'" concluding that "è soprattutto nei testi più tardi che la lettura individuale viene talvolta indicata come possibile modo di fruizione del genere."[53] *(E) nota che* is one such form of authorial address to the reader. It occurs in virtually all works of Andrea and once in *Ansuigi*. Examples of *nota che* in his work illustrate a transition from the plural (public audience) to the singular (private reader) within his corpus: the probable early *Reali* includes the only reference in the *tu* form to a listener: "Nota, uditore, che . . ." (509). Whereas *nota che* is not in the realm of typical *cantari*, often destined for oral performance, the phrase may be found in actual fourteenth-century chronicles.[54] The distinctive abbreviation formula *sotto brevità* in several of Andrea's works is echoed in *Ansuigi*.[55] Since this expression is never used in other chivalric texts nor in the *Tre Corone*, it should be recognized as indicative of a particular author's style. Given its scattered appearances in Andrea's cycle, the connection to *Ansuigi* is too significant to be coincidental.

This lexical examination of *Ansuigi* has thus far revealed numerous examples of words and phrases that scarcely occur in contemporary literature, but that are regularly used by Andrea da Barberino. A still more convincing test would be to isolate extremely rare words and expressions in *Ansuigi*, and then see if they also exist in Andrea's epic romances. In fact, *Ansuigi* shares a handful of words and expressions with Andrea's texts.

Andrea's eye for detail extends also to the chivalric landscapes he portrays. Francesco Flora effuses over how, in Andrea, the "senso dei paesaggi, con brevi tocchi, è reso nei modi più ariosi."[56] One such "breve tocco" is the rarely used *ghiaia del fiume (fiumiciello)* found scattered throughout Andrea's cycle and twice in the short *Ansuigi*.[57] The noun *ghiaia* alone is found just once among other texts examined (*Dec.* VI, 10).

The very unusual *mamaluccho*, an apparent synonym for Saracen, is found in *Ansuigi* (13r). Variants appear in *Aiolfo* (*mamaluc*, 2: 193) and in *Guerrino* (*malmaluc*, **B** 41v).[58] There is also the probable misspelling *armalucchi* in *Ugone* (**Z** 1: 163). These are earlier appearances of the noun than those registered by the Crusca (9: 749). "Mamluk," from the Arabic for slave, was the name given the Egyptian dynasty that originated in 1250 when the Turkish bodyguard usurped power from the successors of Saladin.[59] Andrea's use of a term foreign to the chivalric canon but belonging to actual history reflects his pseudo-chronicle style. The word appears in the Venetian romance *Paris e Vienna*, which may postdate Andrea (228, 230), and in *Morgante* (XXIV, 141, 2).

The verb *affossare* comes into narrative play as a prelude to siege operations for either defensive or offensive purposes. Although sieges are a major convention in chivalric literature, this verb is used only once in control texts (Melli, XLIV, 27, 7) and not by Dante or Petrarch. However, it is used by Giovanni Villani and in Boccaccio's *Rime* (*GDLI*, 1: 223), and in the anonymous *Diario* (118). The verb appears once in *Ansuigi* as well as in *Reali* and *Nerbonesi*.[60]

Bigordare, to joust for sport with a light lance, is found in *Filocolo* (160, 176), *Fioravante* (357, 457), and the *Diario* (55).[61] The verb was used by Francesco da Barberino, Fazio degli Uberti, and Sacchetti and in *Fiore di virtù* (*GDLI*, 2: 228). The related noun *bigordo,-i* occurs in Melli (VII, 24, 7, XXVI, 12, 5), *Filocolo* (160), *Fioravante* (457 [2]), *Tristano riccardiano* (19), and *Tavola ritonda* (I: 331). However, the variant *biordare* is not found in the control texts. This form occurs in *Ansuigi* (2v) and in *Nerbonesi* (2: 238).

Let us now turn to significant phrases. The Gallic *apendu per la gorga* appears in *Ansuigi* (4r). This indicates without doubt the author's access to French models, since most *cantari* and the *Diario* (218) feature the Tuscanized *impiccare per la gola*. The French version does not appear in Dante, Petrarch, or Boccaccio, yet the works of Andrea display a spectrum of variants ranging from *appenduti* and *impendu* (or *impenduti*) to the more common *impiccare*, and from *gorga* to *gorgie* and *gola*.[62] The occasional appearance of this phrase in Andrea may indicate a certain phase of his career, a unity of source material, or simply an expression that struck his fancy and was consciously conserved from a French model. Its appearance in *Ansuigi* marks a definite link to Andrea's rich lexicon.

The unusual *bontà di*, meaning "thanks to" or "because of," is found in *Ansuigi*, as well as in *Reali*, *Aspramonte*, and *Nerbonesi*.[63] This wording does not appear in any of the control texts or concordances cited.

Prospero vento, an unconventional expression employed in Andrea's texts, occurs eight times in *Ansuigi*.[64] This locution is not found in chivalric texts checked, in the *Commedia*, or in Petrarch's *Canzoniere*, but may indicate a linguistic influence from Boccaccio (*Tes.*, I, 20, 4; *Dec.*, II, 6, V, 2).

Stylistically, Andrea brought a sense of historical verisimilitude to the conventional *cantastorie* narration. To achieve this, he reached beyond the vocabulary of *cantari* to include terms and expressions from non-chivalric literature. Many of these later entered the chivalric canon and may be found in the works of Pulci and Ariosto. Among those specialized martial terms *Ansuigi* shares with Andrea's lexicon are words used by Dante (*intronare*) and Matteo Villani (*guanto sanguinoso, carriaggio, fanti da piè*). Other words (*bussine, spallaccio, sinestrare*) occur only sporadically in epic romances by Andrea and in *Ansuigi*.

Certain rare military terms are used in *Ansuigi* and by Andrea to describe armor or the body: *camaglio dell'elmo, forciella del petto, guanto sanguinoso, gorzerino (gorgerino)*, and *spallaccio*. *Camaglio dell'elmo* (var. *dell'elmetto*) appears in *Ansuigi* and in several works by Andrea.[65] *Forcella del petto*, a part of the body, occurs in *I Fatti di Cesare* and Varchi (*GDLI*, 6: 156), but not in the chivalric control group. It does appear in Andrea's *Aspramonte*, *Nerbonesi*, and *Guerrino*, as well as four times, with the variant spellings *forciella* and *forcilla*, in *Ansuigi*.[66] The expression *guanto sanguinoso*, a sign of challenge to battle, occurs in Matteo Villani and was used later by Pulci (*GDLI*, 7: 105). The gesture of hurling a bloodied glove announces the commencement of combats in *Nerbonesi*, *Aiolfo*, and *Guerrino*.[67] This motif appears once in *Ansuigi*—"il ghaggio della battaglia" (4r). The only similar usage is "il guanto della battaglia" (*Fior.* 348, 361, 398; *Diario*, 22; **N** 2: 683; **B** 37r). The two extremely rare nouns for parts of armor are *gorzerino (gorgerino)* and *spallaccio*. For the first, a metal piece protecting the throat, the *GDLI* (6: 984) cites Burchiello, *Aiolfo*, and the variant *gorzarino* in *Cantari cavallereschi*. This noun also appears in *Reali*, *Nerbonesi*, and twice in *Ansuigi*.[68] *Lo spallaccio*, a part of the armor covering the shoulder, is used once each in *Ansuigi* (24v) and in *Nerbonesi* (2:83). No other literary text surveyed used this term, but it may be found in the 1456 inventory of the Medici "arme da piazza": "uno paio di spallacci forniti d'ariento."[69]

A second group of nouns found in *Ansuigi* and in texts by Andrea describes the paraphernalia of war (weapons, instruments, infantry, and troop movements). Only two of these terms occur in the chivalric control texts; others predate Andrea and were used in actual chronicles. Several of these words are shared by *Ansuigi* and Andrea's texts. The noun *pondo* (weight, pressure, force) used alone is common in medieval literature, but its special application to battle narration as *pondo della battaglia* seems particular to *Aspramonte, Nerbonesi,* and *Ansuigi.*[70] *Steccato,* a barricade constructed around a besieged city for either defensive or offensive reasons, or to mark the competition area for a tournament, occurs rarely in texts not by Andrea (*Tes.,* I, 92, 2; *Spagna,* XVIII, 8, 7; Melli I, 24, 7, XXXI, 14, 8). It is employed with both meanings in the anonymous Florentine *Diario* (118, 139). This historical term is used in *Ansuigi* and frequently in all epic romances by Andrea.[71] *Stretti e serrati* describes the orderly march of a brigade approaching an encounter. This expression and variants are found only in Fassò, *Reali, Nerbonesi,* and *Ansuigi.*[72]

Martial music is often recalled in *cantare* literature, but the term *bussine* (antique war trumpets) is found only in *Aspramonte, Nerbonesi, Guerrino,* and *Ansuigi.*[73] It is not registered in the *GDLI,* the Crusca, or in any of the concordances consulted. The reader will recall the cyclical proximity of *Aspramonte, Ansuigi,* and *Nerbonesi:* the similar lexicon suggests a proximity in dates of composition.

Three terms that *Ansuigi* and Andrea's works share with actual chronicles are *carriaggio, disutile gente,* and *fanti a piè. Carriaggio,* referring to military baggage and supplies, is used in *Reali, Aspramonte, Ugone, Aiolfo, Guerrino,* and *Ansuigi.*[74] The *GDLI* (2: 800) records a variant spelling in Matteo Villani. Strangely, the word is not found in the *Cantari* edited by Fassò, despite that poet's penchant for rhymes in -*aggio.* The lowly infantry is remembered in Andrea's texts, and in *Ansuigi,* with two rare terms that impart authenticity to these narrations. The adjective "disutile" to describe worthless troops was used in *Prima Spagna, Reali, Nerbonesi,* and *Guerrino.* It is found twice in *Ansuigi:* "la giente disutile" (9r, 9v). An even more unusual term for the infantry is the somewhat redundant *fanti a piè* found in *Ansuigi* (19v) and in *Nerbonesi* (2: 236). Although the noun *fante* alone is very common in the *Decameron* and elsewhere in medieval literature, parallels for this reinforced version occur in contemporary non-chivalric sources: *fanti da piè* in Matteo Villani and *fanti a piede* in Sacchetti

(*GDLI*, 5: 655). The expression *fanti a pie(de)* appears in the Florentine *Diario* (112, 142, 170).

Other battlefield terms are not found in control texts, nor in Dante, Petrarch, or Boccaccio, yet are shared by *Ansuigi* and texts by Andrea. The historically accurate manner of supporting a lance during a knight's charge is recorded by two expressions found in all works by Andrea and in *Ansuigi* as well: *lancia arrestata* and *lancia in (a) resta*.[75] *Verrettoni*, defensive weapons used by the besieged to stave off attackers, are mentioned in *Reali*, *Nerbonesi*, *Aiolfo*, and *Ansuigi*, but appear nowhere among chivalric control texts.[76] They are mentioned in the *Diario* (99). Finally, an extremely unusual description of the deployment of troops in the shape of a crescent moon occurs once in *Ansuigi* and in *Aiolfo*:

feciono di loro chom'una luna per mettere in mezo e' cristiani . . . (**S** 23r)
feciono della loro gente una luna con due corni . . . (**E** 2: 81)

Although both individual combats and full-scale battles are the mainstay of Carolingian cycle literature, it is possible to distinguish in Andrea and in *Ansuigi* a series of verbs and expressions associated with the preparation, execution, and aftermath of battle. These add color and specificity to martial actions portrayed: *metter(si) in punto*, *intronare*, *mescolarsi*, *(ri)fare testa*, *indrieteggiare*, *sinestrare*, *schianciare*, and *attender(si) a medicare*. Andrea uses *metter(si) in punto* repeatedly to illustrate preparations for battle, and it appears in *Ansuigi* several times.[77] *Intronare*, with the Dantesque meaning "rimbombare," is found once among chivalric control texts (*Add.*, 143). However, its usage in *Ansuigi* corresponds to the meaning found elsewhere in Andrea: "tramortire con percosse, con colpi."[78] The verb *mescolarsi* describes the clash of opposing sides in battle. It is found in all Andrea's epic romances and occurs in *Ansuigi*.[79] The term *(ri)fare testa* referring to the formation or reformation of the point is scattered throughout *Reali*, *Aspramonte*, *Nerbonesi*, and *Guerrino*. Although the word is not in chivalric control texts, it does appear in *Ansuigi*.[80]

In every epic romance by Andrea, *indrieteggiare* (*indietreggiare*) indicates retreating troops. It appears eleven times in the short *Ansuigi*, not including the variant *adretegiare*, which occurs once.[81] This unusual verb also provides a first clue to an attribution of authorship for the anonymous *Storie di Rinaldo da Montalbano*. Its presence in that unedited work was recorded by Lionardo Salviati for the *Vocabolario degli Accademici della Crusca*. Lexical samplings in Salviati's own hand copied from a lost

Rinaldo in prose identify this verb: ". . . la gente di Mambrino *indie-treggiava; e' saraini indietregarono* per modo che 'l campo era del pari" (Ricc. 2197, 108r; emphasis is Salviati's).[82]

Sinestrare is another verb used in the narration of combats. The action of pulling or swerving leftward may be by either combatants or their mounts. The verb is found in *Nerbonesi, Ugone, Aiolfo,* and *Ansuigi*.[83]

The verb *schianciare* refers to glancing sword blows. The *Enciclopedia Dantesca* (5:64) registers its use once in *Il Fiore*, and the variants *schiancire*, in the *Storia della guerra di Troia* by Guido delle Colonne, and "andò a schiancio," in *Orlando* (XLIII, 21, 2). *Schianciare* is found only in *Ansuigi* and in *Ugone:*

> Menògli un cholpo insul'elmo e schianci[ò] via e sciese la spada (**S** 24v)
> schianchiò la spada da llato mancho. (**U** 46v [**Z** 1: 295])

A final example of the close lexical relationship between *Ansuigi* and Andrea is an odd amalgam of two verbs common in medieval literature: *attendersi a medicare.* This expression routinely describes the aftermath of battles in all Andrea's epic romances and in *Ansuigi*.[84]

This chapter has argued that the anonymous *Storia di Ansuigi* of BNCF II.I.15 must have been composed by Andrea da Barberino. The preponderance of philological evidence cited, when considered in conjunction with codicological documentation and with textual and motivic symmetries of the *Prima Spagna*, strongly points to Andrea as the author of *Ansuigi*. Words sampled from both *Ansuigi* and from other texts by Andrea show the same linguistic influence of Boccaccio and, to a lesser extent, of Dante while exhibiting almost nothing in common with the Petrarchan lyric. The author of *Ansuigi* was, like Andrea, a person who did not limit his reading to the *cantare* and romance literature popular in his day, but absorbed specific lexical elements from nonfictional genres. Like Andrea, he preserved details from French models that did not have currency in the larger Italian chivalric tradition. Even though the action of *Ansuigi* centers largely on military encounters and maneuvers, its author possessed the same capacity as Andrea to enliven his narration with richer linguistic and stylistic texture than was the norm, as well as to vary it by including insights into the characters' emotional states. The overall effect of the brief narrative is not without that "certa ambizione d'arte" Boni noticed in Andrea's prose.

The Case for *Le Storie di Rinaldo da Monte Albano* in Prose

The preceding chapters have demonstrated that the lost *Prima Spagna* and the extant *Ansuigi* ("Seconda Spagna") were in all likelihood written by Andrea. These two texts fill the noticeable gap in the huge narrative cycle formed by his previously attested works. Considering Andrea's demonstrated cognizance of both French models and Italian reworkings of chivalric material, it seems unlikely that he would have ignored perhaps the most popular Italian hero of all time, Rinaldo.

The figure of Rinaldo, though of French origin, has been hailed as the closest to an Italian national hero of all the knights and paladins in chivalric discourse.[1] He was so popular that in Boiardo's day he rivaled Orlando, as shown by a debate within the Este court on the relative merits of the two heroes.[2] By the sixteenth century the hero had lent his name to the literary genre of *libri di battaglia*, as seen in the generic term *Rinaldini*, which was applied to all stories of this type.[3] More recently, in the folklore of the nineteenth and early twentieth centuries, Neapolitan *cantastorie* were referred to as Rinaldi by association with the ever-popular protagonist whose adventures they frequently recounted.[4]

Scattered references to Rinaldo and his exploits in *Reali* and *Nerbonesi* affirm Andrea's knowledge of this hero. A genealogical passage detailing the House of Chiaramonte names Rinaldo among the sons of Amone: "del secondo figliuolo, ciò fu Amone, nacque Rinaldo, che fu chiamato poi Rinaldo da Monte Albano, e Alardo, e Guicciardo, e Ricciardetto, tutti e quattro frategli" (**N** 1: 358). Despite the many adventures of Rinaldo *fuorilegge*, in one passage Andrea numbers him among the "signori cristiani" who represent the most admirable knightly qualities of liberty, humility, humanity, and mercy (**N** 2: 135). Rinaldo and his family are again listed honorably in the long genealogy at the end of *Reali:* "Del duca Amone nacque Alardo, Rinaldo, Guicciardo e Ricciardetto. Di Rinaldo si dice che nacque due madornali e due bastardi: l'uno de' madornali fu Ivone, e l'altro Amonetto; e' due bastardi furono questi: Guidone Selvaggio e Dodonello di Mombello" (565). A third bastard of Rinaldo is identified as "Rinaldo, figliuolo di Rinaldo da Monte Albano, non ligittimo" (**N** 2: 406). He is mentioned elsewhere in *Nerbonesi* under the name Rinaldone. Although he plays only a minor role, he acquits himself well by killing a Saracen champion (**N** 2: 417) and commanding a Christian battalion alongside three other notables: Bernardo di Busbante, Folco di Candia, and King Louis himself (**N** 2: 435). A fourth bastard, Rinaldino da Montalbano, was probably a later invention by an anonymous Quattrocento author. Concerning this character, Carlo Minutoli states: "In tutta la storia della cavalleria non ci è avvenuto mai d'incontrare questo nome di Rinaldino."[5] The fact that the diminutive form of the name never appears in Andrea's genealogies is another indication that he did not compose *Rinaldino*, as was once supposed.

A search for a *Rinaldo* written by Andrea logically begins with the lengthy, unedited prose text found in five manuscripts in Florence. This text is bound in two parts, the first containing five books (so labeled in the manuscripts) and the second made up of three long books. Of these last three books, the first presents an anomaly, being called "el quinto libro." Laur. Plut. XLII, 37 contains Books I–V; Laur. Plut. LXXXIX, inf. 64 (mutilated) contains only Books I, II, and most of Book III. Three extant, though imperfect, manuscripts contain Books V*bis*, VI, VII: Laur. Med. Pal. CI, 4; Plut. LXI, 40; and Ricc. 1904. This *Rinaldo* is well known, though critics citing it refer most often to only the two manuscripts that contain the first five books.[6] The question of authorship has not been examined, and recent critics continue to cite the prose *Rinaldo* as an anonymous text. Albertazzi cites Andrea *en passant* as compiler of *Le Storie di Rinaldo*;[7] however, I cannot discover the basis on which he has proposed this attribution other than its prose register and length, traits shared with Andrea's known texts. Before I offer new evidence for Andrea as the author of this text, I must briefly examine earlier critical comments that point in this direction.

Rajna considered many aspects of the prose *Rinaldo*, focusing primarily on Books I and II. Despite Rajna's recognition of the anonymous author's originality and ability as a compiler, traits reminiscent of Andrea, he does not raise the issue of authorship. Rajna praises the originality of the latter books, finding that only Books I and II can with certainty be traced to an "origine antica" (that is, French models): "Gli altri [libri] tutti—e sono parecchi—sono intieramente invenzione italiana." In the course of grappling with the problem of dating, Rajna notes certain "analogies" with *Reali*: "Non si potrebbe rimuovere troppo verso la fine del Trecento la versione in prosa, se dev'essere contemporanea ai *Reali di Francia*, coi quali mostra molta analogia. Anzi non sarebbe forse audacia l'affermare il *Rinaldo* anteriore ai *Reali*." In seeking to establish an order of composition for Andrea's complete cycle, Rajna does include this text among Andrea's works, though without offering precise reasons for this attribution.[8] Following Rajna's lead, Isola lists an otherwise unidentified *Rinaldo da Montalbano* among Andrea's works;[9] Gaston Paris, on the other hand, overlooked the prose *Rinaldo* entirely in his analysis of Andrea's output.

Numerous studies of the Rinaldo textual tradition by Melli, including one that specifically treats a lost exemplar of our text, failed to raise the question of authorship for *Rinaldo*; however, this question was not central to his research.[10] Following in Melli's wake is Andrea Morosi, who studied the entire Rinaldo tradition, with emphasis on the rhymed versions. His discussion of *Rinaldo* is again limited to the two manuscripts that contain the first books. He offers convincing evidence (traces of rhyme still to be found in the prose) that "la prosa rimanda, dunque, ad un testo in rima, toscano e non franco-veneto come pensava il Rajna"; yet other elements "sono comuni alla prosa e al *Renaut*" of Bodleian Douce 121. This indicates the *prosatore*'s equal awareness of earlier French texts and contemporary Italian ones, a trait well exemplified in Andrea's other works.[11] Forni Marmocchi also had the occasion to examine these two manuscripts of *Rinaldo* and recognized "la vasta cultura che possedeva [il romanziere]," an observation that brings to mind Andrea.[12]

Apparent anonymity—often the case with extant medieval texts—should not deter us from seeking to establish authorship for the *Rinaldo* in prose. In speaking of lesser-known Trecento texts such as *L'Acerba*, *Il Dittamondo*, and *Il Quadriregio*, Dionisotti has rightly observed: "Già qui, ma molto più nel genere cavalleresco, i titoli prevalevano sugli autori."[13] Such is the case with several exemplars of Andrea's known works that do not bear his name, including the *Ansuigi* of BNCF II.I.15.

The question of dating the composition must be resolved before proceeding further with an attribution of authorship. Margaret Tomalin calls Ricc. 1904 "an early 15th century manuscript," although she does not provide details. Pulci explicitly referred to "il *Danese* e *Rinaldo*" in a letter to Lucrezia Tornabuoni. Ageno has pointed out certain remarkable plot similarities between *Il Morgante* and the *Danese* section of Laur. Plut.

XLII, 37 and LXXXIX, inf. 64, debts confirmed by Morosi.[14] Such evidence indicates a date of composition for *Le Storie di Rinaldo* prior to the 1460s. Could it have been composed still earlier, perhaps during Andrea's lifetime?

A first clue is found in Ricc. 2197, an autograph manuscript of Lionardo Salviati's, which includes *Rinaldo* among a lexical sampling of "libri della miglior favella cioè, dall'anno 1300, o poco addietro sino all'anno 1400" (1r). Later in the same manuscript Salviati describes his now-untraceable exemplar as "un libro, che secondo me fu scritto ne' tempi buoni, e 'l carattere pare anche antico, ma non quanto la dettatura" (108v).

Andrea's epic romances were still being copied by hand in the sixteenth century. Of the five *Rinaldo* witnesses, three demonstrate similar continuing interest in lengthy prose "battle books": Plut. XLII, 37 bears an internal colophon at the end of Book IV (115r) with the date "primo giugno 1503" and a final one that shows it to have been finished in April 1506 (195v). Although the scribe's name has here been obliterated and replaced with "Istradino," the hand matches that of another *Rinaldo* exemplar, Ricc. 1904.[15] Similarly, Plut. LXXXIX, inf. 64 was probably produced in the late fifteenth or early sixteenth century, to judge from hands and watermarks (datable ca. 1475–1513).[16] Furthermore, household accounts added later in blank spaces in a different hand are dated 1508 and 1519 (103r–v). A third exemplar, Med. Pal. CI, 4, also owned by Stradino, dates from 1472 or later, judging once again by the watermarks.[17] It was copied before 1505, the date written on the first flyleaf by a reader.

The last two exemplars are more helpful for pinpointing the text's date of composition. Plut. LXI, 40 was copied prior to March 4, 1455, the date added by a reader (51r). Its watermarks range from 1397 to 1430, thus indicating a manuscript that may have been produced within Andrea's lifetime.[18] Finally, watermarks for the bulk of Ricc. 1904 date from the late Quattro- or early Cinquecento, a date that tallies with the hand of the principal portion.[19] The Riccardian exemplar bears no colophon, but dates for the paper of folio 1 (which originally belonged to a different exemplar of the same text) range from 1426 to 1445.[20] Given the paper used for the entire Plut. LXI, 40 and for the first folio of Ricc. 1904, it is feasible to assume a date of composition for the prose *Rinaldo* during Andrea's lifetime.

Rinaldo presents another case of multiple ownership of Andrea's texts. Numerous copies of works by Andrea were owned by Stradino, a bibliophile, minor academician, and soldier who served Giovanni delle Bande Nere. His library, which after his death went to the Medici, contained two copies of *Reali*, two of *Nerbonesi*, the BNCF *Ansuigi, Ugone d'Avernia*, and a probable *Aiolfo*.[21] Among his many "Rinaldini" were three and possibly four of the extant *Rinaldo* exemplars: Plut. XLII, 37; Plut. LXI, 40; Med. Pal. CI, 4; and perhaps Ricc. 1904.

More revealing is information regarding the scribe of Plut. XLII, 37 and Ricc. 1904, two manuscripts that, when taken together, form a complete set of all eight books of *Rinaldo*. The hand, date of production, style of rubrication, and spelling norms of these two manuscripts also match those of an extant *Ugone*, BNCF II.II.59. Its undamaged colophon shows the name of the scribe, "Giordano di Michele Giordani," and date of completion, "1511" (83v). Giordano may have been an aficionado of Andrea who was assembling a complete cycle for his own use, or, as indicated by his crisp book hand, he may have been commercially producing these texts. At any rate, the evidence of a single copyist for *Rinaldo* and *Ugone* suggests another link to Andrea's corpus.

Beyond the question of dating, a stylistic analysis shows that *Rinaldo* closely resembles the known narratives of Andrea. Divisions into books, relative length of chapters, division into chapters based on content, style of rubrics, narremes, figurative language, and lexicon, all point to Andrea. Mixing of verse and prose genres and citation of actual or invented authors for source materials are other traits *Rinaldo* displays. It not only features many of the same Carolingian cycle characters, but its genealogical details match those found in Andrea. Itineraries of voyages in its earlier books are generally brief and simple, but later books contain passages that are toponymically more detailed à la *Guerrino*.

The compositional process used in *Rinaldo* reflects the compilation techniques used by Andrea. Andrea has long been recognized as a compiler or adapter, which modernists tend to equate with being unoriginal or derivative. Nonetheless, Rajna astutely noted a relationship between the individualistic *Rinaldo* and Andrea's *Reali:*

> Questo primo libro del Rinaldo, degno di somma attenzione, . . . [è] forse il più singolare esempio della mescolanza di elementi disparatissimi tra loro. L'antico cantare si trova qui accoppiato al racconto di nuova invenzione, l'epopea francese si frammischia al romanzo italiano, i poemi di Malagigi, di Buovo e di Rinaldo si congiungono in un tutto, e la Tavola Rotonda invade il sacro recinto del ciclo di Carlo. . . . Quindi nella storia della letteratura cavalleresca italiana . . . *si può . . . porre insieme coi Reali*, dove noi troviamo similmente accoppiato e confuso il nuovo col vecchio.[22]

Numerous critical studies besides Rajna's have examined the relationship between known source texts in French, Franco-Italian, and Tuscan and Andrea's prose compilations.[23] On more than one occasion, the author of *Rinaldo* explicitly demonstrates just such an awareness of earlier texts, although with Petrarch-like scorn he dismisses "verse confabulations" while privileging the more "authentic" French sources:

> Diciesi in questa storia, cioè nell'usitata discritta in rima . . . e altra confabulazione assai, le quali non si trovano negli *autori franciosi parigini*. (**RM1** 174r)
> Son molti che dichono che Rinaldo segli manifestò e poi fuggisse choi chonpagni. Questo non è verisimile. Et non lo dicie *il testo francioso*, ma achostò molto meglio al detto di sopra, e que[s]to è ssuto tradotto de' libri di Turpino che ssono in San Dionigi inchatenati *in lingua franciosa*, e di quivi sono ritratte di dette *cronache*. (**RM1** 154r)
> secondo il libro *francioso* . . . (**RM1** 178v)
> secondo *le croniche parigine* che trattano di questa materia . . . (**RM1** 187r; emphasis added here and above)

These multiple references to chronicles, and not only to French but specifically to Parisian ones, resonate perhaps more than coincidentally with the "cronica di Urmano di Parigi" Andrea cites in *Reali* (63). Andrea may even have consulted *Les Grandes Chroniques de France*, the official monarchical chronicle maintained at the Abbey of Saint-Denis. No other chivalric author before Pulci mentions "Urmano" or Parisian chronicles as his authority.[24]

In contrast to ubiquitous, generic "l'autore dice" statements, Andrea cites other sources—real or fictive—by name. Besides Urmano, he mentions "Folieri, medico d'Amerigo di Nerbona" as the supposed author of *Nerbonesi*, Books I–III (**N** 1: 28), "Uberto duca di San Marino" as author of Books IV–V (**N** 1: 366), and "Giovanni Vincenzio isterliano" as poet of the verse insertions in *Ugone*, Book IV (**Z** 2: 83). In similar fashion, *Rinaldo*'s author cites "l'autor Maestro Michele" as poet of a short *cantare* at the beginning of Book V*bis* (**M** 2v).

With respect to formulae, one common device used by *cantimbanchi* of Andrea's day was to refresh the listeners' memory by reprising material from the section just completed or to pique the listeners' interest by previewing material to be narrated in the next section.[25] Following contemporary practice, Andrea does this at times: "Come la storia farà menzione" (**F** 470). More interesting are his references to material found in chapters or books earlier in the same work:

come conta al primo libro, a capitolo XXV . . . (**F** 567)[26]
secondo che tratta Folieri . . . nel Terzo Libro della sua opera, dove
tratta de' Nerbonesi . . . (**N** 2: 481)
come si dimostra . . . a' capitoli sei di questo libro nel primo comin-
ciamento d'Elia e d'Ajolfo . . . (**E** 1: 225)
cioè a' chapitoli xxvij di questo libro . . . (**B** 33v)

Such references imply both a readership and a written text, since it would
not have been possible to check recited material. This type of reference to
previously narrated material is even more explicit than the formulaic *come
di sopra è detto* Andrea frequently employs. Since similar auto-citation is
not found in control texts, it appears to be another of Andrea's characteristics shared by the *Storie di Rinaldo:*

come detto è di sopra al fine del primo libro . . . (**RM1** 34r)
Chome appare nel terzo libro di questo vilume . . . (**RM1** 115r)
chom'è scritto nel libro di Monbello a' chapitoli 22 . . . (**RM2** 11v)
chome si tratta al fine di chapitoli nove di questo . . . (**RM2** 62v)
chome fa menzione in questo libro a' chapitoli xvij. (**RM2** 113r)

In terms of narrative order, the prose *Rinaldo* follows *Aspramonte* and
precedes the war in Spain, thereby fitting neatly into Andrea's cyclical
"chronology." With respect to *Rinaldo,* Rajna noted that "il racconto venga
a rannodarsi . . . ai tre libri dell'Aspramonte," although he rejected any
suggestion that the two texts could form part of a single work or be by
the same author. Morosi reaffirms his authorial intent: "Il prosatore [di
Rinaldo] mostra di volersi riallacciare alle vicende contenute nel romanzo
di Andrea da Barberino."[27] The *Rinaldo* author himself announces this
relationship in the *incipit* of Book I: "Nel tenpo che Carlo magnio re di
Francia e imperadore di Roma e della fede cristiana haveva sotto posta la
superbia di Ghirardo da fFratta" (**RM1** 1r). References to events and characters of the *Aspramonte* narration abound:

Disse Manbrino: "Se' tu quello che uccise lo re Almonte, figliuolo del
re Agolante, e ttagliasti le mani al re Traiano, e ppartisti la fronte a
pPantalisse?" (**RM1** 47r)
Dicievano alchuni di loro essersi trovati in Aspramonte chol re Agho-
lante, e avere veduto Orlando e Almonte e Ulieno et Balante e Don
Chiaro . . . (**RM1** 81r)
"O singniore, chome poteste chredere che Filidoro avesse sogioghato
Charllo, che rre Agholamte passò chon xliiij re di chorona e Almonte
e Troiano suo figliuolo e uno milione di saraini, e tutti vi furono morti?"
(**M** 13v)

The now-deceased principal Saracens of *Aspramonte*—*Agolante,*
Almonte, and *Troiano*—are remembered throughout the several books of
Rinaldo: Agolante (**RM1** 17v, 47r, 57r, 81v; **RM2** 68r, 70r, 113r; **M** 1r, 13v);
Almonte (**RM1** 47r, 57r, 58v, 81v; **RM2** 18v, 68r, 70r; **M** 1r, 13v); and
Troiano (**RM1** 47r, 57r, 58v; **M** 1r, 13v). Other characters from *Aspramonte*
who participate, or are remembered, in *Rinaldo* include Ansergi (**RM2**
53r); Avino and Avorio (**RM2** 53v); Balugante (**RM1** 44r, 57v, 178v, 179v,
185v); Druon di Buemia (**RM1** 44r–v, 58v); Gano da Pontieri (**RM1** 35r);
Grandonio (**RM1** 185v); Dus Namo (**RM1** 33r); Salamone di Brettagna
(**RM1** 31v); and Terigi/Teris (**RM1** 78v). Yet these references *grosso modo*
to the *Aspramonte* tradition are not positive proof of a connection to
Andrea's prose version, given that several versions of that legend circulated in his day. More convincing evidence does exist.

A cursory comparison of characters in *Rinaldo* with those in Andrea's
attested epic romances reveals the *Rinaldo* author's probable cognizance
of Andrea's *Spagna* cycle. Of fifty-three distinct characters in *Prima*
Spagna, twenty-seven also appear in *Rinaldo.* With respect to *Ansuigi,*
the percentage of correspondence is much lower. A comparison of characters in Andrea's *Aspramonte* with *Rinaldo* is less conclusive because of
the preponderance of traditional figures and generic names. The name of
Mazzarigi's son is noteworthy, however. Various forms are found: Ysoré
in *Chanson d'Aspremont* (ed. Brandin) and *Anseïs* (ed. Alton), Isoré in
Entrée (ed. Thomas), Isolieri in the verse *Spagna* (ed. Catalano), but Iseres
in the *Prima Spagna* rubrics, *Ansuigi,* and *Rinaldo,* Book V. If we allow
for spelling variants, the author of *Rinaldo* subscribed to the norms of the
two texts that we attribute to Andrea.[28]

Detailed genealogical passages are another hallmark of Andrea's style.
He often embeds such listings within the narrative rather than appending
them at the end, as in *Reali.* Like Andrea, the *Rinaldo* author manifests
the inclination to introduce a character with his or her complete pedigree:

"Io sono Rinaldo da Monte Albano, figliuolo del nobile ducha Amone
di Dordona, chugino charn[al]e del conte Horlando e d'Astolfo
d'Inghilterra; nato sono della francha giesta di Chiaramonte per
anthiqui del sangue del nobile e degnio Costantino, mantenitori di
Sancta Chiesa Romana." (**RM1** 82v)
"Io ò nnome Asstolfo, ducha<cha> d'Inghilterra e ffui filgliuolo de rre
Ottone che ffu filgliuolo del ducha Bernardo di Chiaramonte; e 'l chonte
Orlando e Rinaldo da Monte Albano è mio chugino." (**RM2** 109r)
Ell'era chiamata Alda bella, figliuola del gran ducha Rinieri, signiore
di tutta la Borghognia che ffu figliuolo del valente Gherardo, ducha

da fFratta, figliuolo che fue del ducha Ghuerrino, signior di Mongrana.
"Et [ha] questa Aldabella . . . un zio chiamato Arnaldo di Borghognia
e un frattello charnale chiamato Ulivieri, marchese di Vienna. Ed è
maritata al valentissimo chonte Orlando, signiore d'Angrante e conte
di Brava, e ghonfalonieri di Sancta Chiesa Romana, ed è fratello chugino
di Rinaldo da Monte Albano e cchugino d'Astolfo, ducha d'Inghilterra,
e di Malagigi e di Viviano, fratelli duchi d'Agrismonte, Alardo,
Ghuicciardo, e Ricciardetto. E' suoi zii son questi, cioè Amone ducha
di Dardona, re Ottone d'Inghilterra, Girardo di Ronsiglione e Papa
Li[o]ne, ed è nipote di Charlo magnio, re de' cristiani, e ffigliastro del
conte Gano di Maghanza. El detto Orlando fue figliuolo del gran ducha
Mellone signior d'Angrante, figliuol di Bernardo che fe' il chastello di
Chiaramonte di chui è discieso il nome di Chiaramonte, el quale oggi
è temuto per t[utt]o el mondo." (**R5** 1v)

Regarding the names of Rinaldo's sons found in the genealogical chapter of *Reali* (565), Morosi notes an important connection between *Rinaldo*
and Andrea:

Andrea da Barberino potrebbe avere attinto i nomi dei figli d'Amone
da un testo francese o franco-veneto; così anche i nomi dei due figli
"madornali" di Rinaldo: Ivone (Yonnet) e Amonetto (Aymonnet).
Ma l'appellativo "dal Bastone" aggiunto al nome del figlio di Buovo
è proprio dei *Reali* e delle *Storie di Rinaldo* . . . perché nei testi francesi la forma del nome è sempre "Viviens" o "Viviens l'aumacors";
e, soprattutto, assenti da quelle sono le vicende dei due figli "bastardi" di Rinaldo, Guidon Selvaggio, e Dodonello di Mombello. Di
quest'ultimo, poi, non è traccia se non nel quarto libro delle *Storie di
Rinaldo* . . . ; in questo stesso libro . . . si narra la nascita di Guidon
Selvaggio.[29]

Since Rinaldo's two bastards are not listed in standard repertoires of proper
names in chansons de geste, one may well assume that they were Andrea's
inventions.

Specificities of plot and language underscore the close connection between *Rinaldo* and Andrea's cycle. "Fra i numerosi tratti comuni alle *Storie
di Rinaldo* e ai romanzi di Andrea da Barberino, segnaliamo poi la stretta
somiglianza che lega le figure dei nani Farlet (*Aiolfo*, cap. xxxi) e Allegrino
(*Rinaldo*)."[30] The last book of *Rinaldo* contains this description of Saracen
actions toward their defeated opponents: "Questi x saraini avevano . . .
rubati e morti qua[n]ti christiani vi trovarono dentro, e arsso e di[s]fatto
el chastello, *e per disprego fecono stare e chavalgli nella chiera [chiesa]*"

(**RM2** 114v). The ultimate disrespect is shown by stabling the victors' horses in the Christians' church, a gesture identical to that threatened in Andrea's *Aspramonte*, Book I (10).

The rare term *fibbia*, found only in the *Prima Spagna*'s rubrics and in *Aspramonte*, makes a single appearance in *Rinaldo* in the plural (**RM2** 102v). The related verb *afibbiarsi* occurs in both *Aspramonte* and *Rinaldo* in dramatic situations fraught with impending doom: a knight, having improperly fastened his armor during an unsuspected attack, will be fatally wounded in the ensuing fight. The two scenes as well as the language used to describe them are virtually identical:

> per la fretta non si afibbiò lo sbergo . . . (**A** 39)
> non si potè per lla fretta fare afibiare lo sbergho . . . (**RM2** 39r)

A narrative nuance shared by *Aspramonte, Nerbonesi,* and *Rinaldo* is the recurrent description of golden images of the gods that, according to medieval narrative convention, the "Saracens" worshiped:

> quattro iddei d'oro massiccio . . . (**A** 10, 82, 97, 101)
> Macone tutto d'oro massiccio . . . (**N** 2: 83; **RM2** 112v)

In one extremely unusual narrative motif, a scrap of material bearing a heraldic device serves as proof of a crime. In *Rinaldo*, false evidence is "planted" at the scene of a highway robbery in order to inculpate Rinaldo:

> Perché Ghano di Maghanza odiava molto Rinaldo, senpre cerchava in che modo lo potesse mettere in disgrazia e 'n mala volontà chon Charlo . . . e mandava certi ladroni e faceva uccidere e rubare e' merchatanti per lo paese di Ghaschongna presso a Monte Albano . . . e una volta furono rubati x grandi merchatanti . . . e fue lascato un pezzo di pennone, in pruova, d'uno lione sbarrato . . . e quando quelgli del paese trovarono quello pennone n'andarono a Parigi; e per questo pezzo del pennone ongnuno dava la cholpa a Rinaldo. (**RM2** 51r)

This passage recalls the ambush of Buoso by Count Flamingon in Andrea's *Aspramonte* in which Maganzese guilt was revealed by a telltale scrap of cloth:

> Fu trovato ataccato a uno broncone di spina un poco d'una sopravesta di divisa, . . . e questa divisa fu conosciuta essere del conte Flamingon di Velangna della casa di Maganza . . . (**A** 261)

This discussion of the connection between *Rinaldo* and *Aspramonte* concludes with the *fatagione di Orlando* scene. In this episode from

Aspramonte, Book III, three warrior-saints appear to the young Orlando, knight him, and give him various gifts. This episode appears in versions of *Spagna*, but Boni has identified three elements that may originate with Andrea: the expression "cavaliere di Dio," the gift that no one will be able to withstand Orlando's blows on the third day of combat, and the names of the three saints (Giorgio, Dimitrio, and Mercurio).[31] These components are also found in *Rinaldo*; however, instead of Saint Demitrius, Saint Dionysius appears to Orlando. This reflects an alternate tradition: "San Donisi" is also found in *Cantari d'Aspramonte* (XXXII, 28–29). Despite the variant of one name, it is clear that the compiler of *Rinaldo* subscribed to the notion of Orlando's enchantment, and that he retained various elements derived from Andrea's individualistic account (**A** 189–90):

> "I'òe udito dire che Orlando fue fatato inn Aspramonte e non può morire in battalgla . . ." (**RM2** 33r)
>
> "Noi sapiamo per tuo detto che ttre santi ti fecono chavaliere inn Aspramonte e choncedettonti grazia che uno chavaliere . . . non ti potesse durare altro che ttre gorni" (**RM2** 18v)
>
> "Non sai tue ch'elgl'è chavaliere di Dio fatto inn Aspramonte per mano di Santo Giorg[i]o e di Santo Dionigi e di Santo Merchurio . . . " (**RM2** 19v)

Resemblances between *Rinaldo* and *Guerrino* have been generally overlooked. This is in part because we lack a scholarly edition of *Guerrino*, and critical awareness of this text is virtually nonexistent. Yet the presence of similar narremes in *Guerrino* and *Rinaldo* strongly indicates a single author. In one situation shared by *Aspramonte*, *Guerrino*, and *Rinaldo*, a character offended by the ignoble or treacherous behavior of another indignantly orders the other to remove himself. *Levamiti dinanzi* is found once in the control group (Melli, XLVI, 19, 4), but the brusque, imperative forms of *togliersi dinanzi* seem to be another of Andrea's trademarks:[32]

> "Toglietemi dinanzi . . ." (**F** 224)
> "Tomiti dinanzi!" (**A** 35)
> "Tomiti dina[n]çi, poltrone che ttu sse'." (**C** 9r)
> "[T]ometi dinanzi!" (**RM2** 4r)
> "Tumeti dinanzi!" (**RM2** 66v)

A related insult from *Guerrino* is echoed elsewhere in *Rinaldo:* "poltrone che ttu sse'" (**RM2** 8r). It is noteworthy that these expressions are found only in the last three books of *Rinaldo*, books that for stylistic reasons seem to have been composed much later than the first five. Such lexical evidence may one day help to establish an order of composition for Andrea's corpus.

In Andrea's *Aspramonte* as in the French *Aspremont*, Carlo sends the head and arm of Agolante's slain son to him as "tribute," but no mention is made of the need for embalming or preserving them (**A** 182–83). Likewise, two heads of slain enemies are sent to an Eastern ruler to signify victory in *Guerrino*, but here, in an apparent narrative refinement, they are preserved with salt:

> mandarono la testa a Guerrino; ed egli subito fecie montare a chavallo xx chavalieri et comandò che portassono le due teste innanzi al soldano ... le quali enpierono di sale; et chavalcarono et andaronne a Banbillonia con le due teste et colla novella della ricievuta vittoria. (**B** 62r)

This detail also occurs in *Rinaldo*, where two corpses are preserved before being sent to Carlo:

> E ffecieno pigliare e' chorppi di Beltramo e di Ramondo, e ffattogli v[u]otare, gl'insalarono molto bene e comandarono che fusseno messi inn una bara et mandarongli a pParigi dinanzi a Charllo, e mandarongli a ddire: "Questa è la vendetta di Buovo d'Agrismonte." (**RM1** 14v)

On a lighter note, both *Guerrino* and *Rinaldo* contain a delightful scene in which a hero pretends to be ignorant of armor and horses in order to disguise his true prowess and identity. In each case, the buffoonery provokes great laughter from the observers:

> Volle el Meschino farsi beffe di loro in questa forma: ch'essendo fuori del padiglione e uno schudiere di loro due gli teneva la staffa, ed egli facieva quattro pontate di salire a cchavallo facciendo vista di non essere uso ne' fatti dell'arme; et quegli saraini facievano grandissime risa, tanto che Lionetto corse a vedere. Allora Allessandro l'aiutò sospingniere a cchavallo con le maggiori risa del mondo ... (**B** 118r)
> Quando Malagigi s'armava, v'era le maggiori risa del mondo perché s'infingieva di non sapere armarsi ... (**RM1** 14r)

The depiction of exotic peoples furnishes more parallels between Andrea's works and *Rinaldo*. One exotic Indian race, the Pandae, had been described by Ctesias as being born with white hair that darkened as they aged. By the late Middle Ages, this race had been transferred to "Albania Bianca" on the basis of the type of punning etymology frequently employed by medieval authors such as Mandeville: "It is clept Albania, because that the folk be whiter there than in other marches there-about."[33]

The protagonists of *Aiolfo, Guerrino,* and *Rinaldo* visit Albania Bianca during their adventures, and all three texts contain parallel descriptions of the exotic people found there:

> In . . . Albania Bianca . . . nascono co' capegli bianchi, e quando invecchiano diventano e' loro capegli neri; e però si chiama l'Albania Bianca . . . (**E** 2: 265)
> Questa gente sono begli uomeni et donne, tutti bianchi, et ànno i chapegli bianchi, et quando invechiano i loro capelli diventano neri per lo contrario de' Greci . . . (**B** 16v)
> Entrato Rinaldo nel[l]'Albania Biancha . . . ttrovòvi un bello vecchione tutto nero di peli per vechieza, inperò che ssono el chontrario di noi; inperò che naschono tutti bianchi chome neve di peli, e quando invechiano diventano tutti neri di peli; . . . e però sono chiamati Albani, c[i]oè bianchi d'Albania Biancha. (**RM2** 87v)

In *Rinaldo,* a description of Ethiopian troops focuses on their potential fighting ability, but includes their physical attributes as well:

> e ttutti neri chuanto charboni, e denti bianchi, labra grosse, li ochi avevano rossi. (**RM2** 10r)

In *Guerrino* a more elaborate description of an African princess includes the identical attributes:

> Era grande di persona e bene informata, nera quant'uno carbone spento, col capo ricciuto, et capelli [innanellati], la boccha grande, molti denti tutti bianchi, occhi rossi . . . (**B** 71v and **G** 117v)

There are detailed observations of Eastern customs in other European medieval genres, but these are not the usual stuff of *cantare* literature, nor do they occur in chivalric control texts. In both *Rinaldo* and *Guerrino* the Christian heroes are revolted by the idea of eating from a common bowl:

> Fu posto loro innanzi un gran piattello da mangiarvi dentro tutti e' quattro, e affettando del pane inel piattello cominciarono a mangiare. (**RM1** 116v)
> "Noi fum[m]o viii intorno a uno piattello et ongnuno peschava . . ." (**B** 20r)

The distinctive turbans worn by Eastern warriors are described in *Ugone, Guerrino,* and *Rinaldo:*

> con tela di panno lino avolto al capo . . . (**Z** 1: 261)

percosse uno Turco sulla volgina del panno lino che aveva avolto al
capo . . . (**Z** 1: 282)
un suo capitano di guerra con uno ciercine di tela lina avolto al chapo
. . . (**B** 21v)
ferìllo sopra l'avolta tela della testa . . . (**RM2** 25v)

The unusual phrase "la reina maggiore" describes the favorite wife of a
Middle Eastern potentate in *Rinaldo* and *Guerrino* (**M** 14v; **B** 39v).[34]

The two texts also have in common the terms *moschea* and *zibibbo*.
Reference to the Muslim house of prayer is not found in Tuscan control
texts; the earliest citation of the word *moschea* recorded by the *GDLI* (10:
986) is in *Morgante*.[35] For the same noun, the Crusca cites first *Morgante*,
then *Ciriffo Calvaneo* and *Orlando furioso*, but no earlier Italian chivalric
texts (10: 583). However, occurrences of *moschea* are found in *Rinaldo*,
Nerbonesi, and *Guerrino*.[36] Furthermore, an extremely rare reference to
the Muslim beverage *zibīb* appears in Andrea's *Aspramonte* (109) and
Guerrino (**B** 44v [2]), where it is called *zibibbo*. This word appears in no
control text, but it is found four times in *Rinaldo*, once with a gloss: "uno
grande barlotto di cibibo, c[i]oè vino fatto chon ispezierie perché nel paese
non si uxava vino, ma per lgli viandanti si faceva di questi cibibi" (**RM2**
43v).[37] The spelling here with the "c" is undoubtedly due to the copyist
dropping a stroke from the letter "ç" which stood for "z." This happened
commonly in the written transmission of manuscripts. Spellings with "z"
appear consistently in **M** and **R5**.

Throughout the course of his narrations, the author of *Rinaldo* reveals
a growing interest in geography, a topic that keenly interested Andrea (as
exemplified by *Guerrino*). *Rinaldo* contains some 250 discrete toponyms.
Despite the length of its eight books, this total still seems high: it names
more unconventional places than do contemporary chivalric texts. Books
I, II, and III contain virtually no geography, only a few isolated toponyms,
and no detailed itineraries; Book IV includes some short itineraries similar to *Reali* and begins to have topographical descriptions (rivers, mountains, listing of cities within larger regions, and so on); Book V contains
very little geography and no itineraries or topography. However, Books
V*bis*, VI, and VII, probably written much later than the first portion, but
before *Guerrino*, contain long, detailed itineraries that include means of
transportation, days traveled, and topographical details such as rivers and
mountains, very much like those in *Guerrino*. For example, both *Guerrino*
and *Rinaldo* include the particulars of a ruler's realm and city in the introduction of a new character:

Re Astilladoro . . . avea xv figliuoli da portare arme, ed era singnore della magior parte di Grecia, ed era a' confini dell'Ungheria, ed [era] singnore di Polana et di Bussina e di Ponpolonia et di Vesqua et di là dallo stretto d'Alispunto. Era singnore di Frigia e di Thurchia e di Ponto e di Bettinia e di Panfrigonia e di Galizia e di Isauria, et de' due [reami] che teneano l'Amanzone, chiamati Panfilia l'uno, e l'altro Ciliccia insino ad Antioccia, et [ad entrare nel mare di Setalia] insino a tTrebusonda insul mare Maore. (**B** 8v and **G** 12v)

Questo Rubione era d'uno reame ch'à nnome Alcimunes, e lla sua città magore si chiama Leucharisste a ppie' de' monti chiamati Vendici, e di questa città e' chorreva un fiume a lato alle mura che ssi chiama Visstules. Questo Vistules entra in mare nel'Uciano Sarmatichun e passa per mezzo e' reame di Cinbrea dond'era e' rre Pondras. (**RM2** 52r)

If we allow for copying errors, several of these fantastic-sounding place-names are indeed found in the northern European section of Ptolemy's *Cosmographia*, table 9: Lacris istule, Venediti montes, Istula flumen, Occeanus Sarmaticus. Furthermore, their spatial arrangement accords with the above description. Thus, the author of *Rinaldo*, like Andrea, had a close knowledge of Ptolemy.

The topography of most Tre- and Quattrocento chivalric literature is generic or bland, but the authors of *Rinaldo* and *Guerrino* shared a concern for verisimilitude in their representation of lands traversed or sites for major battles. These passages contain references to bodies of water and configurations of land, in addition to copious lists of place-names. As part of this more detailed depiction of topography, the same term, *giogo*, is used to describe mountain passes in *Aiolfo*, *Guerrino*, and *Rinaldo* (**E** 2: 121; **B** 76v, 77r; **RM2** 98v).

Many of the chivalric texts examined and certain of Andrea's works use abbreviated voyage formulae of the "And they rode so much, they arrived" type. However, itineraries in the later books of *Rinaldo* become much more elaborate, resembling the geographical complexity found in *Guerrino*:

Rinaldo . . . si mosse e per la Turchia n'andò, e passò per questi reami: per rengno di Xauria, per Ghalazia, per Ixia ver[so] Frigia, per Punto, e per Bettina, e g[i]unse in Frigia dove fue la grande terra e ccit[t]à di Troias; e indi n'andò per terra verso el Mar Maore, e passò la città di Riccea e sXalonima, e g[i]unse al Gholfo d'Alispunto, e fecesi porre a

Ghostantinopoli; e indi si partì ed entrò per la Grecia verso Trazia per andare in Texalgl[i]a e per andare verso l'Ungheria. (**RM2** 111r)

Rinaldo abounds with motifs characteristic of Andrea. The notion of characters confronted with a dilemma, from *Prima Spagna* and *Ansuigi*, is also found in *Rinaldo:* "Chi dicieva sì e cchi no" (**RM1** 193r); "Charllo fue in tra due d'armarsi [o no] . . ." (**RM1** 77v). Andrea's healing-bath motif, with all its related components, is repeated several times in *Rinaldo:*

> Questo durò insino alla sera che 'l sole era andato sotto, e g[i]urarono di tornare l'altra mattina alla battalglia . . . e tornaronsi ongnuno alla sua gente. Rubione non avea arme nè schudo magangnate niente, e' suoi baroni fecono gran festa. . . . E la sera si fece fare un bangno e poi ch'ebe cenato, andò a dormire. (**RM2** 72r)
>
> Or questo fue terribile assalto, ma non durò molto perch'elgl'era presso alla sera; e Dianesta, chome fue sera, gli fece lasc[i]are la battalglia. . . . Rinaldo montò a Baiardo e andòssene al palago de' rre Pantalione . . . e andòssene alla zanbra chol nano e disarmòssi . . . e 'l nano fece che 'l si[ni]schalcho di chorte gli mandò due medici, e ffue fatto a Rinaldo un bangno. E ccenato, andò a dormire . . . (**RM2** 105v)[38]

Concern for cleaning battlefields was a constant in Andrea. This sentiment, not found in contemporary chivalric texts, is repeatedly expressed in *Rinaldo* with language virtually identical to Andrea's:

> l'aria si chominciò a cchorronpere per gli tanti morti . . . (**RM1** 114v)
> già sentia di chorritione . . . (**RM1** 55v)
> a chonsumar cho' fuocho e chorpi morti acc[i]ò non chorronpessin l'aria. (**M** 171r)

Furthermore, Andrea's idiosyncratic specification of burial as a means of disposing of Christian corpses and cremation for the Saracen dead is reiterated in *Rinaldo:*

> chomandò che i corppi de' cristiani ch'erano morti fossero seppelliti, e ' chorppi de' saraini fossero consumati per fuocho e per altri modi, acciò che non corronpessono l'aria . . . (**RM1** 49r)
> chomandò . . . che ssotterassono tutti e' corppi de' cristiani ch'[erano] morti, e ' chorpi de' sara[i]ni chonsumassono chon sepulture e chon fuochi p[erch]é non chorrompessino l'aria. (**M** 169r)

The motif of justly dividing spoils of war among victorious troops, and the accompanying observation that all become rich as a result, is found throughout Andrea's works and in *Rinaldo:*

"Noi siamo tutti ricchi: la vettoria è nostra!" (**RM1** 20r)
tutta la roba istribuì e partìlla sì che ogni uno si chiamò contento.
(**RM1** 24v)

Another motif apparently unique to Andrea is baptism without chang-
ing the name of the new convert. This appears in *Aiolfo*, *Ugone*, *Ansuigi*,
and *Rinaldo:*

> E tTurpino fecie rechare l'acqua, e col debito hordin[e] lo batteçò et
> non gli mitò [*sic*] nome. (**RM1** 72r–v)
> battezzòllo . . . e nnolgli mutò nome . . . (**RM2** 20r)
> Charllo la fece battezzare a Turpino e nnolle mutò nome. (**RM2** 30r)

Three distinctive motifs that Andrea apparently introduced into chivalric
literature also occur in *Rinaldo*. These are a ruler's bodyguard, the deployment of troops in a crescent-moon shape, and Orlando's vow of chastity. In *Rinaldo*, "Fiore, filgluolo de rre Baldras" is accompanied by "sua
guardia ch'erano senpre quattro milia" (**RM2** 17v). Troops are arranged
in the same manner as in *Ansuigi* and *Aiolfo:* "fecono di questa schiera
due schiere e da due lati, c[i]oè a chorni" (**RM2** 40r). Orlando's vow not to
consummate his marriage until he has crowned Alda queen of Spain (**A**
296), also found in the prose *Spagna*, probably originated in Andrea's
Aspramonte.[39] This motif, with variants, occurs in different books of
Rinaldo. The sentiments expressed and the language chosen echo directly
those passages in Andrea's works:

> Orlando . . . tolse quella famosa Alda la bella per moglie e mai non
> prese druderia con lei. (**RM1** 111r)
> [Orlando] chontògli il saremento fatto quamdo la tolsse e la chagione
> perché non s'era achonpangniato a matrimonio cho' lei, che lla avea a
> 'nchoronare di Spang[n]a . . . (**M** 8r)

Le Storie di Rinaldo mirrors Andrea's narratives in their most minute
details. The motif of a quintain is used in one control text and in Andrea
with an important difference in language. In *I Cantari di Rinaldo* (XVIII,
28, 7), the construction is called "una quintana," but Andrea and the
Rinaldo author consistently call it "uno 'dificio":

> uno 'dificio di legname . . . il quale pareva uno cavaliere armato . . . (**F**
> 391)
> uno 'dificio d'uno uomo armato, grande di comune statura, a cavallo;
> ogni cosa di legname . . . (**E** 1: 132)
> edificio di bronzo in forma d'un uomo a chauallo . . . (**RM1** 129v–30r)

'difizio del lengname ... (**M** 7v)
uno 'difizio chome uno omo. (**RM2** 71r)[40]

Faville used alone is unexceptional in late medieval literature; among texts surveyed, only Boccaccio and Andrea employ the dazzling image of a knight's blow that literally makes sparks fly off his opponent's armor. Unlike Boccaccio, Andrea frequently pairs the noun *faville* with the verb *riempire*.[41] This motif occurs several times in *Rinaldo*, twice with wording identical to passages in Andrea: "l'aria si riempiè di faville" (**F** 319; **A** 289; **RM1** 47v, 127r).

According to the chivalric canon, heroes are normally strong and heroines beautiful, both being conditions predicated on good health. An unusual motif in Andrea presents protagonists who are ailing for reasons other than poison, old age, or lovesickness (**F** 551; **S** 14r, 20v). A principal cause for these uncharacteristic ailments is the hardship of travel. In *Guerrino*, for example, the normally stalwart hero becomes sick in one exotic location: "a questa ciptà ebbe el meschino otto giorni la feb[b]re" (**B** 33r). In *Ugone*, protagonists are forced to postpone the continuation of their voyage because of *mal de mer* (**Z** 2: 139). In an analogous scene in *Ansuigi*, a ship puts in to port when the heroine becomes seasick: "Giunssono al porto di Ghonbre[s], e smontati a terra, tesono ' loro padiglioni per amore di Galdina ch'era travagliata dal mare" (**S** 14v). In *Rinaldo*, this singular motif is reworked again when the hero delays a challenge to combat by feigning seasickness in order to have time to seek appropriate armor: "'El mare m'àe un pocho noiato'" (**RM2** 47r). Elsewhere, another hero suffers the ill effects of imprisonment in a dank tower: "Orlando, per la maninchonia ed el luogho humido e schuro dov'egli stava, chominciò a ssentirsi alchuno riprezzo di febbre con grandissimi duoli di testa, per modo che mangiare niente non voleva e tutto il dì si rammarichava" (**RM1** 166r). Given the number of captured knights imprisoned "in fondo di una torre," it is remarkable that such sufferings are not described by other chivalric authors.

Another distinctive motif in Andrea may owe its inspiration to Boccaccio.[42] In *Aspramonte* and *Nerbonesi*, the depiction of hawking furnishes a narrative pause, a "calm before the storm," before plunging the story into violent action. For example, Almonte "aveva uno astore in pungno" when he discovers the approaching Christian army. He gives the bird to a squire and goes to investigate (**A** 97). Other passages from *Aspramonte* and *Nerbonesi* explicitly capture the contrast between carefree pastime and ensuing danger, which informs the motif:

Buoso, che sanza paura cavalcava, sanza arme e sanza sospetto, entrò nel mezzo de' tre aguati con uno astore in pungno . . . (**A** 258)

[Folco] andossene nella zambra di sua madre con uno falcone da campagnia in pugno. E andava cantando una canzona di nuovo fatta. . . . E quando entrò nella camera, la madre, piangendo, gli si fecie incontro, e disse: "O figliuolo mio, non è più tempo di potere uccellare, né di portare uccello in braccio; ma egli è tempo di portare lo scudo in braccio, e la ispada in mano, e l'arme indosso." (**N** 2: 182)

The *Rinaldo* author employs the same image of a carefree knight carrying a hunting bird and expresses it in identical language. The term *falchon da chanpangna*, for example, parallels the citation from *Nerbonesi*:

gittò un falcone che aveva in mano . . . (**RM1** 34v)

gittò uno astore ch'egli avea in pungno . . . (**M** 6r)

andava a uccellare a falchon da chanpangna ed erasi fermo chome vide venire questo messo. . . . Quando Malagigi udì queste parole, gittò via el falchone . . . (**RM2** 48v)

In Andrea's works, several instances of unrequited love culminate in the suicide of a noble damsel who realizes her beloved is unattainable, a reaction that recalls Bellices' death in *Tavola ritonda* (1: 61).[43] In each case, the chosen means of death—falling on a sword—reminds us of Vergil's Dido:

E quando Fegra intese questa novella, addolorata se n'andò nella sua camera, e prese una spada, e apoggiò il pomo in terra, e per me' 'l cuore si misse la punta e misse uno grande grido, e finí sua vita. (**F** 127)

[Oripida] prese la spada, e pose el pome al muro e la punta al cuore, e caddevi sue, e trasse un grande strido. (**E** 1: 72)

Quando Rampilla si sentì chosì cacciare, si volse indietro et uscì del padiglione; et prese una spada et pose il pome in terra, e per mezzo il cuore si pose la punta. Et gridò una grande vocie . . . et caricòssi insulla spada et per lo petto si la ficchò, et di presente morì. (**B** 72v)

The tragic scene is repeated in *Rinaldo:*

Quando questa novella venne, ella [Personida] se n'andò in chamera piena di dolore . . . e prese una spada e ppose la punta per mei el chuore a ssé e 'l pome misse in terra e gitovesi sue e morì traendo un grande strido. (**RM2** 98v)

Lexical choices in the *Rinaldo* passage ("pose," "misse," "per mei") con-
cord exactly with those by Andrea, as opposed to the terms found in *Tavola
ritonda* ("pone," "diritto al cuore suo"). Yet such passages in *Rinaldo* have
not been slavishly copied verbatim from the texts by Andrea (as is the
case with *Acquisto* or *Rambaldo*); rather, their small permutations of a
theme indicate the pen of a single author.

The above considerations on the text's structure, style, and narremes
demonstrate clear connections between *Rinaldo* and Andrea's chivalric
narratives. When lexical criteria are applied, the argument for Andrea as
author of the *Rinaldo* becomes still more convincing. The lexical sampling isolated in preceding chapters as representative of Andrea's voice
forms a virtual checklist of *Rinaldo*'s vocabulary. Words found in multiple works by Andrea also appear in *Rinaldo* and include *a (di) buon'ora*
(**RM1** 65r, 75r, **RM2** 18r; [var.] *a una buonissima hora:* **RM1** 36v),
(al)lattare (**RM1** 57r, 169r, 171v), *alloggiamento* (**RM1** 115v, 149v, **RM2**
43r, 57v, **M** 147v; [plur.] **RM1** 156v, 176r, 192r [2], 192v [3], **R5** 1r, **RM2**
42r, 38r, 56r), *alloggiarsi* (**RM1** 86v, 116v, **RM2** 10r, 11v, 65v, 77v),
alloggiare (**RM1** 122r, 130r, 131r, 134r, 148r, **RM2** 15r, 54v, 69r, **M** 171r;
[part.] **RM1** 42r, 76v, 166r, **RM2** 54v, 114r), and *bontà di* (**RM2** 66r, 85r).
One likewise finds the superlative *asprissimo* (**RM1** 48r, 120r, 121r, 152r,
RM2 16v, 31v, 33v, 64v, 66r, 74v, 102v, **M** 8v, 11r) and the Dantesque
dibatter(si) (**RM1** 147v, 152r, **RM2** 21v, 78v; [part.] **RM2** 111r).

Three nouns outside the usual chivalric canon that occur in several
works by Andrea are also in *Rinaldo: chollazione* and variants (**RM1** 77v,
117v, 154r, **RM2** 18r, **M** 15r, 163r); *gioielli,* here used generically and not
referring to armor decorations (**RM1** 1v, 91r, 96r; [var.] *goelgli:* **RM2** 109
[2]); and *petrone,* for dismounting (**RM2** 51v).

Two adjectives frequently used in Andrea are also found in *Rinaldo:
deretano (diretano)* (**RM1** 50v, 93r, 114r, **RM2** 35v, 39r, 69v, 74r, 76v, **M**
170r; [var.] *dretana:* **RM2** 81v, 118v, **M** 170r, 170v) and *maninconoso* (**RM1**
30r [2], 53r, 116r, 164v, 184r; [var.] *malinchonoso:* **RM2** 43v, 54v).

A handful of rare words that occur in *Ansuigi* and just one or two works
by Andrea also turn up in *Rinaldo: affossata* (**RM2** 62r), *carissimo* used
as a form of address (**RM1** 47r, 83v, 121r, 149v, 167v, 186r, **RM2** 15v [2],
19r, 19v, 36r, 75r, 87r), and the extremely rare *mammaluccho* (**RM1**
93r, **RM2** 75r; [var.] *manmaluc:* **RM2** 8v, 65v). Related to the unusual
biordar(si), schianciare, and *fanti a piè,* found in *Ansuigi* and works by
Andrea, are the forms *bigordando* (**RM1** 34r), *a schiencio* (**RM2** 24v, 68r),
and *gente a ppié* (**RM1** 8r).

Numerous terms Andrea uses to create a realistic depiction of warfare make their appearance in *Rinaldo* as well: *camaglio dell'elmo* (**RM1** 19r, 24r), *spallaccio* (**RM1** 167v; [var.] *spallacciuolo:* **RM1** 109r; [plur.] **M** 1v), and *forc(i)ella del petto* (**RM1** 84r, 101r, **RM2** 39r). The phrase *gioielli dell'elmo* does not occur in *Rinaldo*, but one finds the related *goelgli dell'arme* (**RM2** 111r). Nouns Andrea uses to describe instruments of war also occur in *Rinaldo: charriaggi* (**RM1** 114v), *steccati* (**RM1** 37r, 103v) and its adjectival form (**RM2** 62r), and *ver(r)ettoni* (**RM2** 10v, 117v). *Mettersi in punto,* very common in Andrea, makes numerous appearances in *Rinaldo* as well (**RM1** 135v, 140v, 164r, 164v, 167r, 186v, 195v, **RM2** 31r, **M** 3v, 7v; [var.] *rimettere in p-:* **RM2** 17v). Certain terms uncommon or nonexistent in other chivalric texts are employed in Andrea and in *Rinaldo: lancia arrestata* (**RM1** 104v, 106r, **RM2** 67v, 84r; [plur.] **RM1** 113v), *a resta* (**RM1** 37r, 94v), and *in resta* (**RM1** 189v, **RM2** 66r, 119r); *indietreggiare* and its variants (**RM1** 44r, 114r, 114v, 190r, **RM2** 31v, 41r, 118r, 119v); *intronare* (**RM1** 14v, 15v, 19v, 94r, 114r, 167r, **RM2** 4r [2], 9r, 19r, 21r, 78v, 104v, **M** 9v; [part.] **RM1** 10v); and *sinestrare* (**RM1** 47v, 121r; [part.] **RM1** 76r). Like Andrea, the author of *Rinaldo* frequently indicates the clash of opposing armies with the verb *mescholarsi:* "ll'una giente si mescholò choll'altra" (**RM1** 189v–90r; [part. as adj.] "la battaglla era mescholata" [**RM1** 191r], **RM2** 28v, 40r, 47v, 79v). After a fierce encounter, Andrea recounts the need to regroup forces and uses the expression *(ri)fare testa.* The identical maneuver is mentioned in *Rinaldo* (**RM1** 190r, 190v, 191r, **RM2** 9r; [var.] *rifare t-:* **RM1** 24v, 46r, **M** 169v). Finally, to portray the aftermath of battle, Andrea uses the idiosyncratic *attendersi a medicare,* a phrase that recurs in *Rinaldo* (**RM1** 98v, **RM2** 11v, 69r).

A small group of significant items, hardly ever found in control texts, appears in the *Prima Spagna,* in other works by Andrea, and in *Rinaldo: bella diceria* (**RM1** 57v); *chapitano gienerale* (**RM1** 22v, 56r, 187v, 193v; [var.] *g- c-:* **RM2** 39v); *notificare* (**RM1** 56v, 128v, 183r); and *disfare insino a' fondamenti* (**RM1** 38r).

As for phraseology, a rather characteristic formula used by Andrea in his *incipits* appears, slightly varied, in the openings of the last three books of *Rinaldo:*

Regnando Carlo Martello, Imperadore di Roma, et Re di Francia, negli anni Domini viij cento lv . . . (**Z** 1: 1)
Mangnificando Charlo mangno, Re di Francia, figliuolo del secondo Pipino, Re di Francia, Enperadore di Roma, rengnando nelli anni del

Nostro Singnor Gesù Cristo 783 . . . (**B** 1v)
Book V*bis:* Regniando Charllo magnio, Inperadore di Roma et Re di
Francia, nella città di Parigi . . . (**R5** 1r)
Book VI: Rengnando Charlo mangno, Inperadore ne' rreame di Franza
. . . (**RM2** 51r)
Book VII: Rengnando Charlo mangnio, Re di Francia . . . (**M** 117v)

Similarly, the expression *tagliare a pezzi,* frequent in most of Andrea's
texts, is also found in *Rinaldo* (**RM1** 7v, 27r, 48r, 56r, 125r, 186v, **RM2** 8v).
Even more striking is the presence in *Rinaldo* of Andrea's distinctive interlace formula *Torna la storia* (**RM1** 94v, 176v).

Other expressions occur infrequently or not at all in control texts, but
are employed often in Andrea's works. These appear with similar regular-
ity in *Rinaldo: andare a vicitare* (**RM1** 5r, 16r, 57r, 131r, 149v, 150r, 153r,
161v, 183r, 187v, **RM2** 14v, 65v, 86r, 96r, **R5** 1v), *una balestrata* (**RM1** 90r,
RM2 8v, 39v, 49r, 60v, 68r, 114v), *ben fare* (**RM1** 112v), *far(si) fare piazza*
(**RM1** 32v, 98r, **RM2** 2v, 34r, 37r, 40r), *giusta mia possa* (**RM1** 117v, 165v),
lamentarsi della fortuna (**RM1** 51v, 62r, 65r, 66v, 86v–87r), and *mortale
nimico* (**RM1** 36v, 41r [2], 45v, **RM2** 114v; [var.] *n- m-:* **RM2** 30v; [plur.]
RM1 38v, 40r, **RM2** 19r).[44]

Several expressions discussed in chapter 4 are not in control texts and
make only scattered appearances in Andrea's work, yet all appear in *Rinaldo:* the Gallic *appendu sia uos por la ghorge* (**RM2** 20r), *atti d'amore*
(**RM2** 6v), *guanto sanguinoso* (**RM1** 58r, **RM2** 104v), *pondo della battaglia*
(**RM1** 102v), and *prospero vento* (**RM1** 138v, **RM2** 42r). Variants of the
highly personal *giungere forza a forza e ira a ira* also occur: "giunse
forza all'i-" (**RM1** 108v); "giugniendo f-sopra f-" (**RM1** 5v); "gunse i-
sopra a i-" (**RM2** 66r); "aggiugniendo i- a i-" (**RM1** 117v); (rel.) "agunse
la vergongna chol[l]'i-" (**RM2** 105v); "mescholòe la vergongna e lla furia
choll'i-" (**RM2** 94v); "mescholò l'i- cholla verghongnia" (**M** 147r). Formulaic expressions preferred by Andrea, such as *come di sopra è detto,
come il fatto (la cosa) stava,* and *(e) nota che,* or their variants, occur regularly throughout *Rinaldo.*[45] The particular phrase *molti religiosi* used by
Andrea to describe processions of clergy is found in *Rinaldo* as well (**RM1**
53r).

Terms thus far discussed were typical of Andrea's lexicon with respect
to the attributions *Ansuigi* and *Prima Spagna.* Next we shall scrutinize
Rinaldo for words and expressions not used by other chivalric authors of
the period, but which are found in texts clearly identified as Andrea's.
Several terms in *Rinaldo*'s descriptions of armor, the body, and wea-

pons reveal the type of verisimilitude Andrea sought. The rare *baviera (dell'elmo)* (**RM1** 98r, 127v, 130v [2]) never occurs in control texts, but appears in *Aiolfo* (2: 282).[46] *La pançiera*, an armorial fitting that protects the abdomen, is mentioned just once in control texts (*Orl.*, XXXIX, 38, 4),[47] but it is used in identical glosses in *Rinaldo* and in *Reali*: "lo sbergo di maglia, cioè la panziera" (**RM1** 64v; **F** 208). The anatomical term *collottola* is not found in control texts yet occurs more times in *Rinaldo* than in all the other texts by Andrea combined. The *GDLI* registers one of the occurrences in Andrea, followed by Pulci and Ariosto (*GDLI*, 3: 300).[48] In some chivalric texts, *palle di metallo* are attached by chains to a mace (*mazzafrusto*). However, in *Rinaldo* and in *Nerbonesi*, such balls are hurled by hand (**RM1** 69r, **RM2** 58v, 90r; [plur.] **RM1** 18v, **RM2** 71r, 89r, 89v, **N** 2: 121).

Castles and fortifications in *Rinaldo* are given the same realistic treatment as in Andrea's works. *Bastia* and *liccia* connote fortification against attack, as does *steccato*. These terms were used by medieval chroniclers such as Compagni, Giovanni and Matteo Villani, and Sercambi, but not by the contemporary chivalric authors I examined.[49] These synonyms are well represented in Andrea and in *Rinaldo*.[50] Although many battles and sieges take place around castles, only Andrea employs the special term *ponte levatoio* to describe the characteristic drawbridge.[51] Another term, *rastrello*, is used regularly by Andrea yet it appears only once in control texts (Melli, XV, 39, 4) and once in Matteo Villani's *Cronica* as *rastello* (IV, lxxxviii, 13–14).[52] Both nouns occur several times in *Rinaldo: ponte levatoio* (**RM1** 49v, **RM2** 55r, 56 [2], 56v [3]; [plur.] **RM2** 65v); *rast(r)ello* (**RM1** 7v, 106v [2], 107r, 108r, 192v, **RM2** 1r [4], 1v, 3r, 3v, 4r [3], 4v, 10v, 31r, 56r, 97r); [plur.] *rastelli* (**RM1** 49v), *rastrelgli* (**RM2** 117v).[53]

The concept of a battle or individual combat being officially judged, *battaglia giudicata* (or its inverse), is expressed in Andrea's cycle and twice in *Rinaldo* (**RM2** 38v, 39r).[54] This expression occurs only once among control texts (*Spagna*, XXXIII, 6, 2). The verb *nimicare* (to treat as an enemy, persecute, vex) or its past participle is found in *Reali, Nerbonesi, Aiolfo*, and *Ugone*, as well as in *Rinaldo* (**RM1** 40r, **RM2** 25v).[55] This verb is common in Trecento Tuscan and appears in the *Decameron*, but I was unable to find examples of its use by any other chivalric author of the period.[56] The concern for equitable division of the spoils of war is a recurrent idea in Andrea's works. The unusual *bottiniere*, related to this concept, refers to the person in charge of booty (*GDLI*, 2: 333). This noun and its variants appear in Andrea's *Aspramonte* and in *Rinaldo*: *bottinieri* (**A** 126n, 135n, **RM1** 24v); *bottoliere, bottoglieri* (**A** 149n).

Several words and expressions (*toccarsi il dente, certificare, capitolare*) fall into a category that might be loosely labeled "protocol." They concern pledges, treaties, and official reports that exemplify the responsibilities of knights and especially of ambassadors. These occur very rarely in our chivalric control texts, at times in Boccaccio, and occasionally in Dante.[57] Many of the examples furnished by the *GDLI* are taken from commercial documents, chronicles, and histories.[58] The fact that *Rinaldo* shares such "real world" vocabulary with Andrea's works indicates the same desire on the part of its author to impart to his narrative a pseudo-chronicle texture. *Toccarsi il dente,* the gesture used to swear an oath in Andrea's texts (**A** 8, **N** 2: 600, **E** 2: 123, 216, **B** 25v 58v), reappears in *Rinaldo* (**RM1** 25r, **RM2** 17v, 33r). *Certificare,* to officially impart crucial information to a concerned party or attest to its veracity, was not used by chivalric authors before Ariosto (*GDLI*, 3: 2; M. Villani, IV, lxxxv, 1). Both the infinitive and its participle occur in Andrea and in *Rinaldo* ([inf.] **B** 46v, **RM1** 154v; [part.] **A** 260, **Z** 2: 188, **B** 2r, **RM1** 142v). *Capitoli* appears in *Aspramonte,* the *Prima Spagna* rubrics, *Aiolfo,* and *Rinaldo* (**RM1** 188r, 188v, 194r, 194v [2], 195r [7]). The related verb *(ri)capitolare,* meaning to stipulate the terms of an agreement, is even rarer in late medieval chivalric literature. This diplomatic verb and its participle are found only in *Ansuigi* and *Rinaldo.*[59]

Certain pragmatic concerns expressed by Andrea, but not by most early chivalric authors, include the need for safe conduct passes and interpreters when traveling, and food testing for the nobility as a precaution against poison. *Salvo condotto* may be frequent in "testi antichi,"[60] but I found only two examples among literary texts examined: in the *Diario* (193) and Melli (XLIII, 26, 4, *salvecondotte*). The masculine singular form used by Giovanni Villani, Sercambi, and Morelli is extremely common in Andrea and in *Rinaldo.*[61] Gerardo Ciarambino praises Andrea's realistic portrayal of the linguistic difficulties that travelers encounter.[62] This is an element found in actual medieval travel accounts. Chivalric texts at times refer to foreign languages, but mention of interpreters is rare (Fassò, XXI, 13, 4). Yet the noun *interpido (interpito)* appears frequently in several works by Andrea and several times in *Rinaldo* as well.[63] *Fare (dare) la credenza* is used by Andrea (**F** 554, **E** 1: 2, 5, 37, 2: 213), and the variant with *fare* appears in *Rinaldo* (**RM1** 1r, 21v, 124r, **RM2** 43v).[64]

Rinaldo also contains numerous examples of the *cioè* gloss favored by Andrea:

alchaliffo, cioè . . . uno sacierdote de' lloro falzi iddei (**RM1** 87r)
uno portante, c[i]oè un chavallo che portava l'anbio (**RM2** 63r)

una archata, c[i]oè ccc bracc[i]a (**RM2** 81r)

A nearly identical gloss involving synonyms for an oak tree appears in *Aiolfo* and *Rinaldo*:

su per le rovere, cioè su per le quercie (**E** 1: 137)
una rovare, c[i]oè una querc[i]a (**RM2** 56v)

An interesting sidelight pertaining to the legendary royal house of France concerns a cross-shaped birthmark borne by the five direct descendants of Constantine. Despite the appearance of this notion in the Old French tradition of *Renaut* and in Andrea's known source *Fioravante*, the use of the lexeme *neo* or *niello* seems to be his own (**F** 143, 144, 337, 362).[65] *Neo* occurs in the *Decameron*, but is unknown in *cantare* literature. It is therefore striking to find *neo* used twice at the beginning of *Rinaldo* (**RM1** 1r, 1v).

Three infrequent terms found in works by Andrea and in *Rinaldo* show an acquaintance with French language, literature, and customs. The suffix of *veritiere* ("truthful") reveals French influence. This adjective is not found in the *Tre Corone* nor in our control texts, but occurs with identical meaning in *Reali*, *Guerrino*, and *Rinaldo*.[66] *Ballate* and *sonetti* are performed by characters in some Italian chivalric texts, but the "lay," a musical lament, is never mentioned.[67] There are occurrences in *Inferno* (V, 46), in Boccaccio's *Rime*, and in various commentaries on Dante (Crusca 9: 38). The form *lais* appears in *Reali* (389 [2]), as noted by the *GDLI* (8: 696). Like Andrea, the *Rinaldo* author included a *lai* in his prose text (**M** 6v). A third term reflects an accurate knowledge of foreign customs: the French "league" exceeded the contemporary Italian "mile." Andrea sometimes uses the adjectives *galeesca* or *francesca* to modify *lega* (**F** 431, 451; **E** 2: 230). These are not found in the *Tre Corone* nor in control texts.[68] Remarkably, one finds examples with both adjectives in *Rinaldo*: *lega alla franzosa* (**RM2** 12v); *legha ghalescha* (**RM2** 119r [2]; [plur.] **RM1** 66v, 132r, **M** 171r).

Other terms used infrequently in Andrea's works have to do with the presence of evil or heresy. At times a character is prompted by a demon to perform some immoral or treacherous deed. *Investigare* is used alone three times in the *Decameron*, but *investigato dal dimonio* is not found in Dante, Petrarch, or chivalric authors of the period except Andrea (**F** 150, 169, 292; **A** 41). The complete expression appears in *Rinaldo* (**RM1** 75v) and elsewhere with a virtually synonymous variant: "investigato ... da Gano" (**RM1** 35r). When confronted by a potentially demonic force, a knight knows his best protection is to cross himself. *Segnarsi il viso* is found only once among control texts (*Fior.*, 472), but occurs in five of Andrea's works as well as in *Rinaldo.*[69] An extended variant, *(farsi) il segnio della (santa) croce*, is found in *Tavola ritonda* (461 [2]), in the *Decameron* twice, and in *Purgatorio* (II, 49). It occurs in all Andrea's major works and several times in *Rinaldo.*[70] *Paterino*, derived from a thirteenth-century heretical sect, is used in *Il Fiore* (*ED* 4: 348), in G. Villani's *Chronicle* (*GDLI*, 12: 808–9), and in *Melli* (XXXVIII, 22, 6). Andrea anachronistically reflects the Church's fears when he uses it to describe characters who have renounced their Christian faith, such as the renegade Gherardo da Fratta (**A** 263, 264, 269, 271, 279). The word occurs in *Rinaldo*, where it also means "heretic" (**RM1** 16v, **RM2** 66v, 67r).

We now consider a final series of words united only by virtue of their novelty. None is found in the *Tre Corone*, and only one occurs (with a variant spelling) among chivalric texts examined. *Abavagliare, bavagliare,* or *imbavagliare* is featured in scenes by Andrea in which heroes or heroines are abducted.[71] The only citation under *bavagliare* in the Crusca (2: 111) is from *Reali*, and its only occurrence among controls is in *Orlando* (XLIX, 6, 3). For the variant *imbavagliare*, the *GDLI* (7: 283) cites *Aiolfo*. These verbs and participles occur several times in *Rinaldo: ab(b)avagliare* (**RM1** 95v; [part.] **RM2** 116v), *bavalglar[e]* (**RM2** 110r [2], 110v), and *'nbavagliati* (**RM1** 115v).

Another rare verb with somewhat nefarious connotations is *alloppiare*, to drug with opium. In *Reali*, sleeping potions are at times administered to the protagonists; at other times helpers drug prison guards and liberate the heroes. For the infinitive, the *GDLI* cites no author earlier than Firenzuola (1493–1543), although for the participle it cites Ser Giovanni (mid-fourteenth century) and then Andrea (1: 334). The term does appear in *Fioravante* (378), a recognized source for *Reali*, Book II. For the related noun *alloppio*, the Crusca (1: 385) cites *Reali* first. Like Andrea, the author of *Rinaldo* seems to have had a fascination for this verb and its related noun, since he uses them in several books.[72]

Intrinsico and *infingardo* are two unusual adjectives not found in control texts; they occur only rarely in Andrea.[73] Each of these makes a single appearance in *Rinaldo: intrinsicho* (**RM2** 96r) and "O traditori infinghardi e da pochi, o codardi" (**RM1** 18v).

Sensitivity toward rank or position is revealed by the expression *bassa condizione*, used in the *Convivio* (IV, xiv, 11) and twelve times in the *Decameron*. Andrea employs the term several times (**F** 309, 477, 479, 500, **A** 123, **E** 2: 179, **B** 1r, 4v, 6r, 27v, **G** 79r). It appears once in *Rinaldo* (**RM1** 81r).

Garbino (*gherbino*) is used infrequently in *Aspramonte* (197), *Guerrino* (**B** 61v, 84v, 87r), and *Rinaldo* (**RM2** 33v) to refer to a southwest direction. For this noun, the *GDLI* registers no chivalric author earlier than Ariosto (6: 587). It is found in Matteo Villani (III, xxxvii, 2).

Rabbonacciare is used by Andrea to indicate the calming of the sea as a tempest subsides: "rabbonacciò un poco la fortuna" (**E** 2: 87), "era rabbonacciato" (**E** 2: 95), "in chapo di v giorni si rabonacciò" (**U** 28v), "il mare che rabonacciava" (**Z** 1: 189]).[74] The concept is not unknown in other chivalric texts, but it is expressed differently: "il mar bonaccia" (*Spagna*, XXVI, 7, 1). For the infinitive with its marine connotation, the *GDLI* (15: 184) offers few citations, but these include *Aiolfo* (2: 87). However, the participle is used in identical phrases in *Reali* and *Rinaldo*: "rabbonacciato il mare" (**F** 232; **RM1** 17r).

As noted in chapter 2, Andrea's figurative language is generally richer and more imaginative than is the norm for *cantari*. Carolingian cycle material in Italy contained various animal similes (*come un drago* or *lione* or *lupo*), but elephant similes were not one of its accepted conventions. These occur only in *Guerrino* and *Rinaldo*: "enmisse un mug[h]io che parve uno leofante" (**RM2** 11r).[75] The unusual comparison of a combatant being pounded by his opponent's blows like an anvil being struck by the smith's hammer appears once each in *Ugone* and in *Rinaldo*:

chome il fabro insull'anchudine quando più ispesso martella lo perchoteva . . . (**U** 60v–61r)
pareva avere mille febbre nella testa che ferro caldo martellasseno sopra all'anchudine. (**RM1** 126v)

Although hammer blows are not unknown in the similes of *cantari* (Melli, XIV, 10, 1), the use of *anchudine* in both instances here is noteworthy. Other similes in *Ugone* and in *Rinaldo* share unusual vehicles:

gittava tanto sanque che ongnuna di per sè pareva una doccia di mulino. (**U** 38r)
si rotò parecchie volte come robechio di mulino. (**RM1** 161r)
chome si gira una macina da nmulino. (**RM2** 64r)

Another rarity, *affettare come rape*, may have originated with Andrea, occurring as it does in both *Nerbonesi* and *Rinaldo*: "come rape gli affettavano" (**N** 2: 54); "affettavano i saracini chome fosseno r-" (**RM1** 190v). Although this phrase was not found in any earlier control text, it was absorbed by Andrea's imitators in *Seconda Spagna* (94), *Acquisto* (245), *Rambaldo* (70v), and *Morgante* (XX, 67, 7).

Classically inspired similes in *cantari* are infrequent and usually elementary—knights being compared to Hector or Achilles, or ladies to Venus or Helen—but two passages from *Rinaldo* suggest its author's heightened awareness of antiquity, similar to that of Andrea: "un *porcho grande e grosso che pareva quello di Chalidonia* . . . " (**RM1** 186r);[76] "bisogniava che *Giove* si turasse gli orecchi . . . " (**RM1** 191r). Further evidence of classical inspiration in Andrea and in *Rinaldo* is in the similes referring to bulls. The *Aeneid,* a work readily available to medieval Italian readers, contains three bull similes; surprisingly, this image did not enter the repertoire of Carolingian cycle authors. There are six examples in Andrea,[77] and one in *Rinaldo:* "sacrificati a Maumetto chome se fusseno tori o montoni" (**RM1** 101v).

Other chivalric authors at times use tower similes to indicate great height—"era lungo venti piedi, sicché parea una torre a vedere" (*Fior.,* 481); "a verderlo [*sic*] parea un piè di torre" (Melli, X, 15, 1–3)—or firmness and immovability ("fermo su 'vi più che torre" [Melli, XXXVI, 33, 8]). However, only Andrea uses the Vergilian image of a structure falling (see *Aeneid,* IX, 711–13). *Rinaldo* employs not only the same unconventional notion of instability but language identical to that of Andrea:

> parve che rovinasse una torre. (**E** 2: 218)
> che parve rovinasse una torre. (**U** 1: 241)
> parve che una torre rovinasse. (**RM1** 106r–v)

As we have seen, Andrea frequently used Dantesque language or images in his similes. In like manner, a unique example from *Rinaldo* resembles several passages in Dante's *Convivio* (*ED* 2: 419): "tagliò tutto come fusse ciera, e come il sole per corpo diafano passano e' razzi chosì passò Frusbertta fiera" (**RM1** 152r). Although no passage identical to this one exists in Andrea's proven works, its Dantesque overtones are remarkable and indicate that its author's register was more exalted than is the norm for chivalric literature of the period.

In sum, this chapter has furnished detailed evidence to show that Andrea was in all probability the author of *Le Storie di Rinaldo da Montalbano* in prose. Anyone acquainted with Andrea's prose notices immediately upon reading *Rinaldo* similarities of content, style, language, and narrative flow; yet without executing a thorough comparison of narrative motifs, nuances, and lexicon, the former resemblances could be dismissed as mere coincidence or as skillful imitation. The wealth of examples cited argues convincingly for Andrea's authorship of the anonymous *Rinaldo,* and even offers clues for establishing the work within a compositional ordering for Andrea's entire output.

The Case against *Il Libro di Rambaldo*

The unedited Florentine prose romance *Il Libro di Rambaldo da Risa* has perhaps not without reason been attributed to Andrea. However, this is an instance that proves the dictum of Guglielmo Gorni that "possiamo, e spesso dobbiamo, togliere credito a certe paternità documentate."[1] The medium-length text (seventy-two folios) is preserved in a single manuscript: Florence, Biblioteca Nazionale, Palatine 578 (old E.5.5.19). The work begins with a proem identical to that of *Guerrino*, continues with a long recapitulation of the *presa di Risa* (Reggio, Calabria) from *Aspramonte*, and includes several chapters and rubrics identical to some found in *Guerrino*, with still other chapters identical to material from *Ugone d'Avernia*. *Rambaldo* did not enter the standard chivalric repertoire. It is not mentioned, for example, among the "required readings" of that aficionado of chivalric literature, Michelagnolo da Volterra (Laur. Med. Pal. 82, dated 1487–88). It is not named in the inventory of Stradino's library, nor is such a title mentioned in other fifteenth- and sixteenth-century book inventories. Literature on this romance is lacking, although a transcription is being published serially by Virginio Bertolini. This chapter examines the too-facile attribution of this text to Andrea and offers new critical insights on its style and more probable authorship.

The similarities between *Rambaldo* and *Guerrino* were first pointed out by Luigi Gentile in his catalog of the BNCF Palatine codices. It was he who proposed *Rambaldo* as a prototype done by Andrea for the more famous work: "Questa istoria di Rambaldo ha tali attinenze col *Guerrin Meschino*, che sembra essere il primo getto di questo; e probabilmente n'è autore lo stesso Andrea da Barberino." Rajna followed Gentile in ascribing *Rambaldo* to Andrea: "Del *Guerrino* è bene da ritenere una forma antecedente il *Rambaldo*, che la convenienza . . . di un prologo spiccatamente personale, porterebbe a credere, nonostante qualche ragione in contrario, opera del medesimo Andrea." Those "reasons to the contrary" should make one wary of proposing an easy attribution of authorship for *Rambaldo*. Modern critics, however, have continued to regard early claims of authorship as an incontrovertible fact. Adolfo Werner observed that *Rambaldo* contained elements of *Aspramonte* and *Guerrino* and believed that it had served as a source for Andrea. Osella provides a detailed comparison of many corresponding rubrics and passages of text that *Guerrino* and *Rambaldo* share. Both Rajna and Boni note the occurrence in *Rambaldo* of the *presa di Risa* scene from *Aspramonte*.[2]

In the wake of opinions by such respected scholars, succeeding literary anthologists have shown little hesitation in including *Rambaldo* among Andrea's works. In a comprehensive study of *Rambaldo*, Bertolini compares certain passages with similar ones in *Aspramonte, Guerrino*, and *Ugone* and examines the language, genealogy, place-names, dates, and characters of *Rambaldo* with respect to Andrea's works.[3] Despite the obvious connections between *Rambaldo* and Andrea's texts, scholars have rather conveniently set aside one glaring piece of evidence: a statement of authorship in the manuscript itself. In a brief opening comment that precedes the *Guerrino*-like proem, the anonymous author has modestly signed his work "chonposto per me .B. citadino fiorentino." A second signature appears within the proem: "Io .b. mi sono dilettato di cierchare di mollte istorie" (**R** 1r). Osella, quoting this passage, rather tentatively suggests the correlation "B. [Barberino?]." Bertolini includes this *incipit* in his description of the manuscript, but does not raise the issue of the identity of the anonymous Florentine "Citizen B," assuming throughout his study that Andrea is the author.[4] However, when one analyzes the text microscopically and macroscopically, beyond the obvious similarities of rubrics, text, and narremes, it appears that *Rambaldo* can hardly have been written before *Guerrino;* in all probability, an anonymous fifteenth-century Florentine imitator compiled it after Andrea's death.

It is instructive to examine names of characters in *Rambaldo* with respect to the works of Andrea. A large percentage of proper names had appeared in passages copied directly from *Guerrino* or *Ugone*. Several major characters from *Aspramonte* are preserved in *Rambaldo:* Agolante, Almonte, Ricieri, Beltramo. The Galiziella of *Aspramonte* becomes Galizella in *Rambaldo*. Some minor characters, such as Marsilio's brothers Balugante and Falserone, occur in several of Andrea's texts, but derive from the larger chivalric tradition. In passages taken from *Guerrino* or *Ugone*, Citizen B fuses the two titular characters, renaming the composite "Rambaldo." Other name changes only partly camouflage their source: Guerrino's opponent Tenaur becomes Tenperano in *Rambaldo*, and his companion Caristopo becomes Chariello. Some of *Rambaldo*'s characters such as Malagrapa (56r), Meridonio (12v), and Angielia (55r–56r) share a name-only relationship to works by Andrea.[5] For instance, the heroine Violante is a rather pallid figure in *Nerbonesi* (2: 36, 86). In *Rambaldo* (**R** 20r), however, her persona is more akin to Amidam in *Guerrino*, Book II. The name Foriello used for a pagan (**R** 11v) "sounds" wrong, according to Andrea's narrative usage. In *Reali*, for example, one finds Fiorello, the king of France, active in Books I and II, and a lesser Fiorello of Chiaramonte in the genealogical closing of Book VI. Both of these are clearly Christian heroes.

During the course of *Rambaldo*'s narration, two popes are mentioned: Papa Adriano (2v) and Papa Lione Secondo (48r–49r). A fictional Papa Arians (var. Aurianus) in A.D.827 appears in *Nerbonesi* (1: 225), but Andrea mentions no Papa Adriano. Papa Lione terzo, not always shown with his numerical indication, appears frequently in Andrea's *Aspramonte* and *Reali*, Book VI, as well as in *Guerrino*.[6] According to Andrea's chronology, and history, this pope elected Carlo Magno emperor of the Holy Roman Empire (**F** 546). Although the date 783 (corresponding to Pope Adrian I's tenure) is mentioned at the beginning of *Guerrino* and repeated in *Rambaldo*, the bulk of the story and the hero's birth occur after this, that is, at the time of the historical Pope Leo III (795–816). The author of *Rambaldo* may have wanted to correct the pope's name with respect to the narrative's opening date; unfortunately, Pope Leo II reigned a full century earlier, from 682 to 683. Thus, Andrea's mention of Pope Leo III was more verisimilar.

Several unusual proper names in *Rambaldo* are apparent inventions or possible scribal errors. These are not found in Andrea's works nor among our chivalric control texts: Ghargaloro (13r), Albateilla/Abbiteile (22v, 23v), Rilitiria (47r), Reina Silisi (5r), Belito (53r), Ulitos (60v), Isbrehe (53r), Changienoua (69r, 70v), Pandrocho di Trabusonda (69r), and Almadeore (70v). In a possible attempt at historical realism or perhaps encomium, Citizen B includes non-Tuscan names that are outside the usual canon of noble families found in Italian chivalric literature of the period: la [c]hasa de' Pitoni da Todi (61v) and, at Naples, Monsigniore Chocia, arcivescovo di Napoli, Messer Bindello degli Aviati, Messer Anselmo de' Butini, and Messer Alaman[n]o (66r).

Given Citizen B's heavy reliance on three of Andrea's works, one might expect to find place-names imported from these texts directly into *Rambaldo*. Much of the action in the early chapters of *Rambaldo* takes place at Organoro, the fictional North African kingdom of Agolante, a place mentioned frequently in the parallel narration of *Aspramonte*. A certain "re di Schondia e Nobiro" participates in *Rambaldo* (4v); this king's territory corresponds to the realm ruled by Andrea's Balante (**F** 545; **A** 4). Some unusual place names were copied within entire excerpts from *Ugone*, such as Boli (**R** 50v < Bolin [**Z** 2: 229]) and Nalbrucho (**R** 51v < Nalbus [**Z** 2: 234]). Like the protagonist of *Guerrino*, that of *Rambaldo* visits Cairo. His route as well as the description of that city, most often written Chario in **R** (14v–15v), are transcribed directly from a passage in *Guerrino* (**B** 59v). The land Bus(s)ina (Bosnia) is named in *Guerrino* (**B** 114r), *Aiolfo* (1: 73; 2: 5, 190), and *Reali* (314) and appears in *Rambaldo* (56r). A large portion of the siege of Media episode in *Guerrino* (**B** 19v–20v) has been transferred into *Rambaldo* (19v–20r), along with that geographical name. Part of *Rambaldo*'s action occurs at an English city called Uliena (61v), probably related to Ulione, also in England, found in *Guerrino* (**G** 161r). The Spanish kingdom of Aragona or Ragona in *Reali* (498), *Aspramonte* (14, 229, 246, 250), and *Nerbonesi* (2: 74, 77, 82, 84) is Raona in *Rambaldo* (71r).

Despite his inclusion of foreign place-names, Citizen B does not fully share Andrea's interest in detailed itineraries and realistic geographical descriptions. In transcribing passages from *Guerrino*, he has on more than one occasion consciously eliminated some places from passages dense with such names, as in the following example:

> Dopo tutte queste chose, demo ordine d'andare a Babillonia dal [so]ldano; e ragunò questo re del suo paese xl mila saraini da molte parti, ma da Polismangnia et da Siennesi [e] da Tripoli e da Polisbere dell'isola [di Tazia] e verso la città detta Tartis n'anda[mo]. (**B** 59v and **G** 96r)
> Dopo queste chose, demo ordine d'andare a Banbilonia dal soldano, e raghunò l'amostante di sua paesi xl mila di saraini. Chaminando [?] inversso la città detta Tartis n'a[n]damo. (**R** 14v)

Much longer excisions occur elsewhere in passages in *Rambaldo* (**R** 25v, 33v–34r) and correspond to those of *Guerrino* (**B** 24r–v, 32v–33r). On folio 38r of *Rambaldo* an entire folio of geographical description from *Guerrino* (**B** 36v–37r) has been omitted. On folio 69v *Rambaldo* omits a section of geography (**B** 23r) used to introduce a new character by describing his realm. In addition to this sort of gross abbreviation of place names, Citizen B often omits Petrea from the correct longer form Arabia Petrea (**R** 16–17; **B** 49v, 62r). This suggests that Citizen B was not aware of the different Arabias—Arabia Petrea, Arabia Deserta, and Arabia

Felice—as found in Ptolemy's *Cosmographia,* a known source for Andrea's *Guerrino.*

Some places in *Rambaldo* are not found in Andrea nor in other chivalric texts. These geographical names are apparently inventions or interpolations by Citizen B: la città Dalmares or Dalmandes or Dalmades (11r–13v); Vilitis (11v–12v); Alma Varentis (14v); Murida or Marida (18v); "uno chastello chiamato Bello Porto" (20v); Mulitas or Militas (56r, 58r–v); Monte Tibelli or Tiboli (23r–v); "la montangia detta Pilitone" (47r); Buabilis (47r); and Biltirano (47r). In two instances in *Rambaldo,* there seems to be a confusion of place and character names with regard to those found in Andrea: Valitor, an African character in *Guerrino* (**B** 71r–72v), appears as a place-name in *Rambaldo* ("Rilitiria, marchese di Valitor" [47r]), and the *Rambaldo* character Abineo (47r) may be derived from Monte Arbineo (**F** 253–54). Despite such minor problems, Citizen B maintains a degree of accuracy. He gives the names of two actual churches in Italy: "Santo Janni . . . la sedia papale" (San Giovanni Laterano) in Rome (48r) and "la chiesa di Santa Maria della Neve i' Napoli" (71r, 72r).[7]

On the microscopic level, places named or invented in *Rambaldo* apparently follow Andrea's praxis; on the macroscopic level, however, Citizen B's handling of geography leaves much to be desired. Those portions of *Rambaldo* that appear to be original reveal no interest in minutely chronicling the protagonists' itineraries as Andrea's works do. These sections utilize the old, abbreviated voyage formula, which goes back to Trecento texts such as *Orlando:* "in poche giornate chavalchò che giunse alla città" (**R** 11v). Citizen B ends one chapter with this type of formula, only to begin the next with an expanded version of the same journey, almost an afterthought:

> e po[i] ongniuno si partì e tornorono a Panpalona, e Ranbaldo [c]holla sua giente tantto chavalchò notte e giorno che g[i]unse presso alla città di Risa.
>
> [New chapter begins] E chossì chaminando Ranbaldo per mollte giornate, tantto chaminò che g[i]unsse i' Lonbardia, e di Lonbardia in Toschana; e andòne a Roma e andò a vicitare il santo papa e da lui si chonfessò. . . . E partitosi n'andò in Puglia, e di Puglia n'andò in Chalavria e pas[s]ò le montangie d'Aspra monte e arivò insulo tereno di Risa presso alla città. (**R** 46r)

Other remarks seem to reveal only a vague knowledge of geography, unlike Andrea's striving for precision or, at least, the semblance of accuracy. Bertolini has remarked more than once that the major part of

Rambaldo's geography is fictitious and its distances improbable.[8] For example, *Rambaldo*'s otherwise detailed itinerary across northern India reveals a strange gap caused by Citizen B's omission of three chapters from the account in *Guerrino* (see map 1). When Rambaldo deserts Marsilio's camp and joins Carlo's, accepting baptism in the bargain, Carlo Magno awards him the duchy of Risa "ne' chonfini della Chalavria a' chonfini di Barberia" (**R** 45v). It seems rather strange to describe this territory as ending across the sea from the Italian peninsula. Other such geographical infelicities include a trip Rambaldo makes from Mecca directly to Spain by sea (**R** 42v) and an invasion of England by Africans (**R** 60r–v). Such long voyages were within the realm of physical reality, but their presentation in *Rambaldo* violates Andrea's geographical logic. Andrea would normally have narrated points along the route, or described the sea voyage, instead of having the hero leap inexplicably from Mecca at the end of one chapter to Spain at the beginning of the next. After the careful topographical descriptions in the passages borrowed from *Guerrino*, such facile narrative transporting of the protagonists is jarring in the extreme.

In fact, the overall handling of geography and its relative importance in the two texts should arouse suspicion of the theory that *Rambaldo* preceded *Guerrino*. Anyone familiar with *Guerrino* cannot but admire the way in which Andrea has framed his narration on the map of the known world. Not only does he mention places visited by classical heroes such as Alexander and Cato, he describes actual trade routes found in contemporary maps and portolan charts.[9] If we trace Guerrino's itinerary on a modern map, the epic expanse of the narrative becomes apparent: the hero wends his way from his birthplace at Durazzo to the Far East, returns westward through Arabia and Ethiopia, across northern Africa, goes north through Europe to England, and arrives finally at his natal city. The final two books of *Guerrino* feature still more journeys in Asia Minor and a return trip to Presopoli in order to be reunited with his betrothed.

By contrast, the map of Rambaldo's voyages is fragmented and incomplete (see map 2). Since many chapters have been copied directly from *Guerrino*, a large segment of Rambaldo's itinerary does follow Guerrino's route. Yet many place names in *Rambaldo* are fantastic—for example, Monte Tibelli—and the author gives no other indication of directions or topographical landmarks as Andrea does. In view of the geographical evidence, it hardly seems possible that an author with enough precise data at his disposal to list detailed itineraries (as in the chapters that correspond to *Guerrino*) would suddenly abandon this approach and grossly abbreviate voyages or make such errors as having Calabria border on Barberia.

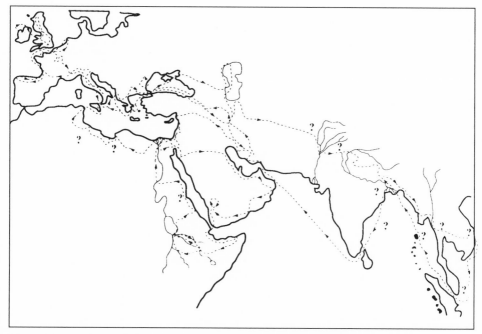

Map 1. Guerrino's travels

On the other hand, it seems probable that an author with a clear interest in geography (*Reali*, an early work, contains many European toponyms, which recur in *Guerrino*) and travel (*Ugone* may more properly be considered a prototype for *Guerrino*) would ultimately have conceived so expansive a work as *Guerrino*.

Formal analysis also reveals great differences between the compositional process of the two authors. Andrea works well in large forms, and structuring on a grand scale is easily discernible within his individual epic romances as well as throughout his narrative cycle. For example, *Reali di Francia* concerns the spread of Christianity across Europe and the rise of the Carolingian dynasty. *Nerbonesi* focuses on a later generation of the same dynasty as it struggles with Maganzesi pretenders to the throne and against the Saracens still present in Spain. *Ugone* pits the righteousness of its hero against the malicious schemes of the immoral Carlo Martello. *Guerrino* is a quest for identity that follows the hero throughout the known world until he regains his patrimony, his parents, and his beloved. Citizen B's work, however, is fragmentary, lacking the sense of purpose that sustains Andrea's narratives and makes possible their larger formal constructs.

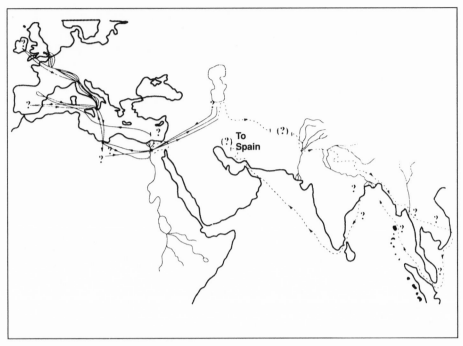

Map 2. Rambaldo's travels

Andrea and Citizen B worked from preexisting models, but Andrea absorbs entire chivalric texts into his own, for the most part fusing borrowed and original material seamlessly and coloring the whole with his personal brand of chivalry and morality. Citizen B uses his model texts differently; as Osella and Bertolini have indicated, he borrows, rearranges, and recasts individual chapters from Andrea into a kind of montage. After quoting the proem of *Guerrino* (see Appendix B), the author of *Rambaldo* began nicely enough by paraphasing *Aspramonte*, Book I, and adding some original ideas. Notably, he selected the references to Galiziella's twins (**A** 32) and the alternate ending to her story—escape, not execution (**A** 43)—as the basis for his romance and to establish the genesis of his protagonist.[10] Yet Citizen B could not sustain the effort of paraphrasing and quickly slipped into verbatim transcriptions of entire chapters from *Guerrino*, though with a slightly rearranged order. Later he also copied verbatim a few chapters from Andrea's *Ugone* (Book IV, chaps. 11–15). Near the end of *Rambaldo*, Citizen B even repeated four of the same *Ugone* chapters, although with a somewhat freer reworking (see Appendix C). It seems evident even on a first reading that Citizen B had no clear structure in mind for his romance and merely patched together one section after another. An authorial intrusion near the beginning of his tale attests to the fact that he himself is not sure where the narration will lead: "*Forse se ne traterà d'Alma la bella in qualche parte in questo libro; p[e]r[ò] al presente no se ne dirà p[e]rché abiano a tratare di Ranbaldo Ricieri, suo fratello*" (**R** 11r, emphasis added). Key episodes repeat themselves (Rambaldo is awarded with a duchy three times; five consecutive chapters treat celebrations), and the length of chapters from Book II, chapter 46, to the end is noticeably diminished as the author struggles to sustain the narrative. By comparison, chapters borrowed from *Guerrino* are very long. Even with omissions and abbreviations of up to two folios, they greatly outdistance the average chapter length of *Rambaldo*. It seems improbable that a single author could have produced both the well-handled and detailed narrations found in the extracts from *Guerrino* or *Ugone* and then failed to sustain them in the latter chapters of the same text.

The poor distribution of *Rambaldo's* narrative content stands in marked contrast to Andrea's works. Redundant use of identical motifs in *Rambaldo* robs them of their dramatic potential and also retards the narrative flow. For example, in Andrea the notion of a disinherited knight winning a *signoria* normally provides a natural closure for a narrative segment, a long series of adventures, or an entire romance. Citizen B recognized the emotional impact of such scenes of ultimate triumph over adversity, but he overused them, thereby ruining both the formal balance and the verisimilitude of his story. In *Rambaldo*, Book II, chapter 12, the protagonist is appointed duke of "la cit[t]à di Risa chon tutto il territoro." He is reaffirmed ruler of "Puglia, Chalavria, e mollto paese" (chap. 28) and again: "Ranbaldo p[e]r merito della faticha fu fatto rre di Puglia" (chap. 46). Not much later, in chapter 48, he is invited to rule the city of Naples, leaving his more substantial realm to his young sons. The triple appointment of Rambaldo to rule Puglia and Calabria most likely occurred because the author borrowed multiple battle scenes from various sources, resulting in the need to reward his hero's victories in each case. Yet the extent of this narrative oversight emphasizes Citizen B's lack of skill: he could at least have changed the names of the kingdoms to eliminate repetition.

Another example of poor distribution of material concerns five consecutive chapters of *Rambaldo*, Book II, that deal with celebrations. Again, Citizen B well understood the emotional climax such a scene represents, but ignored the need for variety, as the following rubrics show:

Chome Ranbaldo, g[i]unto a Risa, ordinò la festa p[e]r mandare pella sua nuova isposa Angielia, figliuola de' re d'Ingilterra. Chapitolj xxviiij. (**R** 55r)
Chome i' Rre d'Ingilterra manda a marito Angielia sua figliuola al du[c]ha Ranbaldo da Risa, e lla festa che si fa. Chapitolj xxx. (**R** 55v)
Chome il ducha Asperante g[i]unse a Risa chon bella chonpangnia ala festa di Ranbaldo suo zio. Chapitolo xxxi. (**R** 56r)
Chome Ranbaldo giaquue chola bella e gientile Angielia sua donna e lla grande festa si fè . . . Chapitolj xxxij. (**R** 57r)
Chome s'ordinò e fèssi una bella giostra a rocieti p[e]r detta festa . . . Chapitolo xxxiij. (**R** 57v)

These chapters do not constitute the only occurrences of festivities in *Rambaldo,* Book II: still others take place in chapters 8 (43r), 19 (49r), 57 (71r), and 59 (71v). By contrast, Andrea most often places weddings or victory celebrations at the end of a single chapter, thus providing a joyous conclusion to a longer episode.

Citizen B does include other narrative commonplaces such as ambassadorial missions, orations, texts of letters, combats, and amorous scenes; yet when compared to the original chapters in Andrea's texts, these reveal certain remarkable divergences in content. In the original portions of *Rambaldo,* the protagonist travels through exotic lands without encountering giants or exotic peoples as Andrea's heroes frequently do. One such example in *Guerrino* is the *geranomachia*—Indian Pygmies fighting against cranes—a topos that had appeared in Ctesias, Megasthenes, and Homer: "Io dissi ad quello indiano: 'Io ò letto che questa ginia [i piccinacholi] combattono colle gruge'" (**B** 30r). Although Andrea would not have had access to these accounts in the original Greek, many such legends had by his day entered medieval culture.[11] Andrea enhances his narrative by weaving the classical topos into his exotic landscape, but Citizen B, though he includes the Pygmies, omits the reference to cranes entirely (**R** 31r).

Attacks by wild beasts are fairly common in Andrea, yet none occur in the original portions of *Rambaldo.* Individual combats in Andrea are normally quite detailed, and his full-scale battles often include information on strategy as well as a large cast of players. By contrast, the combats in *Rambaldo*'s original sections lack detail and are restricted to a small number of participants, making them less complex than corresponding scenes written by Andrea. A notable example is the duel between the Saracen-raised Rambaldo, newly joined with Marsilio's camp in Spain, and the well-known Christian champion, Orlando. Such encounters of champions of the two faiths have enormous dramatic potential, as other chivalric texts demonstrate. One recalls the classic duel between Orlando and Ferraù, which stretches over eighteen chapters in the lost *Prima Spagna* (rubrics for chaps. 15–32) or the various treatments of the same duel in *Spagna* (ed. Catalano, and its appendixes). Yet in *Rambaldo*, Book II, the encounter is only in chapter 9, which is short and consists mostly of dialogue. It is clear that the author of *Rambaldo* lacked Andrea's sense of drama and perhaps even his knowledge of chivalric literary conventions. Osella, although he argues that *Rambaldo* served as a prototype for *Guerrino*, admirably summarizes the stylistic differences of the two works:

> Il Rambaldo presenta un grado minore di perfezione stilistica . . . e minore abilità di variare l'espressione delle stesse idee e la narrazione di fatti poco diversi. Così descrive le battaglie e i duelli quasi sempre nello stesso modo e colle stesse parole, . . . ripete gli stessi motivi quasi nella stessa guisa, non curando di riprodurre. . . . Invece il *Guerrino* ha, per una parte, maggiore sicurezza di periodo, e per l'altra, molto maggior varietà, non ripetendosi quasi mai o rimaneggiando gli stessi fatti in modo da renderli quasi irriconoscibili.[12]

Another stylistic difference is even more noteworthy. Just as *Guerrino* abounds with place names, the Otherworld journey of *Ugone* and the *cantare* discovered by Branca are saturated with classical personages and allusions. However, nothing of the sort appears in the original portions of *Rambaldo*. Once again, the absence of an important ingredient of Andrea's style in these sections indicates that *Rambaldo* was not by Andrea.

To turn the authorship question on its edge, since some chapters of *Rambaldo* are identical with some in *Ugone*, should we also consider *Rambaldo* to be its prototype? The same issue of naive simplicity versus mature complexity applies in *Rambaldo*'s relationship to *Ugone*, yet no one has suggested that *Rambaldo* was a prototype of this later work by Andrea. On the contrary, the presence of material from these more complex, better-handled works, in addition to passages that correspond to Andrea's *Aspramonte*, indicate that *Rambaldo* was an unskilled imitation of Andrea by a later writer.

The apparently original passages of *Rambaldo* furnish stylistic evidence of Citizen B's lack of writing skill when compared to Andrea. He is, for example, notoriously clumsy in the use of direct discourse, as the following speech of Alma la bella shows:

"Fratelo mio Ranbaldo, io mi sono partito [*sic*] del mio Reame, ed ò are[c]hato tantto oro e argiento e gioielli che vagliono più che questa città. Io òne sentitto tutto il fatto dal prencipio alla fine de' fat[t]i nostri, chome tu se' batezato che [sei] fatto singniore della città che teneva nostro padre. Chon[o]scho avere presso buono partito a farti cristiano e credere in Giesù Cristo, vero figliuolo di dio; onde io voglio batezarmi anchora io e credere in Giesù Cristo. E chon questo pensiero mi parti' del mio reame, inperò ch'io veggio ch'egli aiuta chi crede i' lui di buono chuore; p[e]r tantto io mi voglio batezare e credere i' lui chome fai tu, siché da modo ch'io voglio ricievere il santo batesimo di Cristo." (**R** 47v–48r)

Here the tangled syntax and redundancies differ greatly from the generally clear and straightforward speeches of Andrea's characters. Another example of Citizen B's inept handling of direct discourse displays a confusion of regal titles within a single line of dialogue: "Disse Ranbaldo: 'O ducha Asp[e]rante, io ti voglio dire, o rre, ongni mio chonvenente'" (**R** 68v). An astounding example of redundant language occurs in a joust scene of *Rambaldo* in which the encounters of various combatants are described with a sing-song alternation of *perchosse . . . gittòllo per terra:* "e p[e]rchosse i' rRe di Portoghallo e gitòllo p[e]r tera e p[e]rchosse i' rRe di Granata e gitòllo p[e]r terra, e p[e]rchosse i' re del Marocho, e anchora l'abat[t]é, e ischontrandosi chon Falserone lo gitò da chavallo; e [c]horendo, urtò i' rRe Dragonagi di Rucia e gitòllo p[e]r terra lui e 'l chavallo, e chossì giostrando l'uno chontro al'a[l]tro p[e]r sì grande virtù che 'l dì gittò p[e]r terra vi rRe di chorona" (**R** 43v).

Andrea's inclusion of foreign languages and the need for interpreters has been noted as one element of his realism.[13] Andrea enumerates the languages his hero learned as a youth; Citizen B does not. In one instance, however, Citizen B attempts to duplicate this facet of Andrea's style, but the results are unconvincing: the hero, who was raised in Africa, leaves Mecca (in "Persia") and goes directly to Marsilio's camp in Spain, where he continues speaking *persiana* (**R** 42v). Given the Islamic presence in Spain, there may be some grounds for this remark, but within the context of the work, it strikes one as out of place.

Although Citizen B includes dates, years, and characters' ages, he does not achieve Andrea's realistic texture. Problems with giving the ages of his protagonists illustrate this: in a single chapter (11r), Rambaldo is twelve, but his twin Alma is fifteen. In a later episode, without a clear indication of time elapsed, Rambaldo's age is given repeatedly as twenty-two (42v, 43v) while his sister is twenty-eight (48v).

The superficial identification of rubrics, content, and style first signaled the connection between *Rambaldo* and the works of Andrea, yet a close, meaningful reading of the text reveals significant violations of contemporary narrative conventions. The gravity and frequency of this type of error show that Citizen B could not have composed *Rambaldo;* he merely copied preexisting texts by Andrea. In more than one instance, Citizen B did not grasp the meaning of Andrea's text, nor did he understand the direction of the overall narration. Other errors reveal Citizen B's limited general knowledge. The *Rambaldo* author does not always quote his source correctly. In one passage copied directly from *Guerrino,* he inserts a remark that the Queen of Saba "profetezò del avenimento di Cristo" (**R** 31v). There may have been a medieval legend to that effect, but according to Andrea's version, the sibyl "Arrichea [Eritrea] . . . profetò di quello advenimento" (**B** 78v). She is decidedly not the Queen of Saba, as Andrea's Sibyl tells *Guerrino.* The passage in *Guerrino* regarding this prophecy is followed immediately by reference to the sibyl Saba d'Arabia. It appears that Citizen B erred in not reading his model carefully.

One apparently conscious alteration by Citizen B of his model—necessitated by the name change of the protagonist—results in lost humor and a weaker replacement text. In *Guerrino,* the Christian hero, finding himself challenged by a Saracen in Mecca, withholds the nickname Meschino, under which he had already wreaked considerable havoc among Saracen armies, and gives the name newly discovered during his visit to an oracle:

> Egli, come singnore, mi domandò come io avea nome. Io per temenza di non essere conosciuto, cielai il nome che ebbi a Gostantinopoli e dissi el propio secondo ch'avea udito dagli alberi [del sole]. Et risposi: "ò nome Guerrino, el quale nome viene a dire 'huomo di guerra.'" Molti se ne risono . . . (**B** 37r)

However, in *Rambaldo,* Citizen B is forced to suppress reference to the hero's youth spent at Constantinople and the name *Guerrino.* Without that name, the pun *Guerrino < huomo di guerra* is lost and so is the reason for laughter. Yet he has maintained the phrase "molti se ne risono," adding "di me delle chosse ch'io avevo det[t]e" in an attempt to repair the oversight:

> "Egli mi domandò chome io avevo nome, ed io dissi: 'Ò nome Ranbaldo.' Mollti se ne risono di me delle chosse ch'io avevo det[t]e, onde io dissi: 'Signore, cholla ispada i' mano lo vo' sostenere,' e l'amansore mi sichurò il chanpo." (**R** 39r)

A more remarkable series of errors concerns the religious orientation of the *Rambaldo*'s protagonist. In passages that correspond to *Guerrino,* several revealing slips show that its protagonist was originally a Christian raised in the West who travels extensively in the Orient and through Africa—such as the hero of *Guerrino*—and could not have been a baptized orphan raised in Africa among Muslims. The first clue occurs when a foreign potentate asks the traveling hero about "i fatti di Ponente" (**R** 30r = **B** 29r). How could Rambaldo be expected to furnish news of the West if he was brought up in Africa? Yet Guerrino, who had been raised at the Byzantine court, could provide such information. Citizen B was apparently copying his model mechanically and failed to eliminate this statement. Similarly, the ostensibly Saracen protagonist of *Rambaldo* (31r–v) is pleased to find a Christian population in one eastern land. There is no motivation in his character for this response because the hero has not yet learned that he was baptized as an infant. For the Christian Guerrino, however, such a response would be entirely natural (**B** 31r).

In the same episode, details of armor again reveal *Guerrino* as the model for *Rambaldo* and not the reverse. According to an established literary convention derived from Old French sources and based in historical practice, Saracens are poorly armed while Christians have excellent armor that covers the whole body.[14] It is obvious that the author of *Rambaldo* did not understand this fundamental notion, one that occurs repeatedly in Andrea's works. The supposedly African Rambaldo should not be wearing Christian-style armor; yet the Monocholi, an exotic eastern race, marvel at seeing a man encased in armor (**R** 30r).[15] Unlike the typical Saracen, Rambaldo is described as *bene armato* (**R** 31v). Later he makes a remark about his "pagan" opponents being *male armati* (**R** 33r). This difference in armor styles was too subtle a point for Citizen B, who again neglected to adjust his source material to fit his Saracen protagonist.

Elsewhere in the same episode, Citizen B does successfully eliminate references to his hero's religion: he omits the word *cristiano* several times (**R** 31v [4], 33r, 54v), drops *idio* where it had appeared in *Guerrino* (**R** 32r; **B** 31v), and elides *pagani* in an attempt to make Rambaldo's point of view conform to that of a Saracen: *i sacierdoti* [*B: pagani*] (**R** 36r; **B** 34v). In a similar reworking strain, Citizen B omits reference to the false gods of the Other: *i loro* [**B***: falsi*] *idei* (**R** 38v; **B** 37r) and *la chiesa* [**G,C.**: *falsa*] *di Maumetto* (**R** 41r, 41v; **G** 61v; **C** 41r). He eliminates the disappointed hero's desire to kill the high priest of Apollo, since now the hero is supposedly of their faith (**R** 37r; **B** 35r). In one place (**R** 37r), he eliminates *cani saraceni* of *Guerrino* (**B** 35v), replacing it with *egli;* in another instance, the Florentine citizen's Eurocentric sentiments are revealed when he inserts the insult *chane* (**R** 40v), not found in the corresponding passage in *Guerrino*. Citizen B does excise a theological dispute between characters regarding the falsity of the "god" Apollo and the supposed idolatrous practices of the Saracens (**R** 37v; **B** 35v). Folio 41v of *Rambaldo* deletes a sacrilegious remark from *Guerrino* about the hero's actions inside the mosque at Mecca: "s'inginochiò non per divozione, ma per vedere" (**B** 38v). In the context of *Guerrino*, the remark was intended to underscore the hero's firm belief in his Christian God. In the same chapter, Citizen B omits Guerrino's disrespectful prayer posture but conserves two comments that a Christian could utter: "chonobi lo 'nghano del *falso* Maumetto" and "la *grossa* giente saraina" (**R** 41v, 42r = **B** 38v). Later in the same scene, however, he remembers to make the hero seem Saracen when he omits Guerrino's disparaging remarks about Muslim beliefs: "Io, ridendo della loro *stoltizia*" and "queste *paz[z]ie*" (**B** 39r).

Another serious error shows that *Guerrino* served as *falsariga* for many chapters in *Rambaldo*, and not vice versa. For a few folios, Citizen B carefully eliminated references to the hero's Christianity from his model, but at **R** 40r–v a major oversight occurs. Here he mechanically copied passages, revealing that Andrea's Christian hero was the prototype for Citizen B's pagan one. The first, "preghai idi<di>o che mi desse vitoria" (**R** 40r), could refer to any god; the next indicates even more strongly that the hero was conceived originally as a Christian. Rambaldo preaches Christian doctrine to defeated Saracens, referring to "le chose . . . che sono fatte dalo somo fatore" (**R** 40r–v).

A final example of this type occurs in a passage *Rambaldo* borrowed from *Guerrino*. A Saracen champion challenges the veracity of the hero's travel tales in the presence of the sultan at Mecca, and the hero must defend his honor (**R** 39r; **B** 37r). During their duel, the hero attempts to convert his opponent and to ask him to receive baptism. Realizing he is alone in a Muslim land, he decides not to raise the subject. Citizen B begins to copy a line in which the Christian hero wants to baptize the defeated Saracen, but then breaks off abruptly: "Io pensai non esere i' luogho [probable deletion] e dissi" (**R** 40v). The resultant phrase makes no sense whatsoever. The text of *Guerrino* had read "i·lluogho da farlo battezare" (**B** 38r). This psychological nuance can only belong to a protagonist who was considered from the first as Christian. It is not the behavior of a Saracen raised in Africa.

The preceding chapters on *Prima Spagna, Ansuigi,* and *Rinaldo* offered evidence that these works belong to Andrea's oeuvre by demonstrating the relation of their vocabulary to Andrea's own. In the case of *Rambaldo,* however, we must modify our method somewhat, since Citizen B has not only extracted large portions of text from *Guerrino* and *Ugone,* but seems to have self-consciously absorbed Andrea's lexicon and phraseology even to the extent of assimilating very rare or specific terms from Andrea's works into his own. For example, the word *limosinieri* appears only once in Andrea (**Z** 1: 97) and once in *Rambaldo* (67r). The learned-sounding phrase "i sagri libri di Maumetto" occurs only once in *Guerrino* (branch β: **G** 40r; α: *sagrati libri* [**B** 25v]), but it obviously struck the fancy of Citizen B, who used it four times in *Rambaldo,* a work less than half the length of *Guerrino* (**R** 2r, 23r, 42r, 58r). *Brivilegi e capitoli,* a highly individual phrase from *Aspramonte,* is assimilated as *charte e brivilegi* in *Rambaldo* (45v), the word *carte* having also appeared later in the same passage (**A** 253). The insulting reference to unworthy troops, *porcinaglia,* which occurs only rarely in Andrea (**Z** 1: 275; **S** 6v), is utilized twice in *Rambaldo* (55r, 65r). The Latinate *isso fatto* found numerous times in *Nerbonesi* and once in *Ugone* occurs several times in *Rambaldo* as well.[16]

For passages that treat courtly images and pastimes, Citizen B could have derived his terminology from either *Aspramonte* or *Ugone:* "E partiti chavalchando, dandosi piaciere e diletti p[e]r via, ucielando, chaciando per solazo e gioia l'una damigiella chol'a[l]tra, chon falchoni isparvieri in braccio, chani, veltri seghugi, amano dandosi grande piaciere e solazo" (**R** 55v).[17] *Bella criatura,* found in *Ugone,* becomes a favorite expression of Citizen B, who rather overuses it in *Rambaldo.*[18] A description of a damsel featuring her golden braid, inspired by a passage in *Ugone,* appears several times with variations in *Rambaldo:*

> Era adorna di ricchi drappi che adornavano sua bellezza, con una treccia di biondi capelli che gli davano sotto la cintura . . . (**Z** 1: 71)
> tantto bella della sua persona, grande, grosa, biancha, bionda, frescha e [c]holorita, gientile e chostumata e valorosa, chon [u]na treza bionda insino in terra [c]he propia mente parevono fila d'oro; mai no si vide la più bella criatura . . . (**R** 6v)
> Ella era grande più che niuno uomo una grossa ispanna, biancha, bionda, cho' le sue trecie insino a' piedi, uno viso angielicho, onesta, chostumata, gientile che mai no si vide la più bella criatura . . . (**R** 48v)
> Angielia, novella isposa di grande belezza, d'età di xv anni, grande, grossa, bionda, chon una treza insino a' piedi che parevono fila d'oro tantto era bella e adorna, bene adobata di roba d'oro e di seta mischiato insieme che propia mente pareva uno angiolo di Dio nato nel mezo

del Paradiso, tantto era bella criatura. (**R** 56r)

When one considers the physical descriptions of characters in Andrea, one notices his temperate use of these "strings" of adjectives, a technique greatly favored by the *Rambaldo* author. In addition, the adjective *grossa*, used in an apparently complimentary way in *Rambaldo*, in Andrea's works means "pregnant," certainly not a desirable attribute for the idealized lady.[19]

Since most of Andrea's characteristic expressions and vocabulary appear in *Rambaldo*, either in passages overtly copied from his works or through a careful assimilation process, it may seem fruitless to apply the lexical approach used in preceding chapters to *Rambaldo*. Despite an apparently identical lexicon, however, glaring differences do exist: some of Andrea's preferred expressions are absent from *Rambaldo*, others are misused, and still other words appear that are never found in Andrea. For instance, the ubiquitous interlace formula *Torna la storia*, found even in the *Prima Spagna* rubrics, is conspicuously absent from *Rambaldo*. Instead, its original portions employ other formulae—"chome in esso si trat[t]erà" (**R** 1r), "[c]home la storia nar[r]a" (11r), "chome nella istoria seghuiterà (seghuirà)" (20r, 42v), "chome nella istoria tratta" (71v), or the exceptionally inelegant "chome udirai nella istoria che seguirà in questo libro di punto in punto si nar[r]erà" (10r).

Some distinctive terms used by Andrea appear in *Rambaldo*, but with an incorrect or distorted meaning. These are not polygenetic copying errors, but seem quite clearly the errors of someone who is familiar with the words, but unsure of their significance. "Venire colla correggia al collo," common in Andrea's works to indicate the humiliated demeanor of a subjugated opponent, is at first used correctly in *Rambaldo* (3r).[20] A far different expression, *il camaglio dell'elmo*, in Andrea and other authors indicates part of the knight's armor. Yet Citizen B has conflated the two when he writes *la choregia de l'elmo* (**R** 5v), a type of psychological copying error that I have not seen occur in other manuscripts of similar texts. The peculiar term *verette* or *verrettoni*, used by Andrea, is incorrectly given as *ventiere* in *Rambaldo*, although Andrea's meaning is preserved (59v).

Another of Andrea's expressions that is misunderstood by Citizen B is *bandire la croce adosso* (to banish as heretic; excommunicate): "Carlo . . . mandò Turpino a Roma a papa Lione e fece bandire la croce sopra a Gherardo e a chi tenesse con lui, e fu scomunicato" (**A** 263).[21] Andrea's use of this phrase in *Nerbonesi* parallels that by Dino Compagni in his *Cronica*: "e sbandì, e scomunicò i Pratesi, e bandì loro la croce addosso"

(Crusca, 3: 1009). Andrea's representation reflects historical practice: heretics were required to wear a yellow cross on their breast and shoulder.[22] However, in an episode of *Rambaldo* in which the Christian armies are mobilizing to stave off a Saracen invasion of Rome, Citizen B improperly applies the expression to Saracens, who would hardly be subject to papal jurisdiction: "Il papa promisse di fare suo isforzo e dimandarlo in aiuto de' Rre d'Ingilterra e di bandire la crocie adosso a' saraini" (**R** 59r).

Other words from Andrea's *Ugone* that are misunderstood or miscopied in *Rambaldo* include *la pressa [di battaglia]* (**Z** 2: 235) > *peste* (**R** 10r), *pesta* (**R** 53r); *ispessissime grida* (**Z** 2: 233) > *ispendisime grida* (**R** 51v); and *la mischia* (**Z** 2: 239) > *la smura* (**R** 52v). These are particularly significant examples, since they occur in long passages copied verbatim from *Ugone*. The first, *la pressa di battaglia*, is not rare in Andrea, but the other two are good examples of *lectiones difficiliores* from *Ugone* that have been corrupted by later copyists or by Citizen B himself.

In addition to these familiar Andrean words that have been misused in *Rambaldo*, one finds a group of words that Andrea did not use. While Andrea's characters generally behave nobly and decorously, the characters in *Rambaldo* can be quite coarse at times. Typical insults in Andrea, derived from Old French models, are of the variety *poltrone, ghiottone,* and, occasionally, *bastardo;* characters in *Rambaldo* call each other *bastardone* (22r [2], 22v, 60r) and *busbatiere* (39r [2]). For characters who have been grievously provoked by their opponents, Citizen B uses certain verbs and past participles that do not appear in Andrea's works: *incipringito* (58r), *ingrongniato contro a lui* (21r), and *ingrungniò cho' cristiani* (58r). The verbs *inciprignire* and *ingrugnare* are found in the *GDLI* (7: 684, 1083), but the earliest usages cited are from the sixteenth century. The verb *spuntare,* with the sense of "to defeat, to undo" (*disfare*), appears in *Rambaldo.* As the Saracens prepare to invade England, they bluster: "Noi ispuntiano l'isola" (**R** 60r). The rare *rifiditure* (n., pl. from v. *fedire?,* n. *fedita?*), meaning to fight off besiegers or stave off attack, occurs once in *Rambaldo* (60v). The author of *Rambaldo* (59v) also employs the noun *istanbehini* (i.e., *stambecchini*) to describe archers who carried a type of bow curved like the horns of a mountain sheep, the *stambecco.*[23] These words do not occur in any of Andrea's works.

Among the expressions used in *Rambaldo* that are not found in Andrea, *signore a bacchetta* (**R** 7r, 8v) appears to be related to Andrea's *bacchetta del reame* (**A** 43).[24] For the noun *bacchetta,* the *GDLI* cites Compagni and Andrea under the meaning "bastone di comando, emblema di comando; segno di autorità" (1: 926). Another Tuscan expression used in *Rambaldo* is *(dire) (tutto) il convenente* (**R** 44v, 45r, 46v, 49v) or the related *dire ongni mio convenente* (**R** 68v).[25] There is no trace of this expression in Andrea.

Working from the hypothesis that *Rambaldo* may have been copied from *Guerrino* and *Ugone* and not the reverse, we should be able to apply the *recensio* process to *Rambaldo* as though it were another exemplar of the *Guerrino* tradition. This study focuses on *Guerrino* instead of *Ugone*, since the passages borrowed from *Guerrino* are more numerous, since the *Guerrino* tradition is more extensive, and since certain newly discovered exemplars of *Ugone* await thorough examination. Nevertheless, a comparison of *Rambaldo* (**R**) to the Zambrini edition of *Ugone*, which was based on a late copy (ca. 1500), reveals that **R** has many of the same corrupt readings. Similarly, when viewing *Rambaldo* from this perspective, one finds many indications not only that it was copied from *Guerrino*, but that the model used was itself of a second and less authoritative branch of that work. Many readings of *Rambaldo* are very close to those of Ricc. 2226 (**G**), dated 1448; other variants are identical to readings in BNCF, Conv. Sopp. C. 1, 720 (**C**), dated 1470, and Laur. Gaddi rel. 50 (**L**). It seems clear that the branch best represented by Bodleian canon. ital. 27 (**B**), Paris, B.N. ital. 491 and 98 (**P**), and Ricc. 2266 (**R1**) is closer to the original. Yet **R** could not be direct copy of **G**, since **R** 31v and 32r contain words that were omitted from **G**, and **R** 32v has a few readings that are probably more authentic than those of **G**. In fact, **R** contains several instances of probable original readings that are no longer found in some otherwise authoritative witnesses. Taken as a whole, however, the "errors" or variants in *Rambaldo* indicate that its author could not have been Andrea. Frequent *lectiones difficiliores* of the *Guerrino* tradition have been simplified or trivialized. In numerous cases, errors in understanding the sense of passages from *Guerrino* occur that could not have been made by Andrea as author. They are more likely from a scribe or an imitator, such as Citizen B, who lacked Andrea's broader literary background. Even if the same type of scribal errors could have entered a tradition of *Rambaldo* as they did that of *Guerrino*, the presence of identical variants linking **R** to the branch represented by **G**, **C**, and **L** points to *Rambaldo*'s dependence on the later *Guerrino* tradition.

R does preserve some probable authoritative readings of the *Guerrino* tradition. In the first example, **R** allies itself with all the most authoritative exemplars of *Guerrino* to conserve the reading *la tramontana* (**B** 26r, **P** 33r, **R1** 45v, **R2** 36r, **R4** 27r, **R** 28r). The second branch of *Guerrino* reveals the effects of the trivialization process: *l'altra montana* (**G** 41r);

alta mo[n]tagna (**C** 27v); *l'altre montangnie* (**R3** 21r); and *l'alte montangne* (**L** 42v). In a passage describing *piccinacoli* (Pygmies), the meaning becomes inverted and distorted in *Guerrino* branch β (represented by **G**, **R3**, **C**, and **L**) while **R** is again aligned with the "better" manuscripts:

> *sono neri et piccoli* **B** 30r, **R1** 51v
> *neri e picholini* **R** 30v
> *sono nigri e piccoli* **P** 37v
> *sono negri e piccoli* **R2** 41v
> *non sono neri e* **G** 47r, **C** 31v
> *non sono ne piccholi ne grandi* **L** 48r
> *non sono ne picholi* **R3** 26v
> *naschono neri e picholi* **R4** 33v

A third passage in **R** preserves a longer description of a Saracen high priest's appearance: "Era vestito di grossi panni ed era ischalzo sanza niente in piede nè in chapo, m[a] avia grande moltitudine di chapegli, i quali chapegli lo coprivono infino alla cintura *e lla sua barba folti e lu[n]ghi insino alla cintura*" (**R** 36r; emphasis added). This fuller description also appears in the other manuscripts of *Guerrino* branch A (**B** 34v, **P** 44v, **R1** 59v), though the portion describing the priest's beard has been omitted, because of a probable homeoteleuton (*cintura-cintura*), in the exemplars of branch β (**G** 55r, **R3** 33v, **C** 37r, **L** 53v, **R4** 41r) and in a later descendant of branch α (**R2** 48r). Finally, **R** preserves a typically Andrean gloss "una corona *ovvero* ghirlanda" as found in the majority of *Guerrino* manuscripts (**P** 44v, **R1** 60r, **G** 55v, **R3** 33v, **L** 55r, **R4** 41r, **R** 36r). Other variants read: "corona et una grillanda" (**B** 34v); "corona & girlanda" (**R2** 48v); and "aveva vna girlanda" (**C** 37r).

The tendency for copyists to substitute an easier, better-known reading (*lectio facilior*) for a lesser-known, unusual one (*lectio difficilior*) is a widely recognized phenomenon of the *recensio* process.[26] Many examples of banalization or trivialization exist in the portions of *Rambaldo* that correspond to passages of *Guerrino*. This crucial evidence supports the hypothesis that **R** was copied from an exemplar of *Guerrino*, since simplification of this type indicates the work of someone who did not always grasp the significance of the difficult language originally chosen, or who substituted a simpler construction for that found in the original. For instance, among provisions for a voyage, *biada* is unanimously represented by *Guerrino* manuscripts (**B** 26r, **P** 32v, **R1** 45r, **R2** 36r, **G** 40v, **R3** 21r, **C** 27r, **L** 42r, **R4** 26v), but is changed, significantly, to *vino* in **R** (28r). Two more examples of simplification in **R** concern learned or unusual words. In the first, *velli* becomes *pelli* in at least two manuscripts of *Guerrino*, a tendency followed in **R**:

choperta di velli **B** 33v, **P** 43v, **R1** 58v, **R2** 47v, **R3** 32v,
   C 36v, **L** 52v
di [?]elli [struck out, illegible] **G** 54r
di pelli **R4** 40r
di pelj **R** 35r

This could also be a case of **R** preserving a late variant of the *Guerrino* tradition. Another example occurs in all manuscripts of *Guerrino*, but in **R** the difficult wording has been neatly excised:

balchone (i)sportato (in) fuori del palagio (palazzo)
   B 37v, **P** 49v–50r, **R1** 65r, **R2** 52v, **G** 60r, **R3** 38r, **C** 40v,
     L 60r, **R4** 46r
balchone del palagio **R** 40r.

In *Guerrino* when a guide dismounts and hides under his horse in defense against an attacking griffon, Andrea represents this action with *chinarsi*. This is simplified in only one exemplar of *Guerrino* (**R2**); the author of *Rambaldo* has found a unique substitution:

chinossi sotto il (al) chauallo **B** 28v, **P** 36r, **R1** 50r,
   G 45v, **R3** 25r, **C** 30v, **R4** 31v
missesi socto **R2** 40r
entrò sotto **R** 29v
eliminated in **L** 46r–v.

In the same scene, the guide warns Guerrino that they should leave immediately because the area may be a breeding ground for griffons. The majority of *Guerrino* exemplars contain an unusual past participle *ànno figliato* (**B** 29r, **R1** 50r, **R2** 40v, **G** 45v, **C** 30v; *filliato* **P** 36r; *filato* **R3** 25v) or the infinitive *figliare* (**L** 46v).[27] One scribe seems to have first misread and then self-corrected while following an authoritative model: "ànno figliuoli, overo figliato" (**R4** 32r). Citizen B has made a similar error, either independently or perhaps from copying a late manuscript related to **R4**: *ànno figliuoli* (**R** 29v).

A clearer example of trivialization occurs in the following admittedly sticky passage describing the pepper trade route:

arrechano a certi porti di molti fiumi
   B 30r, **P** 38r, **R1** 52r
di fiume **R2** 42r
a molti porti di fiume **R4** 33v
a molti porti di questi fiumi **G** 47v
si rechano a molte parti di certi fiumi **C** 32r
sono chome certi fiumi **L** 48r, **R3** 27r
e a cierti porti venghono **R** 31r.

R has both abbreviated the topographical details of the *Guerrino* tradition and simplified the verb: *arrecare* < *venire*. Two similar errors occur later in **R**, where there are gross morphological and semantic simplifications:

vettuvaglia **B** 31v, **R1** 54v, **G** 50r, **R3** 29r, **C** 33v, **L** 50v,
   R4 36r
uictuallia **P** 40r
uectuuaria **R2** 44r
but
roba **R** 31v

Tarteria (Tartaria) **B** 32v, **P** 42r, **R1** 56v, **R2** 45v,
   G 52r, **R3** 31r, **C** 35r, **L** 51v, **R4** 38r
but
terra **R** 33v

The first case shows Citizen B's excision of a word common to all of Andrea's epic romances.[28] The second is not only a simplification, but an example of Citizen B's apparent disinterest in geographical detail.

Another example of Citizen B's lack of concern for detailed description—in sharp contrast to Andrea—is noted in this passage from *Guerrino*, which includes details of a Saracen's armor and horse: "s'armò di cuoio chotto e uno grande ischudo, e montò a uno chavallo molto grande e possente, e prende (prese) una lanc[i]a lunga e ssottile" (**B** 23r, **P** 28v, **R1** 40r–v, **R2** 32r, **G** 35v, **R3** 17r, **C** 24r). The more complete description appears in all the *Guerrino* exemplars I examined with two exceptions: **R4** (22r) describes the lance as *grande e sottile*, and **L** (37r) omits mention of the lance. By contrast, in *Rambaldo* the passage has been greatly simplified: "s'armò e montò insun uno grosso chavallo e pres<s>e una grossa lancia" (**R** 69v).

Probable errors in understanding the sense of the model, *Guerrino*, occur numerous times in *Rambaldo*. Such errors can be of scribal origin, but in *Rambaldo* their nature and frequency combined with other traits already discussed (simplified vocabulary, lack of literary background, lack of narrative skill) suggest that they originated with Citizen B. Several of these errors in meaning occur in the work's proem (1r, except as noted). In the first, the reading in **R** seems to belong to a point in the *Guerrino* tradition by which time the adjective *novelli* had disappeared and the change to a possessive article *degli* had emerged. More important, the variant in **R** contains the semantic change from "authors" to "others":

> *si dilectano dudire nouelli autori* **B, R2**
> *nouelli altori* **R1**
> *nouelle li aucturi* **P**
> *novelle degli autori* **G**
> *novella degli autori* **L**
> *dilettino degli altori* **C**
> *dudire delle altruj* **R**

Another semantic change, present only in **R**, again occurs in the proem:

> *intrar(r)ompe* **B, P, R1, R2**
> *interronpe* **G**; *interrompe* **C, L**
> *interpone* **R**

A rather complex musical metaphor is mangled in **R**, perhaps because of the mechanical process of copying:

> *soniamo* **B, R1** 1v, **G** 1v, **C, L** 1v
> *siamo* **R2** 1v, *s[i?]amo* [damaged] **P** 1v
> *siano* **R** 1v

> *consonanze* **B, R1** 1v, **R2** 1v, **G** 1v, **L** 1v
> *consonancie* **P** 1v
> *chondonaze* **R** 1v
> *condanare* **C**

While unique readings (*lectiones singulares*) are not always entirely useful in the *recensio* process, such drastic alterations in meaning seem to show that *Rambaldo* could not have served as a model for *Guerrino*.[29] Another example of misunderstood meaning in the proem concerns the author's task of writing. Only *Rambaldo* (**R**) has lost the clear sense of the original:

> *scrivere* **B** 1v, **P** 1v, **R1** 1v, **R2** 1v, **G** 1v, **C** 1v, **L** 1v
> *s(er)vire* **R** 1v

A final example refers to the apparently uneven distribution of benefits from Fortune, which shines more in one place than in another:

> *risplende* **B, R2** 1v, **L** 1v; *ressplende* **P** 1v
> *risprende* **R1** 1v, **G** 1v
> *riprende* **R** 1v
> *risponde* **C**

Here Citizen B (or the copyist of **R**) seems not to have grasped the significance of Andrea's message.

Admittedly, the proem of *Guerrino* is rather verbose and linguistically more akin to moralizing treatises than to the usual chivalric tales. Where errors occur in other *Guerrino* manuscripts, these are more often *sauts du même au même* than gross semantic errors of the type found in **R**. However, two examples taken from decidedly chivalric passages in the text reveal that even when dealing with the most conventional language, **R** is not free from errors in meaning. The first of these occurs during the blow-by-blow narration of an individual combat. Although the words *bastone* and *scudo* are repeated elsewhere in the passage, and so do not rule out the possibility of copying the wrong word from an adjacent line, the two objects are confused only in **R**:

> *peso del bastone* **B** 23r, **R1** 40v, **R2** 32r, **G** 36r, **R3** 17v,
>   **C** 24v, **L** 38r; *delu* **P** 28v; *petto* **R4** 22v
> *peso delo ischudo* **R** 70r

A second example concerning chivalric language demonstrates that Citizen B (or perhaps a copyist) anticipated the direction of his model's plot when he writes first *chamino* and then adds a gloss to correct the reading:

> *prese il (el, lo) suo chavallo* **B** 26v, **R1** 46r,
>   **R2** 36v, **G** 41v, **R3** 21v, **R4** 28r
> *prese el chauallo* **L** 43v
> *riprese il chavallo* **C** 24v
> *prese il suo chamino e prima gli tolse il suo chauallo* **R** 29r
> [lacunose] **P**

Another misreading occurs only in **R** and in no manuscript of *Guerrino* examined:

> *all'ora di terza* **B** 26r, **P** 32v, **R1** 45v, **R2** 36r,
>   **G** 41r, **R3** 21r, **C** 27v, **R4** 27r
> *a ora di* **L** 42v
> *al'atro dj a terzza* **R** 28r

The next errors offer indisputable evidence of misunderstanding the model because of ignorance of travel topoi, especially those concerning topography and exotica. In this passage from *Guerrino*, an extremely arid climate is portrayed:

non piove (gia)mai e bangniasi (bangniosi) la terra
   (le terre) di rugiada **B** 25r, **R1** 43r, **R2** 34v,
     G 38v, **R4** 25r, **L** 40v; *ruciada* **C** 26r; *rojata* **P** 31r
e bangniesi le teste **R3** 19v

Despite spelling variants and one semantic error (*le teste*), all *Guerrino* manuscripts preserve the verbs *piovere* and *bagnarsi*. *Rambaldo*'s author (or copyist), however, at first misread his model and then attempted to correct his error by adding a gloss: "Non può mai bangniarsi le terre che no uj pioue bene alchuna rugiada" (**R** 26r).

A passage in *Guerrino* describes the confluence of rivers that form the Indus: "Questo fiume s'agiungnie con un altro fiume e da questa congiunzione ingiù è chiamato Indus" (**B** 28v). All exemplars of *Guerrino* but one maintain some form of the same noun: *congiunzione* or *coniuncione* or *congiuntione* (**P** 35v, **R1** 49v, **R2** 39v, **G** 45r, **R3** 24v, **C** 30r, **R4** 31r; section omitted from **L**). On the other hand, Citizen B has apparently misunderstood his model, writing *chondizione* instead and again creating a gloss to adjust his mistake: "Quvesto fiume s'agiungia, ed à quvesta chondizione che chore mollto forte che da quvi in giù è [c]hiamato Indus" (**R** 29r). Later in the same passage, Andrea describes India's location: "vede prima il sole che altra *provincia* della terra ch'è abitata" (**B** 28v; emphasis added). The reading with *provincia* (*provincie*) is preserved in most *Guerrino* manuscripts (**G** 45r, **P** 35v, **R1** 49v, **R2** 39v, **R3** 25r, **C** 30r, **R4** 31r).[30] Here the author or scribe of **R** has erred by anticipating or misreading his model, and has again added a quick gloss to fix the slip: "altra *prsona cioè* prouincie" (**R** 29r).

A final error of sense in **R** shows that the author or copyist lacked a rudimentary knowledge of legendary exotic races. He is not aware of the people who live by smelling apples (*pome, pomi*) and that ignorance betrays him when he writes *pane:*

vivono di pome **B** 28v, **P** 35v, **R1** 49v, **R4** 31v
del pome **L** 46r
di pomi **G** 45r, **R3** 25r, **C** 30v
di poma **R2** 40r
di pane **R** 29r

Andrea, on the other hand, was clearly familiar with some medieval travel accounts, such as that of Friar Odoricus or Mandeville, where he could have learned of these people.[31] A more complete explanation and the name of the race (Pomadossi) follows, after which **R** does conserve one reading found in part of *Guerrino*:

> *vivono solamente dell'olore et d'anasarle* **B** 28v
> *del(l)'odore* **G** 45r
> *del'odore e d'anasare* **R3** 25r, **R4** 31v, **R** 29r
> *del odor e d'anasarele* **P** 35v; *dello hodore* **R1** 49v
> *non mangiano mai se nnone uno solo di loro et donaselo* **R2** 40r
> *solamente d'odori cioe dello olore di fiutarle* **C** 30v
> omitted in **L**

The last category of textual errors in **R** reveals definite links to the later *Guerrino* manuscripts. The first of these variants in **R** may be either an abbreviation derived from **C** or another instance of banalization:

> *el sottoro* **B** 29r, **R1** 50r
> *il sotor(e)* **G** 46r, **R3** 25v, **R4** 32r
> *il soctare* **P** 36r
> *quello di soctora* **R2** 40v
> *la ghuida da sotora* **C** 30v
> *la ghuida* **R** 30r
> [omitted in **L**]

Later in the text, a small interpolation in **R** is identical to one found only in **L**: *di netto* (**R** 70r, **L** 38r). The next error both serves as an example of simplification and connects **R** to the least authoritative witness of *Guerrino* branch α:

> "Per qual(e) chagione?" **B** 26r, **P** 33r, **R1** 45v,
>   **G** 41r, **R3** 21r, **C** 27v, **R4** 27r
> "De,' dimmi la chagione" **L** 42v
> "Perché?" **R2** 36r, **R** 28v.

A final example, which contains the difficult toponym *Fugnia*, offers evidence that *Rambaldo* was in all probability copied from a later descendant of *Guerrino* and as such could not have served as a prototype for *Guerrino* regardless of its authorship. Place-names have a tendency to produce multiple variants and therefore are often inconclusive in establishing textual relations, yet ample surviving testimony in *Guerrino* manuscripts shows that the name of this city was meant to be *Fu(n)gnia*. The

first occurrence of this name was often misspelled in *Guerrino* manuscripts, but its repetition three times later in the same chapter allowed
most copyists to eventually record it accurately. In later manuscripts of
Guerrino, however, the adjective *ricca* has been fused to the proper name,
a corruption found also in *Rambaldo:*

chiamata fungnia richa e bene appopolata **B** 31r
Fugnia richa e **R1** 54r
Fungniarica & **R2** 43v
[???] fu gia richa e **R3** 28v
Fugrina fu ga richa e **G** 49v
Fugaricha e **R4** 35v
Fugiaricha bene **C** 33v
Frigia riccha e **L** 50r
Fugiaricha e **R** 31r
Fugniaficha et e bona **P** 39v

Another troublesome passage concerns the hero's orders for battle. Here
the unusual syntax coupled with the tendency to abbreviate *per* has led to
the substitution of the verb *percuotere* for the original *assalire.* **R** seems
to stand between the two:

p(er) coste da ongni parte assaliray **B** 32r, **R2** 44v
et da omne parte **P** 40v
per chosta da **R1** 55r
p(er) choste p(er)choterai **G** 50v
per chosta perchoterai **R3** 29v
p[e]rchotette da ongni parte **R** 32v
dua perchosse e da due parte **R4** 36v
da due parte gli assalimo **C** 34v
omitted due to an abbreviation in **L** 51v

In the following examples from the proem, **R** clearly maintains variants of the principal members of branch β (**G**, **C**, and **L**) (1r, except as
noted):

tutti figliuoli del padre **B, R1, R2**
tutti d'uno padre **G, R**
tutti d'um **C, L**
tucti fighioli de patri **P**

sug(g)ietto a lleggie di punizione **B, R1** 1v, **R2**
sugetto alli sue punicione **P**

sug(i)etto di p- **G** 1v, **C, L** 1v, **R** 1v
la fortuna mia mi fa **B, P, R1** 1v, **R2**
la fortuna mi fa **G** 1v, **C, L** 1v, **R** 1v

Several other variants in the *Rambaldo* proem are identical to the corrupt *Guerrino* exemplars **C** and/or **L**, or show characteristics that indicate such a derivation.

vivere e stare e fare peggio **B, P, R1, R2**
vivere stare e fare **P**
vivere e istare peggio **G**
dire e (i)stare peggio **C, L, R**

p(er) li loro pecchati o p(er) li pecchati paterni **B,**
     P, R2
pe' loro pechatj ho pechati paterni **G**
p(er) lli loro pechati patternni **R1, L**
pe' loro pechati paterni **C**
pe' pehatj paterni **R**

liberalita (liberta) del pieno albitrio spechiate nella
     prima liberta data al primo padre **B, R1**
liberta del primo albitrio **G**; *arbitrio* **P**
pienita del libero albitrio **R2**
     [abbreviated, probably because of *sauts*]
liberta data al primo padre **C, L** 1v
liberta datta del primo nostro padre **R** 1v

cioè bestiali **B, P, R1** 1v, **G** 1v
ciechi bestiali **C, L** 1v, **R** 1v
non bestiali **R2**

Thus, the very proem that once seemed to indicate that *Rambaldo* was the progenitor of *Guerrino* contains evidence to prove its derivation from the later *Guerrino* tradition.

To conclude this Lachmannian analysis of *Rambaldo*, we must point out that **R** preserves some original readings from *Guerrino*, but in many instances simplifies probable original *lectiones difficiliores*. Numerous errors in understanding the sense of the model indicate that **R** was most likely copied from *Guerrino* and not vice versa. Some of these may have been polygenetic scribal errors, but the apparently limited circulation of **R** argues that they were closely related to the original. Other frequent and consistent errors in misunderstanding most likely originated with

Rambaldo's author, since one finds no such readings being produced by various copyists of *Guerrino*. The overall preponderance of variants in **R** that are identical to second-branch manuscripts of *Guerrino* (**G**, **C**, or **L**) is too striking to ignore. Finally, the presence in **R** of these late variants from the *Guerrino* tradition seems to be convincing proof that the composition of *Rambaldo* postdated that of *Guerrino*.

Having posited the improbability of *Rambaldo's* being composed by Andrea, we must consider its possible date of composition. BNCF, Pal. 578 does not bear a date or scribal signature. From scattered marginal notes in a different hand and the generally worn condition of the folios, we can surmise that the exemplar had at least a limited readership. As indicated by watermarks, the codex was certainly copied after Andrea's death. The first, a scissors (fols. 2, 8, 41), is similar to but slightly shorter than Zonghi, 620 (Fabriano, 1430). The second mark, found throughout the rest of the manuscript (fols. 1–72), is eyeglasses surmounted by a cross similar to Zonghi, 1433 (Fabriano, 1443) or Briquet, 10624 (Perpignan, 1457; var. simil. Perpignan 1457–66, Palermo, 1460), but with a double crossbeam. From this it appears that the copy was made at mid-century or later, well after Andrea's death. The text itself may have been compiled after 1431. It was probably copied before the proliferation of the printed *Guerrino:* with the availability of printed copies of the original, interest in reading a reduced version set within original chapters may have diminished.

Less speculative data concern the appearance of late *Guerrino* variants within *Rambaldo*. We have noted the points of contact between **R** and three branch β manuscripts (**G**, **C**, **L**) of *Guerrino*, two of which preserve dated colophons. **G** was completed September 30, 1448 (208v), and **C** was finished on March 2, 1470 (153r). Although lacking its final folio and any colophon it may have contained, **L** may also be dated as relatively late by means of its two watermarks. The first, a ladder (fols. 1–90), most closely resembles Briquet, 5910 (Florence, 1473–74). The second, a cardinal's hat (fols. 91–209), perfectly matches Briquet, 3387 (Florence, 1465). Thus the late variants of *Guerrino* contained in **R**'s model probably emerged by or during the third quarter of the century.

One may also discern stylistic parallels between *Rambaldo* and the *Seconda Spagna* and *Acquisto* (ed. Ceruti). All three of these imitative works are in Tuscan prose, are considerably shorter than the average length of Andrea's epic romances, show evidence of having been written by romance aficionados who were not professional authors, accurately cite titles of Andrea's works, and include Andrean language. The compositional process used was also similar: some passages are copied verbatim from Andrea's works while other sections are loose paraphrases of Andrea interwoven with original material. From these parallels, one may hypothesize that in the decades after Andrea's death, there was a continuing interest in his style of epic romance. Amateur writers may have attempted to satisfy this demand—their own, if not that of a larger "market"—by creating close imitations of Andrea's more successful texts. Pulci's *Morgante* is, in part, a satire of the continuing mania for chivalric romances. The appearance of printed editions of *Guerrino* in 1473, followed by *Reali* in 1491, together with the growing vogue for *ottava rima* romances, probably satisfied this demand and precluded the composition of more such imitative texts in prose. By combining these narrative, codicological, and cultural clues, one may conjecture that *Rambaldo* was composed toward the mid-fifteenth century or, more likely, during the third quarter of that century.

In conclusion, although *Rambaldo* abounds with similarities to Andrea's narrative content, language, and syntax, these mostly result from the close paraphrasing of portions of *Aspramonte* and from many direct borrowings from *Guerrino* and *Ugone*. However, these superficial similarities are outweighed by negative proofs that point to an author other than Andrea, not least of which is the unknown author's auto-identification at the beginning of the manuscript: "B cittadino fiorentino." This anonymous Florentine lacked Andrea's narrative skill—witness his narrative infelicities, poor distribution of content, and failure to sustain the long narrative form. The *Rambaldo* author's general lack of culture—distortion of Andrea's vocabulary, simplification of difficult language, failure to employ classical allusions, misunderstanding or abbreviating geographical descriptions, inclusion of somewhat vulgar colloquial expressions—further argues against the work having been written by Andrea. The dearth of verisimilar details—hallmarks of Andrea's pseudo-historiographic style—discloses an authorial ethos distinct from Andrea's. Finally, a careful textual comparison of *Rambaldo* with respect to the surviving witnesses of the *Guerrino* tradition manifests the conservation of some probable original readings, but more significantly reveals numerous simplifications of *lectiones difficiliores* from *Guerrino* that the *Rambaldo* author misunderstood. Further, there are the variants from less authoritative *Guerrino* manuscripts that appear in **R**. This ensemble of data indicates the improbability of Andrea as author of *Rambaldo* and points instead to its composition by a nonprofessional imitator. One should not regret the reduction of Andrea's oeuvre because of the elimination of *Rambaldo*, a text that, when studied in its proper context, furnishes a valuable example of the late medieval compilation process; instead, the very production of this text testifies to the status of Andrea's works and the impact they had on the culture.

Toward a New Perspective

This study has presented cumulative information about all aspects of Andrea da Barberino—his life and works and the criticism of those works—in order to propose an objective reevaluation of his true position in Italian literary history in general and to determine his importance to the chivalric tradition in particular. The resulting accumulation of evidence suggests the need for a revised view of this author and his works, since many past studies were narrowly focused (examining only one or two of his texts), methodologically flawed (using late, corrupt manuscript copies or inadequate modern editions), or generically prejudiced (favoring French models over Italian reworkings, or verse over prose). Romantic and early twentieth-century critics' misunderstanding of, and insensitivity to, late medieval literary norms account in part for the poor critical reception of these texts; indeed, many of the stylistic "flaws" ascribed to them were actually standard practice or desirable attributes in the vernacular writings of Andrea's day.

To appreciate what may have been Andrea's contemporary importance, one must acknowledge the extent of his influence on later, sometimes better-known chivalric authors. Available codicological evidence suggests that the area of production for handwritten copies of Andrea's texts was apparently concentrated in Florence and Tuscany, with little extant evidence to argue for international transmission. The notable exception to this phenomenon was *Guerrino*, a text that was published numerous times throughout the Italian peninsula, and that exerted its influence over a wide geographical area and on an equally wide range of later authors and translators (Florentine, Venetian, Spanish, French).

This study has also attempted to address the need for a better understanding of Andrea's narrative by analyzing his style in greater depth than had previously been done. An examination of his language shows its affinities to that of Dante, Boccaccio, and Florentine chroniclers, and that it surpasses the stock vocabulary of contemporary *cantari*. Appendix A presents the results of manuscript-hunting efforts carried out during initial research, a task that uncovered several exemplars unknown to the nine-teenth-century editors of Andrea's works. The enlarged census of manu-scripts itself argues for reevaluating Andrea's cultural and literary impor-tance, and the variants contained within them should enhance future philological studies and new editions of the texts themselves.

Most important, this study has addressed the question of several attri-butions made to Andrea but never definitively argued. By scrutinizing the remaining codicological, lexical, and narrative evidence regarding the now-lost *Prima Spagna*, we can determine that this work—important to the overall cycle—was probably Andrea's. On the basis of such investiga-tion, we may assert that the extant, unedited *Ansuigi* was in all probabil-ity identical to the lost Albani text, and that this prose narration of the second war in Spain was no doubt composed by Andrea. Application of the same methodology allows us to propose that the unedited prose *Storie di Rinaldo* contains strong evidence of Andrea's style, follows the same mode of compilation/translation, and contains lexicon and narrative de-tails favored by him.

On the other hand, a close examination of content, structure, and lan-guage of the unedited *Rambaldo* suggests that it was most likely a mid-fifteenth-century imitation of Andrea's *Aspramonte, Guerrino,* and *Ugone* that was composed after Andrea's death and based on late exemplars of at least two of those texts. This is another piece in a growing body of evi-dence that suggests the existence of a mid-Quattrocento Tuscan vogue for prose romances written directly in imitation of Andrea, an area that has not thus far been studied.

The resulting assemblage of data regarding authorship, contemporary readership, transmission, and critical history of Andrea's texts clarifies and enhances his role as a cultural exponent. Andrea's various activities—compiling, translating, and reshaping of preexisting chivalric legends and conventions, and passing them on to later medieval Italian audiences and authors—argue for a reevaluation of his position in Italian and European literary history. He is a missing link between the early Italian reworkings of chansons de geste and the Renaissance epic masterpieces. The ultimate goal of this study is to increase modern awareness of Andrea's contribu-tion to the chivalric literary tradition. The newly established vastness of the cycle alone invites more varied critical approaches than have been taken in the past, and the determination of authorship for four of these texts will enable previously "anonymous" texts to be analyzed in their proper literary and stylistic context. It is hoped that the information presented here will encourage more thoughtful and comprehensive critical treat-ments of this author and his works.

Appendix A: Exemplars of Andrea's Texts by Title and Date

Library, Shelfmark	Date
Reali di Francia	
Bodleian, Canon. ital. 129*	XV (cited by Vandelli, xv)
BNCF II.I.14	XV-3
Former Phillipps 929*	1736
Aspramonte	
Ricc. 2308	mid-XV
Moreniana, Frullani 12	XV-3
Angelica 2313 (fragment)	XV-3 (f. 123 of Frullani 12)
Angelica 78*	XV-3
BNCF II.I.14	XV-3
Ricc. 2309	1455
Angelica 2263	1460
BNCF II.II.56 (fragment)	1467
Ricc. 2410	1472
BNCF Pal. 677	1473
BNCF Pal. 583	1475
Marc. Ital. cl. 11, XXXVIII	1493
Lost Albani MS	ca. 1508 (cited by Michelant)
Lost Milan, Bibl. Melziana MS	XIX (cited by Boni, xxvi)
Rome, BNC, V. Emanuele MS 232*	XIX (BNCF II.I.14)
Prima Spagna	
Lost Albani MS	1508 (cited by Michelant)
Ansuigi	
BNCF II.I.15	XV-2d half; before 1504
Lost Albani MS	1508 (cited by Michelant)

Nerbonesi

Ricc. 2327 (Book VIII)	XV
Corsiniana, Rossi 62 (43 C 22)*	XV-2d half
BNCF Panciat. 35 (fragment)	XV-3
BNCF II.IV.35 (2d part)	1474
Laur. Ashb. 530 (Books IV–VII)	1487
Ricc. 2933	1490
BNCF II.I.15	XV-2d half; before 1504
Laur. Plut. XLIII, 18	1504
Parma, Pal. 32	1509
Vatican, Barb. lat. 4101	1515
BNCF II.I.16	XV-2d half; before 1517
BNCF II.IV.679	1519
Laur. Redi 177	1520–22
Ricc. 2481	1521–22
BNCF II.VII.3	1534
Rome, BNC, V. Emanuele MS 231*	1852 (copy of BNCF II.IV.35)

Ugone

BNCF II.II.58	XV
BNCF Panciat. 34	mid-XV, before 1472
Parma, Pal. 32	1509
BNCF II.II.59	1511
Vatican, Barb. lat. 4101	1515
Laur. Redi 177	1520–22

Aiolfo

Laur. Ashb. 537	1433
Laur. Plut. LXII, 27	mid-XV(?)
BNCF Magl. Cl. XXIV, 146*bis*	1460–61
Laur. Plut. LXI, 34	1474
Parma, Pal. 35	1484
Laur. Plut. XLIII, 9	mid-XV
Ricc. 1912	XV-3
BNCF II.II.54	XV-3
Crusca 64	XV-3 (with modern additions)
Ricc. 1812	XV-exeunt or XVI-ineunt
Ricc. 1909	XVI-ineunt

Guerrino

Bergamo, Civica MA 297*	1468
Bodl. Canon. ital. 27*	XV-ineunt

Ricc. 1921	XV
Ricc. 2266	1444
Ricc. 2226	1448
Parma, Pal. 30	XV-3
Former Phillipps 6654*	mid-XV
Ricc. 2267	mid-XV
Paris, B.N. fonds ital. 491 and 98*	mid-XV(?)
Former Dyson Perrins 71*	1462
BNCF C. S., C. 1, 720	1470
Laur. Gaddi reliqui 50	XV-3
Ricc. 2432	XV-3
Univ. of Penn., MS Codex 16	1472
Vatican, Barb. lat. 3988	XV-3
Vatican, Chig. G.VI.162	XV-2d half

Rinaldo

Laur. Plut. LXI, 40 (fragment)	XV-2; before 1455
Laur. Plut. LXXXIX, inf. 64	XV-exeunt; before 1508
Laur. Med. Pal. CI, 4	XV-exeunt; before 1505
Laur. Plut. XLII, 37	1503–6
Ricc. 1904 (except f. 1)	XVI-ineunt

*Not personally examined.

Appendix B: *Guerrino,* proem

Diplomatic transcription according to the reading of Bodl. canon. ital. 27.

[1r] . . . n ATURALMENTE pare che sia di consuetudine che gli uomeni si dilectano dudire nouelli autori. Osse antiche fossono non sieno suti palesatj alla uolgar giente perche cose antiche e non palesate paiono noue alle menti di coloro che non lano piu udite/ Per questo mi sono dilectato di cierchare molte storie nouelle et auendo piaciere di molte storie trouay questa leggienda che molto mi piacque ondio non uoglio esser ingrato del benificio ricieuuto da dio e dalla humana natura. benche lamia natura ricieua da ciely piu che dengno merito perche sono di bassa conditione e pure Io mi conforto perche io ueggio molti di maggiore natione di me viuere e stare e fare peggio di me./ O che sia per liloro pecchatj / o perli pecchatj paternj questo non giudico ma rimangna nel primo factore. Anchora veggio perlo contrario moltj dipiu uile conditione sormontatj e fanno e stanno e uiuono meglio di me Questo miconforta chenoy siamo tuttj figliuoli del padre

criati dauno solo factore che lucie delle sue grazie piu e meno secondo che per noy sacquista chy innuna opera et chi inn unaltra et dotato da dotatj ciely ogni uno nelgrado suo. puote venire vertudioso che resta in questa uita nella quale per questa puoy acquistare inprendere virtu e uizio. bench' ame pare che la maggior parte seguitj la piu faticosa di questo/ inpero che doppia faticha ene affare il male a rispecto del bene Solo la dilectanza intrarrompe e auiliscie lanimo nostro et tirato per la sua uilta al male piu che al bene. Manessuna cosa per la liberalita. delpieno albitrio/ Spechiati nella prima liberta data al primo padre adamo che contutto che dio gli comandasse non pecchare/ nolgli tolse pero il pieno albitrio di fare chome alluy piaciesse. e chosi non tolse may anessuno. Et pero siamo chiamatj animaly razionaly cioe bestialj/ Et pero si conuiene anoy la punizione del fallo. per questo niuno altro animale e suggietto alleggie di punizione chennoy . perche non anno la ragione.. e per questo siamo chiamatj animaly inragioneuoly cioe sanza ragione. Et perche alchuno dicha la fortuna mia mi fa chosi chapitare/ questo non e uero. i(n)pero chella fortuna e chosa giusta et diritta. Ma noy siamo indiritti nelle nostre operationj. che uiuendo noy tutti con la ragione la fortuna sarebbe comuna e pero nonne incolpare la fortuna ma incolpa noy medesimj. et sella risplende piu et meno innuno luogo che innunaltro/ Questo aduiene perche noy soniamo diuersi stormentj almondo/ Et pero ingnuno singiengnj dinparare a sonare buono stormento e la fortuna gliele intonera di perfecta musica: ma guarda chelle corde nonsieno false Inpero chelle consonanze non risponderebbono. Et non ui sarebbe pero colpa se non di te prop(ri)o che uay sanza ragione e non cholpa della fortuna. ondio chiamo il [1v] nome didio e tutte le forze dalluy ordinate necielj chemi conciedino non per debita ragione ma per gratia di scriuere questa piccola opera sipotra piu di fructo e didiletto.

Appendix C: Content of *Rambaldo* Compared to Andrea's Works

A *Aspramonte*, ed. Boni
G *Guerrino*, Ricc. 2226
R *Rambaldo*, BNCF Pal. 578
Z *Ugone*, ed. Zambrini

Rambaldo Passage   Relation to Andrea's Texts

(Roman numerals refer to books, arabic numbers to chapters)

Rambaldo Passage	Relation to Andrea's Texts
Book I	**G**, Book I
Invocation	**G**, Invocation
Chap. 1, Proem	**G**, Proem
Chap. 2, lines 1–3	**G** I, 2 *incipit*
Chap. 2, body	**A** I, 3–4, 10, 13–15; II 46, paraphased and reordered.
Chap. 3	**A** I, 11–12, 17–19, (22), 30, 42.
Chap. 4	Much original, based on **A**; ending paraphases **A** I, 30–31.
Chap. 5	**A** I, 31–32 paraphased; some original.
Chap. 6	**A** I, 31–33, 38–41 paraphased plus some original portions.
Chap. 7	**A** I, 41–43 plus original portions.
Chap. 8	**A** I, 43; two-thirds is original.
Chap. 9	Two-thirds is original; then **A** III, 158, 161–62, 202.
Chap. 10	Half original; **A** III, 202–3.
Chap. 11	Mostly original; Agolante's death = **A** II, 91–92; boys' sports = **G** I, 8.
Chap. 12	All original, two new characters; uses Andrea's phrases and lexicon.
Chap. 13	Original, in style of **G**.
Chap. 14	**G** IV, 5, paraphased; plus half original material.
Chap. 15	**G** IV, 6 verbatim.
Chap. 16	**G** IV, 7 verbatim.
(lost ending)	[probably followed **G** IV, 8]
Chap. 17 (lost)	
Chap. 18	**G** IV, 9 ending.
(lost beginning)	
Chap. 19	**G** IV, 10.
Chap. 20	**G** IV, 11, paraphased; ends with a version of **G** II, 9.

Chap. 21	Similar to **G** II, 10, abbreviated, simplified, some verbatim.
Chap. 22 (very long)	**G** II, 11, reworked: **R** adds character Violante and motif of jealous half brother; continues with a seductress and her castle à la *Bel Gherardino*.
Chap. 23	
Chap. 24	Inspired by **G** I, 29 and 31, loosely paraphased.
Chap. 25	**G** V, 1–3; conflated two *indovini* into one; **G** V, 4 paraphrased, reworked.
Chap. 26	Original *incipit*; then follows **G** II, 14 verbatim.
Chap. 27	**G** II, 15 verbatim, but abbreviated: **R** omits geography.
Chap. 28	**G** II, 16 verbatim.
Chap. 29	**G** II, 17 much verbatim; some abbreviation and rewording.
Chap. 30	**G** II, 18 and 19 combined plus one original interpolation.
Chap. 31	**G** II, 23 verbatim.
Chap. 32	**G** II, 25 verbatim; one folio of **G** text omitted.
Chap. 33	**G** II, 28 verbatim.
Chap. 34	**G** II, 29 verbatim.
Chap. 35	**G** II, 30 verbatim.
Chap. 36	**G** II, 31 verbatim.
Chap. 37	**G** II, 32 verbatim.
Chap. 38	**G** II, 33 abbreviated opening; the rest verbatim.
Chap. 39	**G** II, 34 verbatim.
	Guerrino Book III begins.
Chap. 40 **R** Book II begins.	**G** III, 1 verbatim.
Chap. 1	**G** III, 2 verbatim.
Chap. 2	**G** III, 3 verbatim.
Chap. 3	**G** III, 4 verbatim.
Chap. 4	**G** III, 5 verbatim.
Chap. 5	**G** III, 6.
Chap. 6	
Chap. 7	
Chap. 8	Proper names from **A**.
Chap. 9	
Chap. 10 (very short)	

Chap. 11 (short)	Name "Fedele francho" derived from **G** VIII, 21.
Chap. 12	
Chap. 13	
Chap. 14	
Chap. 15	
Chap. 16	
Chap. 17	Name "Papa Lione" in **F**, **A**, **G**, *Rinaldo*.
Chap. 18	
Chap. 19	
Chap. 21	A bit from **Z** IV, 9 (p. 218).
Chap. 22	First half is original transition; then **Z** IV, 11, abbreviated.
Chap. 23	**Z** IV, 11, divided by an original rubric, now continues verbatim with a few omissions and name changes.
Chap. 24	Original rubric; **Z** IV, 12 complete, nearly verbatim.
Chap. 25	Original rubric; **Z** IV, 13, complete, verbatim.
Chap. 26	Original rubric; **Z** IV, 14 complete, verbatim.
Chap. 27	Original rubric; **Z** IV, 15 complete, verbatim.
Chap. 28 (very short)	Original conclusion to above chapters. Here departs from **Z** plot.
Chap. 29	
Chap. 30	
Chap. 31	
Chap. 32	
Chap. 33 ⌐ Chap. 34 ⌐	Inspired by **G** I, 9–15, much simplified.
Chap. 35	
Chap. 36	
Chap. 37	
Chap. 38	
Chap. 39	
Chap. 40	
Chap. 41	
Chap. 42, rubric lines 3–4 body	Original; from **Z** IV, 12 again; half original; half from **Z** IV, 12. Several purposeful wording changes, changed names, slight abbreviations.

Chap. 43	Original rubric; then as **Z** IV, 13 plus one extended original insertion; original closing.
Chap. 44	Rubric, brief opening are original; most is from **Z** IV, 14.
Chap. 45	Original reworking of **Z** IV, 15.
Chap. 46 (short)	Original conclusion to above events in a style highly imitative of Andrea.
Chap. 47	
Chap. 48	
Chap. 49 (very short)	
Chap. 50 (very short)	
Chap. 51 (short)	
Chap. 52 (short)	
Chap. 53 (short)	
Chap. 54	Ending summarizes **G** II, 10.
Chap. 55	**G** II, 13, complete, mostly verbatim with name changes.
Chap. 56 (short)	Opening inspired by **G** II, 14.
Chap. 57 (short)	
Chap. 58 (short)	
Chap. 59 (short)	Ending inspired by **G** VIII, 44.
Chap. 60 (short)	**G** VIII, 44, paraphased and amplified; half original material.

Notes

Introduction

1. Rajna, "L'onomastica"; Castellani, *Prosa italiana*, vol. 1 passim.

2. D'Ancona, "*Il Tesoro*," 228–41.

3. Roland (*Inf.*, XXXI, 18; *Par.*, XVIII, 43); Charlemagne (*Inf.*, XXXI, 17; *Par.*, VI, 96, XVIII, 43); Ganelon (*Inf.*, XXXII, 122); William of Orange (*Par.*, XVIII, 46); Renoart (Rinoardo) (*Par.*, XVIII, 46); King Arthur (*Inf.*, XXXII, 62); Guinevere (*Par.*, XVI, 15); Lancelot (*Inf.*, V, 128); Gallehault (*Inf.*, V, 137); and Tristan (*Inf.*, V, 67).

4. Petrarca, "Triumphys Cupidinis," in Rime e Trionfi, ed. Apollonio and Ferro, IV, 66; Equicola, *Chronica di Mantua*, cited in Dionisotti, "Fortuna," 234.

5. Equicola, in Dionisotti, "Fortuna," 234.

6. Boni, "I manoscritti marciani," 257, on Andrea's reworking of *Aspramonte*; Schmidt, "Ein Vergleich," 47–56, 152, on *Aiolfo*; Vitale-Brovarone, "De la Chanson de *Huon*," 401, on *Ugone*.

Chapter 1

1. "Andrea di t[i]eri de magna botti da barberino di valdelsa maestro di chanto" (BNCF, Magl. Cl. XXIV, 146*bis*, 150r); "andrea de magiabotti da barberino di valdelsa" (**C** 153r).

2. ASF, Catasto 19, 167r.

3. ASF, Catasto 339, 90v.

4. Osella, "Su Andrea," 363–64.

5. ASF, Diplomatico Normale 1376 10 nov. S. Maria Nuova.

6. For transcriptions, see *Reali*, ed. Vandelli, 2: cii–vi.

7. Catalano, "La data," 84–87.

8. Levi, "I Cantari leggendari," table 1 and p. 1.

9. Dionisotti, "*Entrée d'Espagne*," 221; *Tav. rit.*, 1: 255, 369, 497, 505, 511, 516, 540.

10. *Spagna*, ed. Catalano, 1: 133.

11. *Romanzi dei Reali*, ed. Mattaini, 23.

12. Osella, "Su Andrea," 366.

13. Paris, *Histoire poétique*, 190; Rajna, *Ricerche*, 1: 326.

14. *Ugone*: Parma, Pal. 32; BNCF II.II.58, Panciat. 34; *Guerrino*: Laur. Gaddi rel. 50; Ricc. 2226; BNCF Conv. Sopp. C. 1, 720.

15. Allaire, "Unedited Epic Romance."

16. *Ajolfo*, ed. Del Prete, 1: xxv.

17. Catalano's claim that "Nerbonesi" is a more accurate title appears unfounded (*Spagna*, 1: 45).

18. BNCF II.VII.3, Panciat. 35; Ricc. 2933; Laur. Plut. XLIII, 18.

19. Hind, *Catalogue*, 302; Harris, "Il Guerino," 97.

20. Ricc. 1912, 1812; Laur. Plut. LXII, 27 and LXI, 34; Ricc. 2244 (da Sangallo inventory).

21. Branca, "Un poemetto inedito," 89; idem, "Una 'schermaglia'."

22. Ludovisi, *L'Ugo d'Alvernia*, 37.

23. Bec, *Les livres*, 33.

24. Osella, in *Pallante*, 114, 121, 147; Renier, "Guerin Meschino," 1.

25. Osella, in *Pallante*, 111, 143.

26. Hawickhorst, "Über die Geographie bei Andrea."

27. Rajna, *Ricerche*, 1: 320.

28. *Les Narbonnais*, ed. Suchier, 1: xxxvi; Colby-Hall, "La géographie."

29. I have examined this exemplar only on microfilm.

30. *Aspramonte*, Marc. Ital. cl. 11, XXXVIII (1493); *Ugone*, BNCF II.II.59 (1511); *Nerbonesi*, Ricc. 2933 (1490); Laur. Plut. XLIII, 18 (1504); Parma, Pal. 32 (1509); Vatican, Barb. lat. 4101 (1515); BNCF II.IV.679 (1519); Laur. Redi 177 (1520–22); Ricc. 2481 (1521–22); BNCF II.VII.3 (1534).

31. Forni Marmocchi, "Reminiscenze"; Boni, "Le *Storie d'Aspramonte* nella *Spagna* in prosa," 40–49, 52–54.

32. La Seconda Spagna e l'Acquisto di Ponente, ed. Ceruti; *Inventario Ceruti*, 3: 141.

33. Mattioli, *Luigi Pulci*, 12–13, 19–20.

34. Graf, *Miti, leggende*, 1: 92–93.

35. Rajna, "Una riduzione," 231–45.

36. *Spagna*, ed. Catalano, 1: 186; Boni, "Le *Storie d'Aspramonte* nella *Spagna* magliabechiana," 133–34; Ankli, "Un problema," 263.

37. Boni, "L'*Aspromonte* [*sic*] quattrocentesco," 46.

38. I am grateful to Juliann Vitullo, who furnished me her own transcription of this poem.

39. *La Discesa di Ugo*, ed. Renier, lxxv; Bendinelli, "Preistoria," 39n.63.

40. MacArthur, "Les versions," 124–25.

41. Ankli, "Un problema," 262; Marchetti, "Sulla 'Gionta,'" 81–103; Mattioli, *Luigi Pulci*, 9, 19–20.

42. Razzoli, *Per le fonti*, 5–6; *Maugis d'Aigremont*, ed. Castets, 324; cf. Rajna, "Rinaldo da Montalbano"; Franceschetti, "L'*Orlando Innamorato*," 524, 527, 529–32.

43. Rajna, *Le fonti*, 529–30, 532–33, 544n.1, 549n.1, 586.

44. Neri, "Le tradizioni," 224.

45. Marinelli, *Ariosto and Boiardo*, 53.

46. Osella, in *Pallante*, 167–68; Cocai, *Il Baldo*, 1: 90.

47. Cordié, "Ancora *Razza*," 283.

48. Foffano, *Il poema cavalleresco,* 2: 212, 129; Boni, *"Le prime imprese,"* 67–68, 80.

49. Osella, in *Pallante,* 166.

50. Martelli, "Schede," 310–11.

51. Wormald and Giles, *A Descriptive Catalogue,* 1: 41–42.

52. Graesse, *Trésor,* 3: 172; *Catalogue of the Choicer Portion,* 154; *Catalogue of the Library at Chatsworth,* 2: 219; *Catalogue des livres de la Bibliothèque,* 3: pt. 2, 281.

53. Henry, *"Berta da li gran pié,"* 136.

54. "Corónica del cauallero Guarino Mezquino. Tr. A. Hernández. G.L. A. d'Burgos: Seuilla, 1548. fol." (Thomas, *Short-Title Catalogues,* 40); Baranda Leturio distinguishes Hernández Alemán from the author of the *Historia parthenopea* (*La* Corónica).

55. Révah, "L'*Auto* de la Sibylle," 175, 183–85.

56. D'Aragona, *Il Meschino,* intro., n.p.: "trouai . . . questo bellissimo libro in lingua Spagnuola."

57. Osella, in *Pallante,* 165–66.

58. Cervantes, *Don Quixote,* 1: 298v (pt. 4, cap. 49).

59. Allaire, "Un ignoto manoscritto," 233–34.

60. Osella, in *Pallante,* 169, 170.

61. Graesse, *Trésor,* 3: 172; Altamura, *I cantastorie,* 21–48.

62. Pitrè, "Le tradizioni cavalleresche," 322, 332–35, 343–45, 348–49; Rajna, "I 'Rinaldi,'" 572; M. Croce, "Manifestations of the Chivalric Traditions."

63. [Beltrami], *L'età eroica.*

64. Ferri, review of *Guerrin;* Renier, "Guerin Meschino," 2.

65. Bufalino, *Il Guerrin Meschino.*

CHAPTER 2

1. Rajna, *Ricerche,* 1: 94, 292–95, 315; *Reali,* ed. Vandelli, 2: lxxi–lxxii; *Les Narbonnais,* ed. Suchier, 1: xxxiii; Albertazzi, *Storia,* 11; Gaspary, *Storia,* 2: pt. 1, 248–49; Palumbo, "Andrea," 343; Paris, *Histoire poétique,* 184; Rossi, *Quattrocento,* 417; Russo, *Compendio,* 139; idem, "La letteratura," 57; Fabio, *La materia cavalleresca,* 48.

2. Grendler, "Chivalric Romances," 67–71; see Cecchi and Sapegno, *Storia,* 634; Russo, "La letteratura," 56; Schmidt, "Ein Vergleich," 118, 153. The new emphasis on individual deeds was true of many Italian reworkings.

3. Grendler, "Chivalric Romances," 70.

4. For the stylistic and political implications of this choice, see Vitullo, "Medieval Epic Romance," 130.

5. Throughout this study, "Saracen" denotes the medieval literary construction of Muslims.

6. Rossi, *Quattrocento,* 417; Gaspary, *Storia,* 2: pt. 1, 246.

7. *Tav. rit.,* 1: 15; *Tris. ricc.,* 18; *Add.,* 146, 168; *Orl.,* VII, 42, 7–8, XXV, 11, 7–8.

8. **F** 248, 253–54, 262–63, 274, 294, 302, 356, 388; **A** 45, 66–67, 228, 257, 280–81.

9. A long list of countries visited by someone who speaks in the first person was a topos of *jongleur* literature. See the anonymous "Erberie" and Rutebeuf's "Dit de l'herberie" (Rutebeuf, *Oeuvres complètes,* 2: 266–80).

10. Gaspary, *Storia,* 2: pt. 1, 249; Paris, *Histoire poétique,* 184; Russo, "La letteratura," 57; Schmidt, "Ein Vergleich," 133.

11. Peters, *Über di Geographie im* Guerrino; Hawickhorst, "Über die Geographie bei Andrea."

12. Ptolemaeus, *Cosmographia,* table 19; Golubovich, *Biblioteca Bio-bibliografica,* 2: 543, 545; Campbell, "Portolan Charts," 379; Vesconte, *Carte nautiche.*

13. The passage in Ricc. 2183 corresponds almost exactly to Bono Giamboni's *volgarizzamento* of Latini's *Tesoro* (chap. LIX, "menticore").

14. Rajna, *Ricerche,* 1: 282.

15. Spiegel, "Genealogy: Form and Function," 48–51.

16. Varanini, "Andrea," 66; Russo, "La letteratura," 59; Schmidt, "Ein Vergleich," 156.

17. Russo, *Compendio,* 139; idem, "La letteratura," 58.

18. Modigliani, "Una nuova redazione," 100; *Ajolfo,* ed. Del Prete, xxxi; *Aspramonte,* ed. Boni, lxxvii; Vitale, review of *Aspramonte,* ed. Boni, 458 (emphasis added).

19. *Romanzi dei Reali,* ed. Mattaini, 23.

20. Rossi, *Quattrocento,* 417; Cecchi and Sapegno, *Storia,* 634; Flora, *Storia,* 1:388.

21. Accame Bobbio, *Profilo storico,* 103.

22. Momigliano, "I Reali," 106.

23. Varanini, "Andrea," 66.

24. Horrent, "Les versions," 248.

25. For example, Freud, *Totem and Taboo,* 141–43.

26. *Reali,* ed. Vandelli, 2: lxxiv; Rossi, *Quattrocento,* 417.

27. Branca, "Una 'schermaglia,'" 645–48.

28. For the difference between medieval and epic rhetoric in chivalric literature, see Kay, "Nature of Rhetoric."

29. *Tes.,* I, 23–35; VII, 3–13; IX, 52–60; and XII, 6–19.

30. Various scholars have remarked upon Andrea's tolerant portraits of the Other (Franceschetti, "On the Saracens," 207; Schmidt, "Ein Vergleich," 148; Allaire, "Portrayal").

31. **N** 2: 40–41, 59–60, 62–63, 77–78.

32. Rossi, *Quattrocento,* 417.

33. Horrent, "Les versions," 98.

34. Pompeati, *Storia,* 1: 709.

35. Boni, "*L'Aspramonte* trecentesco," 46–47.

36. Cabani, *Le forme,* 80–82, 92.

37. Cf. **A** 37; **N** 1: 302, 2: 323; **E** 2: 29, 72, 255n.

38. See also **A** 57, 84; **N** 1: 12, 379, 504 nn. 1, 2: 263, 300, 482, 580; **U** 65r; **E** 1: 195.

39. In a fourteenth-century *cantare,* "cioè" was frequently found with words derived from northern Italian dialects that the author then "translated" into Tuscan (Melli, "Riecheggiamenti," 83).

40. *Torna la storia:* **F** 161, 413, 532; **A** 129, 217, 232, 250; **N** 2: 400n.1, 546n.3, 621n.2; **E** 1: 8, 50, 57, 64, 112, 129, 133, 138, 2: 5, 38, 70, 88, 104.

41. "Ora ritorniamo" (*Add., FU, Orl.*); "Ora dicie lo conto" (*Add., Fior., Tris. ricc.*); "Ora rinforza la istoria/el cantar/'l bel dir" (*OF, Rotta, FU*); "Or udirete" (*Spagna*); "Li mastri delle storie pongano (e divisano)," "Tutte le storie pongano," "Divisa la (vera) storia" (*Tav. rit.*). On the function of such formulae, see Heijkant, "L'emploi des formules."

42. *Reali,* ed. Vandelli, 2: lxxi–lxxii.

43. See Giannozzo's criticism of idleness in Alberti, *Della famiglia,* Book III.

CHAPTER 3

1. Reinhard, *Die Quellen,* 84–85.

2. Rajna, *Ricerche,* 1: 325–26.

3. Ranke, "Zur Geschichte." Melzi speaks of receiving a copy of the *Aspramonte* that the Albani manuscript contained, but he does not mention the other two texts (*Bibliografia,* 58).

4. For a detailed history of the Albani library, see Pinto, *Storia della Biblioteca,* 13–18.

5. Michelant, "Titoli," 191.

6. *Aquisito,* ed. Ceruti, 19.

7. See my "Due testimoni" and "Un manoscritto rediano."

8. Michelant, "Titoli," 406.

9. For detailed information on copyists, owners, and readers of Andrea's texts, see my "Chivalric 'Histories,'" chap. 3.

10. BNCF, Poligrafo Gargani, packet 601: fol. 124; packet 602.

11. Stussi, *Nuovo avviamento,* 120.

12. *Spagna,* ed. Catalano, 1: 159–60.

13. Rajna, *Ricerche,* 1: 13; Forni Marmocchi, "Reminiscenze"; Boni, "Le *Storie d'Aspramonte* nella *Spagna* in prosa."

14. A fact I ascertained to my satisfaction by consulting the manuscript. For sample citations, see Boni, "Le *Storie d'Aspramonte* nella *Spagna* in prosa," notes.

15. Quoted in Forni Marmocchi, "Reminiscenze," 166.

16. It is not found in repertoires of proper names by Langlois, Flutre, nor Moisan. Under the special meaning "stolido, miserabile" the *GDLI* (1: 227) cites only *Aiolfo.*

17. *Spagna,* XXIV, 2, 8; XXVI, 16, 26–50.

18. Branca, "Una 'schermaglia,'" 645.

19. "L'arme proprio d'Orlando a quartiere" is borne by Ansuigi in *Spagna,* XXXVII, 26, 8; also by Ugone de Fioravilla and his brother, Ansuyxe, in *Fatti,* 69 and 71.

20. *Fior.,* 403; *Rotta,* VIII, 5, 1–3; 21, 8.

21. **F** 75, 109, 141, 384; **N** 2: 585, **B** 48r.

22. **N** 2: 23, 55, 65n, 69, 105, 456, 457; "dato sepoltura a' morti cristiani, e' corpi de' saraini furono arsi" (2: 526); **E** 1: 165.

23. Forni Marmocchi, "Reminiscenze," 178–80.

24. Fassò, XV, 20, 1; Melli, II, 33, 3–4; XVIII, 31, 5; XIX, 13, 3–4.

25. Cf. **F** 489–90, 494; **E** 1: 37, 289, 290, 293.

26. *Alloggiar(si)* and part.: **F** 33, 73, 169, 277, 297, 351, 365, 415, 511, 551 (2); **A** 53, 72, 104, 108, 120, 121, 151, 167, 219, 250; **N** 1: 309, 496, 2: 199, 284, 355 (2), 356; **Z** 1: 115, 166, 2: 222 (3), 226 (2), 256; **E** 1: 156, 179, 2: 111, 152, 163, 215; **B** 11v, 20v, 25r, 33v, 37r, 74r, 87v, 110r.

27. *C(h)ollazione, col(l)ezione:* **F** 163, 339; **U** 55r, 61v; **Z** 1: 136; **E** 1: 280, 305, 2: 258, 291; **B** 37v, 74v, 75r.

28. *Capitolo, -i: Dec.* (sing., 3; plur., 1); (plur.) *Diario,* 27, 28 (2), 29, 34, 35, 130. With the meaning "articolo di una legge; paragrafo di un documento," *GDLI* includes G. Villani (2: 694).

29. *Notificare:* **N** 2: 133; (ger.) **F** 78, **N** 2: 111, 372, 415, **B** 62v; (part.) **F** 266. *ED* (4: 79) registers one occurrence each in *Vita Nuova* and *Convivio.* For *notificato,* Bartoli is the earliest citation in *GDLI* (11: 579).

30. *Bella diceria:* Fassò, XXIII, 20, 2; **A** 127, **PS**, chaps. 66, 67, 86, 89, 120, 121, 124, 154, **N** 2: 702n.2; (plur.) *Diario* 74; (var.) *b- diciaria:* Orl., XL, 7, 4.

31. *Metter(si) in punto:* **F** 214, 266, 279, 404, 416, 446, 469; **A** 29, 35, 66, 165 (2), 178 (2), 182, 209, 227, 256; **N** 1: 79, 103, 126, 177, 2: 70, 72, 112, 162, 223, 231, 317, 387, 388, 415, 433, 437, 443, 577 (2), 589, 611n.1, 647n; **Z** 1: 257; **E** 1: 50, 90, 117, 123, 201, 219 (2), 273, 276, 2: 290; **B** 40v, 48v, 105r, 111v, 118r. Phrase and variants are in Morelli's *Ricordi* (Trolli, "Il lessico," 153–54). See also *GDLI,* 14: 999.

32. *Capitano generale: Spagna,* XVII, 12, 7–8; *Tav. rit.* 1: 520; **F** 205, **A** 45, **Z** 1: 66, **B** 25v, 60r; *g- c-:* **F** 430, 519, **E** 2: 111, **B** 21v, 119v.

33. *Gioiello,-i: Dec.* (6); **F** 476, 507, 511, 546, **A** 8, 53 (2), 58, 59, 90, 255, **N** 1: 511, 2: 227, 310, **E** 2: 95, 131, 140, **B** 36r, 45r.

34. Rel. *rafibiata:* Fassò, VIII, 31, 8; *sfibiato:* Fassò, VIII, 32, 3; *afibbiaua:* Orl., LVII, 19, 8; *afibbiata:* **F** 319. *GDLI* registers no chivalric author prior to Andrea (5: 926).

35. *Disutile: d- della persona* (**F** 448); *gente d-da battaglia* (**F** 519); "gente saraina molto d-" (**N** 2: 344); "persiani . . . disutili" (**B** 46v).

36. *Disfare (disfatta) . . . infino a' fondamenti:* **F** 173, 249, 270, **N** 2: 6n, 8, 175, 662n.1; **Z** 1: 16–17, 120, **E** 1: 177, 180, 185, 283, 2: 79, **B** 70v, 117r; (var.) *ne' fondamenti* (*Tris. ricc.,* 17).

37. *Tagli(are) a pez(z)i:* **A** 202, **N** 1: 47, 2: 10, **U** 44v, **E** 1: 45, 201, 2: 151, **B** 67v, 133r, **G** 152v, 200r; *Dec.,* IX, 5; *a p-tagliati: Spagna,* XXIV, 38, 2; *in p- tagliati: Rotta,* V, 30, 8; *a p- tagliarono: Add.,* 238.

38. *Come (tutta) la cosa stava:* **F** 531, **A** 295, **N** 1: 94, 2: 461, **Z** 1: 128, **B** 20r; *ista:* **N** 2: 357; *tutta la c- come sta:* **E** 1: 291; (rel.) *la c- com'era andata:* **E** 1: 21; *tutta la c- come era stata:* **F** 463; *la c-com'ella stava:* **F** 451.

39. *La c- come stava:* Melli, XXXII, 7, 4; *dire che la c- stava male: Dec.,* II, 1; *Tutta la c- come (i)stava:* **F** 154, 531, **N** 2: 349, **E** 1: 272, 304, 2: 104.

40. Cabani, *Le forme,* 100.

41. Chaps. 20, 25, 29, 52, 53, 75, and 101.

CHAPTER 4

1. I first hypothesized these correspondences in "The 'Spain' Cycle." I am currently preparing this text for publication.

2. Brettschneider, Anseïs de Cartage, 13.

3. Rajna, Ricerche, 1: 325; Brettschneider, Anseïs de Cartage, 12; Spagna, ed. Catalano, 1: 84–85n.1.

4. Michelant, "Titoli," 191.

5. Paris, Histoire poétique, 181, 190; idem, "Anseïs de Carthage," 175.

6. See, e.g., National Union Catalog 1973–77, 104: 209.

7. Rajna, Ricerche, 1: 323–25.

8. Gautier, Les épopées françaises, 3: 31, 4: 32–33; Ruggieri, review of Anseïs, ed. Brettschneider, 139.

9. Albertazzi, Storia, 16; Nyrop, Storia, 257; B. Croce, Spagna, 8; Spagna, ed. Catalano, 1: 15, 84.

10. Ranke, "Zur Geschichte," 172n.

11. Rajna, Ricerche, 1: 311.

12. Guis: Anseïs, ed. Alton, ll. 7552, 11422, 11428, 11535ff., 11583, 11588, 11592; Guidone as son of Ansuigi: N 1: 41, 383, 396, 399.

13. Spagna, Fatti, Sec. Sp., Acquisto, Add., and Fassò.

14. Anseïs, ed. Alton, Jehans (l. 7552), Tieri (l. 11241); Moisan, Répertoire, 1: pt. 1, 525, pt. 2, 923; 2: pt 3, 590.

15. Morant de Rivier: Anseïs, ed. Alton, ll. 2759, 2883, 3192, 5196; Morand: Entrée, l. 11307; Moisan, Répertoire, 1: pt. 1, 715; 2: pt. 3, 471, pt. 4, 348.

16. Fatti, 62, 69, 71; Spagna, XVIII, 42, 2–3, XIX, 38, 1–2; Michelant, "Titoli," 229.

17. Fatti, 62, 70, 71; Spagna, XVIII, 45, 1–6, XX, 8, 3 and 22, 3–7; XXI, 32, 7–8 and XXXVII, 30, 8.

18. F 125, 204, A 96, 103, 105, 220, N 1: 139, "fu partita tutta la roba guadagnata de' saraini" (N 2: 618); "tutti i Cristiani furono ricchi della roba de' Saracini" (Z 1: 166); "tutti furon ricchi della roba de' loro nimici" (Z 1: 300; E 1: 156, 2: 79, 9); "sarete tutti ricchi del tesoro de' nostri nimici" (B 46r).

19. Rajna, Ricerche, 1: 8–113.

20. Texts of letters: F 78–79, 112–13, A 50, 91, N 2: 371–73, 626–30, E 1: 61–62, 72, 2: 109, 128–29; Tris. ricc., 29; Tav. rit. 1: 162–63, 368–69, 411, 518–19; Novellino, story 82.

21. The only other occurrence falls outside the Tuscan control group: "Voialtri frati cristiani de lo ponente che io oldo dire che è sì grande posanza de citade, de avere e de baroni, e che avette lo sancto padre etc." (Paris e Vienna, ed. Babbi, 226).

22. (Tutti) i religiosi: Diario 33, 55, 59, 61, 73, 87 (2), 95–96, 99, 105, 141, 148, 168, 170, 178, 180, 212. Andrea also uses an unmodified form: vestito come religioso (F 471); parente e religioso (A 68); molti si faranno religiosi (B 99r).

23. See Bendinelli ("Preistoria," 43), citing Godefroy: "'Trainas' si può mettere in relazione con il francese 'traîne,' o 'traînée' nel senso di strascico."

24. See Diario, 101, 132–33, and esp. 206.

25. *Torna la storia:* **S** 2r, 3r (2), 3v, 9r, 9v, 20v, 21v, 22v.

26. *E poco vantaggio vi fu:* **F** 101, 501, **A** 236, 242, 289, **N** 2: 422, **E** 2: 122, **B** 9r; *e poco v- v'era:* **E** 1: 204; *non vi fu v-:* **A** 277; *non vi fu alcuno v-:* **F** 241, **N** 1: 51; *non fu ... alcuno v-:* **B** 125v; (var.) *nessuno v- vi fu:* **E** 1: 265.

27. *Giung(ere) ira a ira e forza a forza:* **F** 285, **E** 2: 197; (var.) *(ag)giunse i- sopra i-* : **F** 125, 496, **B** 82v; *giugnendo f- a f-:* **F**492; *aggiunse l'una i- sopra all'altra:* **F** 105; *aggiunta l'una i- coll'altra:* **Z** 2: 245; *radoppiava i- sopra i-:* **A** 278; *i- sopra i- sì gli s'accese, e le forze sue si raddoppiavano:* **N** 2: 116; *gli montò un'i-, e la f- gli crebbe coll'i-:* **E** 2: 106.

28. *Tagliare a minuti pez[z]i:* **S** 2r; *taglieremo tutti a p-:* **S** 5v–6r; *tagliati a p-:* **S** 25v.

29. *Asprissimo:* **F** 92, 118, 381, 405; **A** 39, 61, 79, 119, 200, 268, 272, 293; **N** 1: 229, 296, 490, 502n, 2: 123, 694; **Z** 1: 122, 125, 274, 283; **E** 1: 223, 270; **B** 2r, 41r, 106r, 109v. Not in *Canz., DC, ED.*

30. *Dibatter(si):* **F** 382, **A** 105, 147, **E** 1: 87, 103, 110, 113; *cadde morto dibattendo e piè in terra* (**E** 1: 191); *poco si dibattè che morì* (**E** 1: 282, 2: 63, 97, 107, 178, 196, 217); *Fior.,* 379; *GDLI,* 4: 342; in the *Commedia: Inf.,* III, 101, and XXVII, 132 (*ED,* 2: 428). Not in *Canz., Dec.* See *dibattuti:* **A** 148, 237.

31. *Maninc(h)onoso:* **S** 3r, **N** 1: 16, 20, 22n, 402, 442, **N** 2: 183, 333, **U** 2r (2), 2v, 11r, 15v, 86v, **Z** 1: 11, 12, 95, 2: 252, **E** 1: 4, 2: 189, **B** 9r (2), **G** 130r, 132r. This spelling occurs in *Spagna,* XXXIX, 21, 7; III, 161; *Tav. rit.,* 1: 493; and M. Villani, *Cronica,* vol. 1, II, xli, 1.

32. *Petrone: GDLI* (13: 437) cites *Reali* with regard to this special meaning; **A** 46 (3); *ismontò al p- dove ismontano i signiori* (**N** 2: 173, **Z** 1: 31); *smontò al p- reale* (**Z** 2: 198); *dismontò al p-* (**S** 4r); *isciesono al p- reale* (**S** 10r); *smontarono al p-* (**S** 20v).

33. *Alloggiar(si):* **F** 277, **A** 72, 104, 120, 121, 167, **S** 7v, 12v, **E** 2: 152; (part.) **F** 458, **S** 7v, 9v, **N** 2: 533, **E** 1: 55, 281, 2: 17, 245, **B** 4v, 21r, 31r, 87v, 105v, 108v.

34. *Alloggiamento,-i:* **F** 25, 122, 156, 169, 172, 199, 233, 283, 352–54, **S** 10r, 14r, **N** 1: 60, 115, 236, 255, 338, 363 (2), 515, 2: 12n, 87 (2), 437n, 453, 603, 673, **E** 1: 3, 17, 51, 77, 199, 2: 104, 152, 179, 240, **B** 37r, 45v, 58r, 102v, 109r, 110v, 123r, 124r, 133r. The first citation in Crusca (1: 381) is from **E**. Used by Ser Giovanni Fiorentino (*GDLI,* 1: 332).

35. *Retiguardo:* **F** 266; *rieguardo:* **A** 96; *riediguardo:* **A** 112, 166, **S** 9r (3), 15r, 16v; *retrighuardo:* **S** 21v; *rietiguardo:* **F** 69, 519, **A** 77. For *rietiguardo, GDLI* cites Andrea first (15: 942). See *Chanson de Roland,* ed. Segre, for *rereguarde* (l. 656) and *rereguarder* (l. 2774).

36. "Sùvi uno elmo di grande adornamento/di ricche pietre prezïose" (Fassò, VI, 17, 6–7); "su l'elmo aguto ... /che n'abaté pietre" (Fassò, XVII, 50, 7–8); "Sopra dell'elmo avea ... /un Macometto/di perle e di zaffiri" (*Spagna,* II, 39, 1–3); "Su l'elmo d'oro avea un Trevigante,/a pietre" (*Spagna,* XXXIII, 13, 5–6).

37. Cf. "Tolse due gioielli ch'erano insull'elmo" (**B** 44r); "gli donai uno de' dua gioielli ch'io tolsi dell'elmo" (**B** 44v); "gli donai l'altro gioiello" (**B** 45r).

38. *A buon'ora:* **A** 30, **Z** 2: 45, **E** 1: 37, 295, 2: 18, 234, **B** 7r, 75r, 79v, 125r; *di buon'ora:* **F** 123, 191, 206, 367, **A** 165, **N** 2: 306, **U** 9v, **Z** 2: 228, **E** 1: 124, 151, **B** 6r, 10v,

G 120v; *in buon'ora:* **Z** 2: 20. Boccaccio and control texts consistently prefer the preposition *a* (*Dec.*, I, 7, VI, 10, VIII, 8; Melli, XXIII, 34, 3; *Tav. rit.*, 1: 183).

39. *Allattare:* **F** 226, 227, 291; *benedetto sia chi t'alattò* (**S** 22r, **E** 1: 193, **B** 3r [2], 42v); (part.) **A** 123, **N** 1: 159, **B** 107v. Cf. *Dec.*, IX, 6; *Tav. rit.*, 1: 48; (var.) *lattare*, in Dante's *Commedia* (*ED*, 1: 150).

40. *Carissimo,-i:* **F** 27, 169, 174, 190, 415, 562, **A** 22 (2), 34, 111, 208, 262, 272, **S** 12v, **N** 1: 190, 268, 271, 335, 368, 403, 2: 3, 4, 192n, 204, 525, 610, 630, **Z** 1: 22, **E** 2: 115, 128, 129, 147, 261, **B** 2r, 7r, 15r, 26r, 42r, 46r, 55v, 69v, 73v (2), 75v; *Tris. ricc.*, 114; *Fior.*, 390. Not in *Canz.*, *DC*, *ED*. See *Dec.* (34); *Filoc.*, 186, 209, 283, 291, 552, 587.

41. *Deretano, diretano: Tris. ricc.*, 386, 388, 389, 391; *Tav. rit.*, 1: 384; *li diretani* (*Inf.*, XXV, 55); *Dec.*, X, 9.

Balestrata: Dec., VIII, 9, 85, X, 6, 6.

Licenziare, to dismiss from royal presence: *Dec.* (19); *s'allicenzia* (*Tav. rit.*, 1: 390); *(al)licenziato* (*Tav. rit.*, 453, 478).

42. M. Villani, *Cronica*, IX, lxxxv, 20; VII, iv, 16; XI, lxxxiv, 43–44.

43. *Deretano:* **N** 1: 398, 2: 128, **E** 2: 282; *diretano:* **F** 105, **A** 20, 29, 155, 191, 193, 194, **N** 2: 336; *diritano:* **F** 120; *dretano:* **F** 107, **S** 9r, 11r, **E** 1: 160, 291; *drietano:* **A** 123.

Balestrata: **F** 96, 481, **A** 16; *pres[s]o alla città a una b-* (**S** 7v); **N** 1: 234, 2: 458, 521, 673, **U** 85v, **E** 1: 42, 65, 108, 129, 183, 2: 12, 226, **B** 26r, 116v, **G** 110r.

Licenziare: **F** 152, **A** 83, 91, 92; *Marsilio gli licienzò* (**S** 22v); **N** 1: 305, 327, **E** 1: 97, 2: 101, **B** 12r.

44. *Ben(e) fare:* in *Commedia* and *Rime* (*ED*, 1: 572–73 [11]); *Canz.* (5); *Dec.* (2). Without article, *per ben f-: Orl.*, XLI, 14, 8. In Andrea: **F** 182, 219, 403, **A** 118, 129, 280, **S** 23r, **N** 1: 226, 2: 128, 507, 702 (2), **Z** 2: 57, **E** 1: 198, 234, 2: 254, **B** 12v, 62v, 126v; (var.) *f- b-:* **N** 1: 272.

45. *Giusta sua possa:* **F** 71, 129, **N** 2: 453, 564, **Z** 1: 189, **E** 2: 280; *g- mia possa* (**S** 2v; **N** 1: 261; **E** 2: 283; **B** 18r); (var.) *g- mia possanza* (**F** 157; **E** 1: 208; **B** 85v).

46. *Come il (el) fatto stava:* **S** 5v, **N** 2: 561n.1, **E** 1: 43, 228, 2: 206, **B** 54v; *come stava el f-* (**E** 1: 153, 2: 131); *(tutto) il f- chome staua* (**F** 516, **A** 266, 296, **U** 21r, **Z** 1: 113); *tutto el f- com'era andato* (**E** 1: 261); *tutto el f- com'era stato* (**E** 1: 280); *tutti e' fatti come stavano* (**E** 2: 68). See *Dec.*, IV, 10, X, 8; *il f- come stato era (era stato)* (*Dec.*, II, 7, II, 9, VII, 4); *come il f- sta* (*Dec.*, IX, 3); *come stava il f-* (Melli, XXXII, 6, 8).

47. *Andare a vicitare:* **F** 122, 123, 207, 221, 359, 378, 459, 537, **A** 127, 239, 273, 275, **S** 15v, 17v, **N** 1: 310, 2: 495, 532, 625n.4, **Z** 1: 70, 2: 227, **E** 1: 40, 116, 139, 167, 238, 241, 266, 320, 2: 16, 137, 150, **B** 25r, 85r, 87r, 136r; *Tav. rit.*, 162, 337, 524.

48. *Fare la piazza: FU* I, 34, 2; *Tav. rit.*, 1: 305, 306, 307; *si facea gran p-* (*Spagna*, XXXV, 9, 8); **F** 72, 283, **S** 8v, 10v, 16v, 18r, **N** 1: 150, 2: 453, **Z** 1: 156.

49. *Mortale nimico:* **F** 91, 293, 405, 491, **A** 281, 289, **S** 5r, **N** 1: 193, 2: 403, 677, **E** 1: 35, 64, 296, 2: 106, **B** 9v, 47v, 125r, **Z** 1: 22, 26; *nimico (nemico) m-:* **A** 9, **N** 2: 469, **E** 1: 35, 249, 292; *m- nimici:* **F** 419, **N** 1: 502, 2: 273, 422, 461, 534, **E** 2: 103, 106, **B** 126r; *nimici m-:* **A** 90, 257, **E** 2: 44, **B** 126r.

50. *Come di sopra è detto:* **F** 11, 178, 231, 386, 503, **A** 14, 15, 25, 36, 167, 218, **S** 25r, **N** 1: 113, 193, 240, 470, 487, 2: 127, 154, 198, 224, 326, 550, 646, 656, **Z** 1: 89, **E** 1: 5,

207, 132, 177, 207, 2: 163, 221, 238, 250, 257, 259, 263, **B** 3r, 9r, 21v, 23r, 24v, 29v, 31r, 117v, 127v; *come è d- di sopra:* **A** 76, 167, **N** 1: 333, 2: 414, 626, **Z** 1: 279, **E** 1: 207, 2: 176, 231; *come d- è di sopra:* **S** 11v, 12r, **E** 2: 232, 248; *come di sopra fu d-:* **F** 49.

51. *Come di sopra dissi* (*Dec.,* IV, 3, 7) and *sì com'egli è di sopra detto* (*Filos.,* VII, 1, 1); *come di sopra in parte è detto* (8) and *come di sopra è scritto* (3) in Morelli's *Ricordi* (Trolli, "La Lingua," 108).

52. *Lamentar(si) della fortuna:* **F** 155, 323, **A** 141, 165, 213, 250, **S** 13v, 15r, 17r–v, 19v, **N** 2: 165, 272, 277, 332, 397, 424n.1, 473, **E** 1: 178, **B** 5r.

53. Cabani, *Le Forme,* 53.

54. *E nota che:* **S** 26v, **N** 1: 21, 42n.2, **E** 1: 282, 2: 113, **B** 26r, 50v; *Nota che:* **F** 566, **A** 81, **N** 2: 393n.3; *Nota, lettore, che:* **N** 2: 421n.1. See G. Villani, *Cronica: e nota che:* 197, 310; *ma nota che:* 266; *e nota, lettore, che:* 317.

55. *Sotto brevità:* **F** 341, **S** 2v, **N** 1: 2, 366, **Z** 2: 124, **B** 64v.

56. Flora, *Storia,* 1: 388.

57. *Ghiaia: g- d'uno piccolo fiumicello* (**F** 70); *la g- del fiumiciello* (**S** 16r); *g- del fiume* (**S** 12v, **N** 2: 158, **Z** 1: 326); *g- di fiume* (**B** 34r). Noun *ghiaia* alone: **B** 109r.

58. *Mamalucchi:* GDLI cites *Aiolfo* for this item (9: 592). For a phonosymbolic study of the later pejorative meaning in Sicilian, see De Marco, "The Sounds of Change."

59. Setton, ed., *History,* 1: 131–32.

60. *Affossare:* **F** 413, 534; "Marssilio, vedendo non potere avere la terra cioè el chastello, diliberò averllo per fame e fecie intornno intorno <e> affossarlo per mod[o] che niuno non poteva andare nè uscire persona" (**S** 19v); **N** 2: 58, 97; "Tibaldo . . . a Oringa l'assediò e affossolla e isteccolla" (**N** 2: 559). Crusca (1: 276) registers one instance from **N**. *Afossata:* M. Villani, *Cronica,* vol. 2, X, xv, 18.

61. See Quaglio, "Parole," 45.

62. *Appenduti per la gorga:* (var.) *inpendu:* **E** 2: 144; *impendu per la gola* (**F** 555); *impenduti per la gola* (**F** 196); *impiccare per le gorgie* (**A** 71).

63. *Bontà di:* **F** 139, **A** 79; "è stato b- de' re Iseres che ci à traditi" (**S** 20v); **N** 1: 447, 2: 591n.4.

64. *Prospero vento:* **F** 279; *chaminando con p- v-*(**S** 2r); *navichando chon p- v-*(**S** 3r, 3v, 4v, 5v, 10r, 14r, 14v); **N** 2: 316, 405n.2, 406n.1, 413, 655, **Z** 1: 147, **G** 162v.

65. *Camaglio dell'elmo (elmetto):* **F** 270, 502; **A** 148; **S** 11v; **N** 1: 231, 2: 697; **E** 1: 39, 2: 107. Crusca (2: 416) cites **F** and **E** for this noun.

66. *Forcella (forciella, forcilla) del petto:* **A** 287; **S** 6r, 17r, 18r, 25v; **N** 2: 417n.1; **B** 13v, 49v; **G** 111v.

67. *Guanto sanguinoso:* **F** 380, **S** 4r, **N** 2: 416, 435n.1, 682n.1, 683, 684, **E** 1: 121, 2: 135, 181, 292, **B** 13r (2); *s- g-:* **B** 13r. The citation from **N** in Crusca (7: 660) is the only one in which "guanto" is modified by "sanguinoso."

68. *Ghorzerino:* **S** 10v, 18r; "gorzerino" (**N** 2: 697n.1); *gorgerino* (**F** 492); *gorgerino di piastre* (**E** 2: 63); (rel.) "gorgera" (**E** 2: 141). For "gorzerino," the earliest chivalric texts registered by Crusca (7: 428) are *Morgante* and *Ciriffo.* The spelling "ghorgerino"

appears in a 1456 inventory of "arme da piazza" owned by Piero di Cosimo de' Medici (Müntz, *Les collections,* 29).

69. Müntz, *Les collections,* 31.

70. *Pondo della battaglia:* **A** 191, 197, 199; **S** 9r; **N** 2: 276, 691, 701.

71. *Steccato, -i,* **F** 364, **F** 413, **S** 8v, 9v, **N** 2: 58, 381, 492, 558, 562, 563, 580, **Z** 1: 30, 2: 260, 261, **E** 1: 189, **E** 2: 18, 62, 132, 135, 291; **B** 12v.

72. *Schierati e stretti:* Fassò, XXI, 8, 3; *stretti e serrati:* Fassò, XXI, 41, 2; *stretto e serato:* Fassò, XXII, 8, 4. *Stretti e serrati:* **F** 98, 187, **S** 11r, 16r, 16v; (var.) *serrati e stretti:* **N** 1: 508; *stretti stretti:* **N** 2: 580n.4; (rel.) "la sua schiera si serrò insieme, e stretti si difendevano" (**F** 265).

73. *Bus(s)ine:* **A** 184, **S** 23r, **N** 2: 46, 210, 331, 416n.1, **B** 122v, 124v, **G** 110v; *busini:* **N** 2: 406, 416, **G** 35r. Glossed as "buccine, trombe guerresche" (*Aspramonte,* ed. Cavalli, 329).

74. *Carriaggio:* **F** 172, 257, 258, 271, 519, **A** 96, **B** 46r, 46v; (plur.) **S** 1v, **U** 79r, 87v, **E** 2: 37. The earliest entry in Crusca (2: 602) is *Orl. Fur.*

75. *Lancia ar(r)estata:* **F** 156, 204, **A** 132, 210, **S** 6r, **U** 83r, **E** 1: 91, 111, 132, 2: 76, 142, **G** 3v, **B** 109r; (var.) *arrestata la l-* (**B** 104v); (plur.) **F** 381, **E** 2: 135, **Z** 2: 242, **B** 6v, 41r. Under *arrestato,* Crusca (1: 707) cites **F** first.

L- in resta: **F** 92, 101, 204, **S** 7r, 9r, 10v, 11v (2), 12r (2), 15r (2), 18r, 20r, 23r, **N** 1: 297, 2: 52, **Z** 1: 275, 289, 2: 250, **E** 1: 203, **B** 54r, 104v, **G** 110r.

L- insulla resta: **F** 281, 375 (2), **A** 28, 40, **N** 2: 53, 82, 582, **B** 23r; *l- a resta:* **N** 1: 130, 297n.5, 485, 2: 13, 706n.

76. *Verettone:* (**F** 214–15); "salirono insulle mura a difendere la terra chon sassi e *verettoni* per modo ch'e' saraini chonvenono tirarssi adrieto" (**S** 11r, emphasis added); **N** 2: 237, **E** 2: 153. Ageno defines it as an "arma da getto in forma di spiedo . . . da lat. *veru* 'spiedo' con intrusione di *ferro*" ("La Lingua," 227).

77. *Mettersi in punto:* **S** 1v, 2r, 6r (2), 10r, 15v, 19r, 20r.

78. *GDLI* (8: 371) cites Andrea. *Intronare:* **F** 159, 283, 319, 489; **A** 268, 272, 291; **S** 16v, 18v; **N** 2: 71, 243, 362, 391, 517n.1; **Z** 1: 39, 150, 234, 241, 295, 2: 18; **E** 1: 110, 163, 2: 49, 196, 278, 282; **B** 134v.

79. *Mescolarsi:* **F** 64, 281, 522, **A** 29, 250, 285; "l'una ischiera si mescholò choll'altra" (**S** 23r); **N** 1: 395, 2: 16, 281, 608, 695, 696n.1, 700, **Z** 1: 286, 2: 263, **E** 1: 204, 2: 77, 228, 255n; (part.) **E** 1: 319, 2: 71, **B** 106v. Several *Guerrino* manuscripts contain the form *mescolatamente.*

80. *Fare testa:* **F** 57, 118, 187, 219, **A** 213 (2), **S** 12v, **N** 2: 275, **B** 41v; (var.) *rifare testa:* **F** 24, 51, **A** 215, **N** 1: 398, 2: 19; (rel.) *rifé capo:* **F** 119. In M. Villani, *Cronica,* vol. 1, III, xix, 8–9. Not in *Canz., Dec., DC, ED, GDLI.*

81. *Indietreggiare, indrieteggiare:* **F** 23, 383, **A** 192, 285, **N** 1: 179, 2: 70n, 101, **E** 1: 160, 318, 2: 82, 235, 256, **Z** 2: 236, **B** 2v; "si tirarono indrettagiando drento alle liccie" (**S** 8r); 9v, 10r, 10v, 11r, 11v, 15r, 16v, 19r, 23v; *indrietegiando:* **S** 17r; *adretegiare:* **S** 17r.

82. Crusca (8: 566) registers both *Rinaldo* and *Aiolfo; GDLI* (7: 800) cites *Rinaldo* and *Reali* as its first two entries.

83. *Sinistrare, sinestrare:* **S** 16r, **N** 1: 53; "s- il chauallo" (**U** 85v); **E** 2: 39, 52. Rarer substantive form: **F** 124.

84. *Attendersi a medicare:* **F** 24, 53, 361 (2), **A** 152, **S** 17r, **N** 1: 216, 2: 314, 450n, 526, 585n, **E** 1: 98, 122, 222, 274, 277, 2: 276, **B** 47v, 111v, 126r; (var.) '*tendeva a farlo medicare* (**Z** 1: 26).

CHAPTER 5

1. Rajna, "Rinaldo da Montalbano," 125–26.

2. Luzio and Renier, "Delle relazioni," 100–107.

3. See "Per ch'io v'ho sempremai voluto bene," in Grazzini, *Le Rime burlesche*, 468, l. 40; Inventory of 1553, ASF, Guardaroba Mediceo 28, 81r–83r, cited in Maracchi Biagiarelli, "L'*Armadiaccio*," 55–57.

4. Rajna, "I 'Rinaldi,'" 558.

5. *Storia di Rinaldino*, ed. Minutoli, xxxvi.

6. Rajna, "Rinaldo da Montalbano," 215; Nyrop, *Storia*, 174; Melli, "Nella selva," 200n; *Romanzo cavalleresco*, ed. Forni Marmocchi, 17.

7. Albertazzi, *Storia*, 16.

8. Rajna, "Rinaldo da Montalbano," 62, 74; idem, *Ricerche*, 1: 326.

9. *Nerbonesi*, ed. Isola, 4: cccvvi.

10. *I cantari di Rinaldo*, ed. Melli, intro.; Melli, "Estratti"; "Rapporti"; "I cantari di Rinaldo"; "A proposito"; "Intorno al testo."

11. Morosi, "La leggenda di Rinaldo," 1: 113, 199. I wish to express my gratitude to *relatore* Mario Martelli for permitting me to consult Morosi's thesis.

12. Forni Marmocchi, "Il romanzo cavalleresco," 54.

13. Dionisotti, "Appunti su cantari," 244.

14. Tomalin, *Fortunes*, 52; Orvieto, *Pulci medievale*, 142; Pulci, *Morgante*, ed. Ageno, 1079; Morosi, "La leggenda di Rinaldo," 1: 269.

15. As suggested by Morosi, "Breve storia," 285.

16. Laur. Plut. LXXXIX, inf. 64, watermarks: fols. 1–80 *aigle*, not encircled. Most similar to Briquet, 89 (Florence, 1501; var. ident.: Pisa, 1513). Similar to designs in Zonghi, 676–90 (Fabriano, 1475–97). Coincidentally, the same paper was used for the first three quires of Ricc. 1904 containing the later books of *Rinaldo*. Folios 81–102 *monts* (encircled, surmounted by cross, crossbar being bent) somewhat resembles Briquet, 11853 (Fano, 1378–90) or 11872 (Pisa, 1420–21), but these dates seem too early. However, the Briquet examples do not have the bent crossbar and are longer than the watermark in question. Cannot be better identified.

17. Laur. Med. Pal. CI, 4: original fols. 3–170 *balance*, similar to Briquet, 2473 (Ferrara, 1472). Newer paper added to fill lacunae is datable 1501–2.

18. Laur. Plut. LXI, 40: (on the fold) fols. 1–86 *lettre M*, most resembles Briquet, 8347 (Palermo, 1397). Folios 87–120 *tour*, Briquet, 15865 (Prato, 1427; var. simil.: Pistoia, 1430; Palermo, n.d.), and Zonghi 1404 (Fabriano, 1430).

19. Ricc. 1904: *huchet*, Briquet, 7686 (Venice, 1426–34; var. simil.: Naples, 1414–35; Udine, 1425; Hollande, 1427; Florence, 1427–35; Pisa, 1430; Lucca, 1438–45). Fo-

lios 3–32 (the principal portion of the MS) *aigle,* similar to Briquet, 89 (Florence, 1501; var. ident.: Pisa, 1513), and Zonghi, 676–90 (Fabriano, 1475–97); fols. 33–110 *chapeau,* not entirely legible. Similar to Zonghi, 963 (Fabriano, 1507) or perhaps 981 (Fabriano, 1494).

20. See my "Un manoscritto inedito del *cantare.*"

21. I wish to thank *dottoressa* Carla Masaro for sharing her identifications of Stradino manuscripts with me. The ASF, Guardaroba Mediceo 28, 82r, entry *Historia di Guido di bacotto,* in all probability was Andrea's *Aiolfo:* Guido di Bagotte is a character whose name appears early in this text.

22. Rajna, "Rinaldo da Montalbano," 240–41 (emphasis added).

23. Boni, "L'*Aspremont* del codice Marciano fr. IV"; Tyssens, "Poèmes," 309, 311, 315; Vitale-Brovarone, "De la Chanson de *Huon*"; Bendinelli, "Preistoria," 58–67.

24. Pulci, *Morgante,* XXVII, 78, 7, XXVIII, 50, 2, and 53, 8.

25. For example, *Spagna,* II, 2, VI, 46, VII, 1. See Cabani, *Le forme,* 42, 50, 55.

26. Another instance survives in two exemplars not chosen as base text by Vandelli: "Come dice a' capitoli 36 di questo libro" (*Reali,* ed. Vandelli, 2: lxxvii). See also **F** 423; **PS,** chap. 33; **N** 1: 369, 2: 440; **E** 2: 165.

27. Rajna, "Rinaldo da Montalbano," 222; Morosi, "La leggenda di Rinaldo," 1: 265.

28. Ysaresse (**RM1** 185v), Iseres (**RM1** 192v [3], 195r), Iserses (**RM1** 194r).

29. Morosi, "La leggenda di Rinaldo," 1: 267. Guidon Selvaggio is, however, mentioned in Melli, XIII, 11, 1.

30. Morosi, "La leggenda di Rinaldo," 266. Cf. **RM1** 22r, 25r–v, 29v.

31. Boni, "Noterelle," 10–11.

32. The closest example from the *Tre Corone* is "Tolsimi dinanzi a voi" (*Vita Nuova,* XXXV, 7), meaning *allontanarsi* (*ED,* 5: 616).

33. *Travels of Sir John Mandeville,* 97. See also Friedman, *Monstrous Races,* 18, 23.

34. See my "Portrayal," 258.

35. (Var.) *meschite:* Dante, *Inf.,* VIII, 70. For mosques in chansons de geste, see Meredith-Jones, "Conventional Saracen," 209–10.

36. *Moschea, -e:* **N** 2: 137, **B** 34r, 38v, 39r; *m- loro tenpio de falzi iddei* (**RM1** 84r); *m- di machonmet* (**RM2** 63v); *due chorpi morti per sopelirg[l]i nelle loro saraine moschee* (**RM2** 116r). See my "Portrayal," 252–54.

37. *Zibibbo:* **RM1** 171r; *cibibo:* **RM2** 6v, 43v. Spellings with *z* appear consistently in **M** and **R5.**

38. Other examples include "Voleva Fiore far fare uno bangno a Orlando" (**RM2** 17v); "fecono un altro fiero asalto, e durò insino alla notte. Allora fecono patto di tornare l'altra mattina alla battalglia. Orlando tornò a ppie' verso e' christiani . . . la sera Malagigi fece un bangno a Orlando" (**RM2** 78v); "la sera era dama Roenza venuta a' padilgloni, e molto lodò Orlando; e ' medici le fecono un bangno d'erbe quando s'andò a letto" (**RM2** 78v).

39. Boni, "Le *Storie d'Aspramonte* nella *Spagna* in prosa," 41–42. Tibaldo and Aiolfo undertake similar vows of chastity (**N** 1: 40; **E** 1: 94).

40. *Dificio:* **E** 1: 132 (12); (var.) *difizio:* **F** 391 (6), **E** 2: 18; *(e)difizio, hedifizio, (h)edificio:* **RM1** 130v (10), 131r (2).

41. *Parea che faville gittasse d'ogni parte* (*Tes.*, VIII, 32, 6–7). *GDLI* cites Andrea (5: 745). *Riempire faville: l'aria si riempieva di f-* (**A** 267; **Z** 2: 243; **RM1** 10v); *diegli un gran colpo sull'e[l]mo che tutto lo 'ntron[ò] e uscinne mille f- di fuocho* (**RM1** 19v); *dieronsi due grandissimi cholpi che rienpierono l'aria di favilgl[e]* (**RM2** 20v); *tutta l'aria rienpiendo di f- ch'uscivano delle perchussioni* (**RM2** 94r); *l'aria era piena di f-* (**RM2** 111r); *f- ch'uscivano de' cholpi* (**M** 8r); *riempieuono l'aria di f-* (**M** 168v); (rel.) *tutta l'aria favillò* (**A** 242); *tutta l'aria sfavillò* (**RM1** 108v).

42. *Tes.*, V, 78–81; *Filos.*, V, 10, 3.

43. On the theme of suicide in medieval literature, see Lefay-Toury, *La tentation du suicide.*

44. (Var.) *giusta nostra possa* (**RM1** 83v); *g- lor possa* (**RM1** 166r).

45. *Come di sopra è detto:* **RM1** 8v, 70r, 91v, 157r, 172r, 174v, **RM2** 4r, 25r, 56r (2), 65r, 70r, 79r, 108r, **M** 169r; (var.) *come d- è di sopra* (**RM1** 34r); *come è d- di sopra* (**RM1** 85v, **RM2** 75v); *come sopra è d-* (**M** 5v); (rel.) *di sopra è d- abastanza e scripto* (**RM1** 148r); *d- di sopra* (**RM1** 148v); *la materia detta di sopra* (**RM1** 149r).

Come il (el) fatto stava: **RM1** 5r, 34v, **RM2** 2r, 5r, 7v, **M** 11r; *a dire tutto il f- stava* (**RM1** 9v); (var.) *chome il f- era stato* (**RM1** 65v); *come il f- sta* (**RM1** 84r).

Chome la chosa staua: **RM2** 86r; *la c- com'era stata* (**RM1** 39r); *la c- chom'ella stava* (**RM1** 88v, **M** 9v); (var.) *la c- chom'era amdata* (**RM1** 65v); *chome la c- era stata* (**RM2** 34r).

E nota che: **RM1** 126r, 134v, 135r, 136v, 137v, 145r, 147v, 149r, 154r, 166r, 173r, 177r, 179r, 181r, 183v, **RM2** 61r, 74r; (var.) *E nota:* **RM2** 59r; *Et nota:* **RM1** 93r; *nota che:* **RM1** 58r, 139v, 165r.

46. Under the definition "parte mobile dell'elmo," *GDLI* (2: 128) first cites *Aiolfo.* Crusca (2: 111) also cites Andrea.

47. *Panziera:* for this meaning, *GDLI* (12: 459) cites no chivalric author before Pulci. See also Müntz, *Les collections,* 31.

48. *C(h)ollottolg:* **F** 409, **A** 70, **E** 1: 164, 2: 170, 211, **G** 190v, **RM2** 24v, 32r, 50r, 55v, 57r, 57v, 64r, 82v; (var.) *c- del chapo:* **RM2** 11r.

49. *Bastia: GDLI*, 2: 99; M. Villani, *Cronica*, vol. 1, III, xii, 21; *liccia: GDLI*, 9: 42.

50. *Bastia:* **F** 404, 405, **S** 13v, 14v, 15r, 16v, 17v, 18r, 19r, **E** 2: 290, 291 (7), 292, 293, 294, **B** 12r, 12v, 13r, 13v, 39v, 85r, 94r, 113r, **RM2** 62r (3); (plur.) **F** 403, 404 (2), **A** 269, **S** 9v, 25v, **N** 1: 432, 2: 574, 575, **E** 2: 284, **B** 32r, **RM1** 15v, 37r, 103v, 104r (2), 107r, **RM2** 5v, 77r.

Liccia: **N** 2: 284 (2), 285, 287, 327, 330, 331, 352, 370, **RM1** 110v, 113v, **RM2** 31r; (plur.) *licc(i)e:* **S** 8r, 19r, **N** 1: 432, 434, 2: 288 (2), 292, 308 (2), 317, 329 (2), 330, 331, 349, 352, 355 (2), 356, 359, 361, 364, 370, 381, 2: 580; **E** 1: 189, **B** 112r, **RM1** 37r, 110v (2), 113v (2), **RM2** 33v, 37v; (var.) *lizze:* **E** 1: 189.

51. In G. Villani and Sercambi (*GDLI*, 8: 1022). In Andrea: **E** 2: 15; (plur.) **B** 12v. Cf. *levare il ponte:* **N** 1: 109.

52. *Rastrello:* **F** 360, **A** 30 (2), **N** 1: 108, 378, 396, 2: 15n.2, 17, 18, 28, 471, **U** 20v, **E** 1: 205 (2); (plur.) *rastregli:* **N** 1: 410, 2: 20, **E** 2: 282. Under the meaning "palizzata,

steccato posto dinanzi alle porte di una fortezza o di una città," *GDLI* (15: 536) first cites *Aiolfo* and then Ariosto.

53. The less authoritative variant *rastello, -i* is a spelling restricted to the **RM1** scribe.

54. *Battaglia giudicata:* **N** 2: 427, 670, 683, **E** 1: 31; (plur.) **N** 1: 203, 307; (rel.) "dovessono giudicare chi avesse vinto, finito la battaglia" (**B** 13r); "furono aletti tre baroni li quali dovessono giudicare" (**B** 4v); "giudicie della battaglia" (**M** 7v).

55. *Nimicare* (v. tr.): *molto ci nimicheranno* (**N** 2: 211, **E** 1: 305); *tu si fieramente el nimichi* (**E** 2: 256); (part.) **F** 120; *io sono lo nimicato Rinovardo* (**N** 2: 525, **Z** 1: 81, **E** 2: 109).

56. *Nimicare: Dec.*, X, 8; M. Villani, *Cronica*, vol. 1, I, xxvi, 9, xci, 16–17, IX, iii, 7; *inimicato: Dec.*, X, 2. Under "nemicare," *GDLI* (11: 339) cites Compagni, G. Villani, Pucci, Sacchetti, Morelli, Ser Giovanni, Piccolomini, and *Reali*. For Morelli, see Trolli, "Il Lessico," 119.

57. *Toccarsi il dente: Add.*, 212. *Certificare:* (part.) *Spagna*, XX, 17, 3; *Par.*, IX, 18; *Dec.* (5).

58. *Capitolare: GDLI* cites Rinaldo degli Albizzi, Giovanni Cavalcanti, and Guicciardini, but no chivalric authors (2: 693). In M. Villani, vol. 2, *Cronica*, XI, cii, 94–95.

59. *Chapitolare:* **RM1** 194v; *si chapitolò:* **RM1** 193v, 194r; *richapitolerebbe:* **RM1** 194r; (part.) **RM1** 188r, 195r. In *Ansuigi*, an ambassador is granted "pieno mandato di chapitolare" (**S** 4r, 3v).

60. Trolli, "Il Lessico," 72.

61. *Salvo condotto:* **F** 284, 532; **A** 279 (2), 295 (2); **N** 1: 305, 316 (2), 2: 6n.4, 8, 430, 473 (2), 474, 678, 679 (2); **E** 1: 166, 184, 206, 207 (3), 211, 212 (3), 314, 2: 205, 247 (4), 290, 294; **B** 12r, 53v, 55v, 63v, 66v, 121v; **RM1** 36r (2), 78v, 79r (2), 92v (3), 93r, 193v (4); **RM2** 30r (3), 30v, 92v, 94v, 103r (2). Not in *DC, ED, Canz., Dec.* Trolli, "La Lingua," 126–27; *GDLI*, 17: 465. It would be used later by Pulci and Ariosto.

62. Ciarambino, *Carlomagno, Gano e Orlando*, 66.

63. *Interpido,-i:* **F** 303 (2), **A** 16, 234 (4), **N** 2: 679, **B** 25v (3), 29r, 31v, 33r, 36r, 51v, 65r, 65v, 66v (2), 67r, 68r, **RM1** 61v, 92r, **RM2** 15r, 15v, 89v, 114v (4), **M** 1v (2); (var.) *interpito, -i:* **A** 8, 98, 110, **G** 91r. Not in *Canz., Dec., DC, ED.* Under "interprete," *GDLI* (8: 261) cites Andrea.

64. Under the meaning "assaggiare," Crusca (3: 963) cites *Aiolfo* first; *GDLI* (3: 942) cites Boccaccio, Ser Giovanni, *Aiolfo*, Masuccio, Pulci.

65. *Fior.* (366) uses *crocietta vermiglia* to express the same idea. Crusca (11: 140) registers *niello* in *Reali*.

66. "Chi dice la 'verità'; adattamento dell'a. fr. *verteier* da *verté*" (*Dizionario etimologico italiano*, 5: 4023). *Veritiere, -o: veritiero parlatore* (**F** 563); *chiam[ò] se bugiardo et me veritiero* (**B** 38r); *veritiera gente* (**B** 52v); *Chi è cholui che dicie che Rinaldo ène bugiardo? Per mia fe' se llo diciesse altrove, gli mosterrei che Rinaldo fusse veritieri!* (**RM1** 72r).

67. Bloch, "The Lay," 181–82; Neri, "La voce 'lai,'" 182.

68. Crusca (IX: 172–75) cites only the unmodified noun.

69. *Segnarsi il viso:* **A** 189, **N** 2: 569, **Z** 1: 206, 312, 2: 188, **E** 1: 3, 10, **B** 77r, 77v, **RM1** 3v, 50r (2), 85r; (rel.) *si segnò di croce:* **Z** 2: 47. Not in *Canz., Dec., DC, ED.*

70. *Segnio della croce:* **F** 11, 483, **A** 176, **N** 2: 600, **Z** 2: 171 (2), 186, **B** 26v, 51v, 54r, 69v, 79v, **RM1** 33v, 71r, 112v, **RM2** 10r; (var.) *s- della Santa C-:* **Z** 2: 112, **E** 2: 266, **B** 100r.

71. *Abbavagliare:* **E** 1: 213n; (part.) **E** 1: 294; *imbavagliare:* **F** 449, 451, 452, **N** 2: 708n.3, **E** 1: 213; (part.) **E** 1: 294n.

72. *Alloppiare:* **RM1** 25r, 87r, 118v, **RM2** 92v; (part. as adj.) **F** 88, 163, 164, 322, **RM1** 25r, 118v; *a- al veleno del serpente* (133r); *confezioni a-* (**RM2** 7r); *ghuardie a-* (108v, 118v); *vino a-* (**F** 89, 120, 331, **M** 10v); (rel. n.) *(a)(l)loppio:* **F** 154, 164, **RM1** 118r, 118v (3); *a- da dormire* (**RM2** 43v [2]).

73. *Intrinsico:* "voglia dio che simile non avengna alla mia ciptà, la quale veggo per li suoi inpedimentire di gustizia chred'io non muta delli *'ntrinsichi* corpi l[angui]re" (**B** 11v, with **G** 17r); *GDLI,* 8: 359. *Infingardo:* **N** 2: 491, **Z** 2: 97; Crusca, 8: 708; *GDLI,* 7: 947.

74. For the sea storm topos in texts of the period, see Orvieto, *Pulci medievale,* 143–53.

75. For examples from *Guerrino,* see my "Language of Chivalry," 71.

76. Cf. "il cinghiaro di Calidonia" (*Filos.,* VII, 27, 2–3).

77. For examples from Andrea, see my "Language of Chivalry," 73.

CHAPTER 6

1. Gorni, "Metodi vecchi," 192.

2. Ministero della Pubblica Istruzione, *Indici e cataloghi, IV: I codici palatini,* 2: fasc. 2, 145–46; Rajna, *Le fonti,* 530; Werner, "L'*Aspramonte* di Andrea," 137; Osella, in *Pallante,* 51–54, 59–63, 67–95; Boni, "Note sul cantare," 294–96n.1.

3. *Romanzi dei Reali,* ed. Mattaini, 26; Renda and Operti, *Dizionario storico,* 100; Bertolini, "Il *Rambaldo.*"

4. Osella, in *Pallante,* 72; Bertolini, "Il *Rambaldo,*" 42.

5. Balugante, Falserone (**F** 474, 485, 509–10; **A** 229, 235, 249, 280–81, 285; **S** 15r); Malagrap(p)a (**N** 1: 287, 294, 299, 324, 2: 480, 491, 512); Milidonio (**B** 40v); Melidonio (**E** 2: 22–24, 26); Angelia (**E** 2: 175, 182, 247).

6. **F** 531, 534, 539; **A** 7, 135, 263; **B** 1v.

7. The existence of this church in the seaport burg of Chiaia was documented on a map of 1566 (De Seta, *Storia della città,* 231).

8. Bertolini, "Prime imprese," 71n.149, 75n.175.

9. Peters, *Über die Geographie im* Guerrino, 8–13.

10. For a transcription of this episode from *Rambaldo,* see Bertolini, "Sbarco dei saraceni," 73–93.

11. Karttunen, *India,* 128–29; Friedman, *Monstrous Races,* 18, 125, 195.

12. Osella, in *Pallante,* 73.

13. Ciarambino, *Carlomagno, Gano e Orlando,* 55, 66, 68. However, the use of foreign languages by characters in chivalric romance was not Andrea's invention, as Ciarambino had believed.

14. See my "Portrayal," 249.

15. Ignorance of Western weapons and military customs was one component in medieval depictions of alien peoples (Friedman, *Monstrous Races,* 32–33).

16. *Isso fatto:* **N** 1: 517, 2: 42, 70, 154, 212, 377, 389, 412, 426 (2), 545n.4; **Z** 1: 88; **R** 3r, 7r, 7v, 22v, 44v.

17. Cf. **A** 180, 181, 183; **Z** 1: 69–70.

18. *Bella criatura:* **Z** 1: 81; **R** 6r, 6v, 13v, 20r (2), 20v, 21r, 26v, 48v (2), 56r, 56v, 67v, 68v.

19. For example, "Io mi credo essere incinta, cioè *grossa*" (**Z** 1: 4).

20. "Correggia in collo," meaning "in atteggiamento umile," appears in Morelli's *Ricordi* and in Andrea's *Aspramonte* (Trolli, "Il Lessico," 132). Cf. **A** 263. As historical practice, see Butler, *Lombard Communes,* 121.

21. *Bandire la croce adosso:* **F** 179; **A** 70, 71; **Z** 1: 135.

22. Sapori, *Italian Merchant,* 34. Cf. *degni della croce gialla:* Pucci, *Centiloquio* (*GDLI,* 3: 993).

23. "Stambecchino . . . nome di un'antica arma, probabilmente una specie di arco che ricordava per la forma le corna dello stambecco. Anche, il soldato armato di tale arma" (Devoto and Oli, eds., *Dizionario,* 2343). Cf. *istranbecchi: Orl.,* XXXVIII, 6, 7.

24. *A bacchetta:* cf. *Diario* 206, 215.

25. The phrase dates from the Trecento (*GDLI,* 3: 714).

26. See Balduino, *Manuale di filologia,* 169; Martelli and Bessi, *Guida alla filologia,* 13, 28–29; Stussi, *Nuovo avviamento,* 106.

27. The unusual verb *figliare* occurs elsewhere in *Guerrino:* "Diciesi che già vi figliavano i grifoni" (**B** 74r).

28. *Vettuvaglia:* **F** 26, 43, 73, 76, 87; **A** 13 (2), 16, 17, 33, 65, 83; **S** 9r (2), 9v, 10r, 13v (2), 14v, 15r (4), 15v, 19r, 20r; **N** 1: 307, 401, 441, 450, 2: 42, 61, 96, 97, 217, 232; **E** 1: 26, 114, 171, 177, 210, 2: 7, 22, 37, 65, 70; **U** 19v; **B** 2r, 19r, 26r (2), 31v, 34r, 46v, 110r.

29. Balduino, *Manuale di filologia,* 137; Martelli and Bessi, *Guida alla filologia,* 118; Stussi, *Nuovo avviamento,* 141.

30. Omitted from **L** 46r–v because of a lengthy abbreviation.

31. Allaire, "Portrayal," 248; *Travels of Sir John Mandeville,* 196. Cf. Friedman, *Monstrous Races,* 11, 28, 160–61.

Selected Bibliography

Principal Texts

Andrea da Barberino. L'Aspramonte: Romanzo cavalleresco inedito (Aspramont: Unedited chivalric romance). Ed. Marco Boni. Collezione di opere inedite o rare, n.s. Bologna: Antiquaria Palmaverde, 1951.

———. L'Aspramonte (Aspramont). Ed. Luigi Cavalli. Naples: Rossi, 1972.

———. I Reali di Francia: Ricerche intorno ai Reali di Francia seguite dal libro delle storie di Fioravante (The Royal House of France: Research on The Royal House of France followed by the book of the stories of Fioravante). Ed. Pio Rajna. . . . Vol. 1. Bologna: Romagnoli, 1872.

———. I Reali di Francia: Testo critico (The Royal House of France: Critical edition). Ed. Giuseppe Vandelli. Vol. 2, pts. 1 and 2. Bologna: Romagnoli, 1892.

———. I Reali di Francia (The Royal House of France). Ed. Giuseppe Vandelli and Giovanni Gambarin. Scrittori d'Italia 193. Bari: Laterza, 1947.

———. I Reali di Francia (The Royal House of France). Intro. by Aurelio Roncaglia, notes by Fabrizio Beggiato. I Grandi Secoli 6. Rome: Casini, 1967.

———. Storia di Ajolfo del Barbicone e di altri valorosi cavalieri: Testo di lingua inedito (Story of Aiolfo del Barbicone and of other valorous knights: Unedited vernacular text). Ed. Leone Del Prete. 2 vols. Bologna: Romagnoli, 1863–64.

———. Storia di Ugone d'Avernia volgarizzata nel sec. XIV (Story of Ugone of Avernia, fourteenth-century vernacular reworking). Ed. F[rancesco] Zambrini and A[lberto] Bacchi della Lega. Scelta di curiosità letterarie inedite o rare dal secolo XIII al XIX, 188–89. 2 vols. Bologna: Romagnoli, 1882; Bologna: Commissione per i Testi di lingua, 1968.

———. Le Storie Nerbonesi: Romanzo cavalleresco del secolo XIV (The Nerbonesi stories: Fourteenth-century chivalric romance). Ed. I. G. Isola. 4 vols. Bologna: Romagnoli, 1877–91; Genoa: R. Istituto Sordo-Muti, 1891.

Secondary Sources

Accademia della Crusca. Opera del Vocabolario. Concordanze del Canzoniere di Francesco Petrarca (Concordance to Petrarch's lyric poetry cycle). Ed. Ufficio Lessicografico. 2 vols. Florence: [Crusca], 1971.

Accame Bobbio, Aurelia. *Profilo storico della letteratura italiana* (Historical profile of Italian literature). 7th ed. Brescia: La Scuola, 1969.

Ageno, Franca. "La Lingua della cronaca todina di Ioan Fabrizio degli Atti" (The language of the Todi chronicle by Ioan Fabrizio degli Atti). *Studi di filologia italiana* 13 (1955): 167–227.

Albertazzi, Adolfo. *Il Romanzo*. Storia dei Generi letterari italiani (The romance). Milan: Vallardi, n.d. [1902].

Alberti, Leon Battista. *I Libri della famiglia* (The books on the family). Ed. Ruggiero Romano and Alberto Tenenti. Nuova Universale Einaudi 102. Turin: Einaudi, 1969.

Allaire, Gloria. "The Chivalric 'Histories' of Andrea da Barberino: A Re-evaluation." Ph.D. diss., University of Wisconsin–Madison, 1993.

———. "Un Codice ritrovato della *Storia d'Aiolfo del Barbicone* di Andrea da Barberino" (A rediscovered codex of the Story of Aiolfo del Barbicone by Andrea da Barberino). *Lettere italiane* 45 (1993): 398–401.

———. "Due inediti di Andrea da Barberino nella Biblioteca Palatina di Parma" (Two unedited exemplars by Andrea da Barberino in the Palatine Library, Parma). *Pluteus*, forthcoming.

———. "Due testimoni sconosciuti di Andrea da Barberino nel codice Barberiniano latino 4101 della Biblioteca Vaticana" (Two unknown witnesses of Andrea da Barberino in the Vatican Library codex Barb. lat. 4101). *Pluteus* 6–7 (1988–89): 121–30.

———. "Un ignoto manoscritto di *Guerrino il Meschino* di Andrea da Barberino nella Biblioteca Apostolica Vaticana" (An unknown manuscript of Guerrino il Meschino by Andrea da Barberino in the Vatican Library). *La Bibliofilía* 96 (1994): 233–41.

———. "The Language of Chivalry: Similes in the Romances of Andrea da Barberino." *La Fusta* 9 (1992–93): 69–84.

———. "Un Manoscritto inedito del *cantare del padiglione* trovato nel cod. Riccardiano 1717" (An unedited manuscript of the octaves on the pavilion found in Riccardian codex 1717). *Studi mediolatini e volgari* 37 (1991): 9–30.

———. "Un Manoscritto rediano delle *Storie Nerbonesi* e dell'*Ugone d'Avernia* di Andrea da Barberino" (A manuscript of the Nerbonesi stories and Ugone of Avernia in the Redi collection). *Studi e problemi di critica testuale* 47 (1993): 43–48.

———. "An Overlooked Exemplar of *Guerrino il Meschino* by Andrea da Barberino (BAV, Barb. lat. 3988)." *Manuscripta*, forthcoming.

———. "Portrayal of Muslims in Andrea da Barberino's *Guerrino il Meschino*." In *Medieval Christian Perceptions of Islam. A Book of Essays*, ed. John Victor Tolan, 243–69. Medieval Casebooks. New York: Garland, 1996.

———. "The Secular Pilgrimage of an Errant Knight: Andrea da Barberino's *Guerrino il Meschino*." *Romance Languages Annual* 5 (1993): 148–52.

———. "The 'Spain' Cycle in Italy: The Case for a *Seconda Spagna* by Andrea da Barberino." *Olifant* 19, (1994–95):5–17.

———. "Tullia d'Aragona's *Il Meschino altramente detto il Guerino* as Key to a Reappraisal of Her Work." *Quaderni d'italianistica* 16 (1995): 33–50.

―――. "The Unedited Epic Romance *Rambaldo* (BNCF Pal. 578): Disproving an Attribution." Paper presented at the annual meeting of the American Association of Teachers of Italian, Atlanta, November 19, 1994.

―――. "Unknown Exemplars of Andrea da Barberino in the Ashburnham Collection of the Biblioteca Medicea Laurenziana." *Scriptorium* 48.1 (1994): 151–58.

―――. "An Unknown Fragment of the *cantare del padiglione* found in Codex C.256 of the Biblioteca Marucelliana in Florence." *Medioevo romanzo* 18 (1993): 277–92.

―――. "The Warrior Woman in Late Medieval Prose Epics." *Italian Culture* 12 (1994): 33–44.

Alle Bocche della piazza: Diario di anonimo fiorentino (1382–1401). (BNF, Panciatichiano 158) (At the entries to the plaza: Anonymous Florentine diary . . .). Ed. Anthony Molho and Franek Sznura. Istituto Nazionale di Studi sul Rinascimento, Studi e testi 14. Florence: Olschki, 1986.

Altamura, Antonio. *I Cantastorie e la poesia popolare italiana* (The singers of tales and popular Italian poetry). Naples: Fiorentino, 1965.

―――. "Il *Romanzo di Francia*" (The Romance of France). In *Studi di filologia italiana*, 67–79. Collana di studi e testi di letteratura 11. Naples: Fiorentino, 1972.

"Andrea da Barberino." In *The New Century Italian Renaissance Encyclopedia*, ed. Catherine B. Avery, 38. New York: Appleton, 1972.

Ankli, Ruedi. "Un Problema di attribuzione sempre aperto: *Il Ciriffo Calvaneo*" (An unresolved problem of attribution: The Ciriffo Calvaneo). In *L'attribuzione*, ed. Besomi and Caruso, 259–304.

Anseïs von Karthago (Anseïs of Carthage). Ed. Johann Alton. Bibliothek des litterarischen Vereins in Stuttgart 195. Tübingen: Gedruckt für den litterarischen Verein in Stuttgart, 1892.

Babbi, Anna Maria. "Jean de Rochemeure traduttore del *Guerrin Meschino*" (Jean de Rochemeure, translator of *Guerrin Meschino*). In *Miscellanea in onore di Elio Melli*, forthcoming.

―――. "Le Traduzioni del *Guerrin Meschino* in Francia" (The translations of *Guerrin Meschino* in France). In *Il Romanzo nella Francia del Rinascimento: dall'eredità medievale all'* Astrea (*Gargnano, 7–9 ottobre 1993*), 145–53. Gruppo di Studio sul Cinquecento francese 6. Fasano: Schena, 1996.

Balduino, Armando. *Manuale di filologia italiana* (Manual of Italian philology). 3d rev. ed. Biblioteca Universale Sansoni. Florence: Sansoni, 1989.

Baranda Leturio, Nieves. *La Corónica del noble cavallero Guarino Mezquino: Estudio y edición* (The chronicle of the noble knight Guerrino Meschino: Study and edition). Madrid: Universidad Nacional de Educación a distancia, 1992.

Bec, Christian. *Les livres des Florentins (1413–1608)* (Books owned by Florentines . . .). Florence: Olschki, 1984.

Becker, Ph[ilipp] Aug[ust]. *Der Quellenwert der* Storie Nerbonesi (The usefulness of the Nerbonesi stories in source studies). Halle (Saale): Niemeyer, 1898.

[Beltrami, Luca]. *L'età eroica del* Guerin meschino (The heroic age of Guerrino Meschino). Proem by Polifilo, pseud. Milan: Cordani, 1932.

Benci, Antonio. Review of *Li Reali di Francia* (The Royal House of France), ed. Gamba. *Antologia* 4 (1921): 98–104.

Bendinelli, M. L. "Preistoria dell'*Aiolfo* di Andrea da Barberino" (Literary roots of Aiolfo by Andrea da Barberino). *Studi di filologia italiana* 25 (1967): 7–108.

Bertolini, Virginio. "Il *Rambaldo* di Andrea da Barberino: Appunti per un'edizione dell'opera" (Rambaldo by Andrea da Barberino: Notes for an edition of the work). *Quaderni di Lingue e Letterature* 16 (1991): 41–90.

———. "Prime imprese giovanili di Rambaldo (cc. 11r–21r)" (The youthful adventures of Rambaldo . . .). *Quaderni di Lingue e Letterature* 20 (1995): 59–78.

———. "Sbarco dei Saraceni in Calabria. Vicende e morte di Galizella (dal *Rambaldo* di Andrea da Barberino: Firenze: Bibl. Naz., cod. Palat. 578)" (The Saracen invasion of Calabria. Life and death of Galizella . . .). *Quaderni di Lingue e Letterature* 19 (1994): 69–96.

Besomi, Ottavio, and Carlo Caruso, eds. *L'attribuzione: Teoria e pratica. Storia dell'arte, musicologia, letteratura. Atti del Seminario di Ascona 30 sett.–5 ott. 1992* (Attribution: Theory and practice. Art history, musicology, literature. Acts of the seminar . . .). Basel: Birkhäuser, 1994.

Bitelli, Giovanni. "Guerrino detto il Meschino" (Guerrino called "Meschino"). *Corriere del Giorno* (Taranto), Dec. 15, 1951, 3.

Bloch, R. Howard. "The Lay and the Law: Sexual/Textual Transgression in *La Chastelaine de Vergi*, the *Lai d'Ignaure*, and the *Lais* of Marie de France." *Stanford French Review* 14 (1990): 181–210.

Boccaccio, Giovanni. *Decameron*. Ed. Antonio Enzo Quaglio. 2 vols. Milano: Garzanti, 1974.

———. *Filocolo*. Ed. Antonio Enzo Quaglio. I classici mondadori. Tutte le opere 1. [Verona:] Mondadori, 1967.

———. *Filostrato*. Ed. Vittore Branca. I classici mondadori. Tutte le opere 2. [Verona:] Mondadori, 1964.

———. *Teseida delle nozze d'Emilia* (Thebaid of Emilia's wedding). Ed. Alberto Limentani. Oscar classici 227. Tutte le opere di Giovanni Boccaccio. Milan: Mondadori, 1992.

Boni, Marco. "A proposito di un personaggio del *Morgante (Dodone, il figliuol del Danese)*" (Regarding a character in Morgante [Dodone, son of the Dane]). *Atti dell'Accademia delle Scienze dell'Istituto di Bologna,* Classe di Scienze morali, Year 79, *Rendiconti* 73 (1984–85): 98–113.

———. "L'*Aspramonte* trecentesco in prosa del ms. Additional 10808 del British Museum" (The fourteenth-century prose Aspramont . . .). *Studi mediolatini e volgari* 1 (1953): 7–50.

———. "L'*Aspremont* del codice Marciano fr. IV e l'*Aspramonte* di Andrea da Barberino" (The Aspremont of Marciana Library French MS IV and the Aspramont by Andrea da Barberino). In *Studi in onore di Italo Siciliano*, 97–104. Biblioteca dell'*Archivum Romanicum*, ser. 1: Storia-Letteratura-Paleografia 86. Florence: Olschki, 1966.

————. "L'*Aspromonte* [*sic*] quattrocentesco in ottave" (The fifteenth-century Aspramont in octaves). In *Studi in onore di Carlo Pellegrini*, 43–59. Biblioteca di Studi francesi 2. Turin: SEI, 1963.

————. "Il Manoscritti marciani della *Chanson d'Aspremont* e l'*Aspramonte* di Andrea da Barberino" (The Marciana Library manuscripts of the Song of Aspremont and the Aspramont by Andrea da Barberino). *Convivium*, n.s., 17.2 (1949): 253–72.

————. "Il Manoscritto Marciano fr. IV e l'Aspramonte trecentesco in prosa" (The Marciana Library French MS IV and the fourteenth-century prose Aspramont). In *Miscellanea di studi dedicati a Emerico Vàrady*, 175–79. Modena: STEM Mucchi, 1966.

————. "Note sul cantare magliabechiano d'*Aspramonte* e sull'*Aspramonte* di Andrea da Barberino" (Notes on the Magliabechian Aspramont verse epic and on the Aspramont by Andrea da Barberino). *GSLI* 127 (1950): 276–304.

————. "Noterelle pulciane: Il *Morgante* e l'*Aspramonte* di Andrea da Barberino" (Brief notes regarding Pulci: Morgante and Aspramont by Andrea da Barberino). *Atti dell'Accademia delle Scienze dell'Istituto di Bologna*, Classe di Scienze morali, Year 71, *Rendiconti* 65.2 (1976–77): 1–15.

————. "Per una edizione dei *Reali di Francia*" (Toward an edition of the Royal House of France). *Convivium*, n.s., 16.1 (1948): 148–56.

————. "*Le prime imprese del conte Orlando* di Ludovico Dolce e l'*Aspramonte* quattrocentesco in ottave" (The youthful adventures of Count Roland by Ludovico Dolce and the fifteenth-century Aspramont in octaves). In *Studi di varia umanità in onore di Francesco Flora*, 67–87. Milan: Mondadori, 1963.

————. "Le *Storie d'Aspramonte* nei *Fatti di Spagna*" (The Stories of Aspramont in the Deeds of Spain). In *Etudes de Philologie Romane et d'Histoire Littéraire offertes à Jules Horrent à l'occasion de son soixantième anniversaire*, ed. Jean Marie D'Heur and Nicoletta Cherubini, 33–40. Liège: n.p., 1980.

————. "Le *Storie d'Aspramonte* nella *Spagna* magliabechiana" (The Stories of Aspramont in the Magliabechian Spain). In *Studi filologici, letterari e storici in memoria di Guido Favati*, ed. Giorgio Varanini and Palmiro Pinagli, 1: 125–34. Padua: Antenore, 1977.

————. "Le *Storie d'Aspramonte* nella *Spagna* in prosa" (The Stories of Aspramont in the prose Spain). *Atti dell'Accademia delle Scienze dell'Istituto di Bologna*, Classe di Scienze morali, Year 75, *Rendiconti* 69 (1980–81): 25–54.

————. "Le *Storie d'Aspramonte* nella *Spagna in rima* e nel *Morgante*" (The Stories of Aspramont in the verse Spain and in Morgante). In *Charlemagne*, ed. Tyssens and Thiry, 2: 683–95.

Branca, Vittore. "Un Poemetto inedito di Andrea di Barberino?" (An unedited poem in octaves by Andrea da Barberino). *Lettere italiane* 42 (1990): 89–90.

————. "Una 'schermaglia' attribuibile a Andrea da Barberino" (A "joust" that may be attributed to Andrea da Barberino). *Italianistica* 21 (1992): 637–50.

Brettschneider, Helmut. *Der* Anseïs de Cartage *und die* Seconda Spagna (The Anseïs of Carthage and the Second War in Spain). *Romanistische Arbeiten* 27. Halle (Saale): Niemeyer, 1937.

Briquet, C. M. *Les filigranes: Dictionnaire historique des marques du papier des leur apparition vèrs 1282 jusqu'en 1600. A Facsimile of the 1907 Edition with supplementary material . . .* (Watermarks: Historical dictionary of paper marks from their appearance . . .). Ed. Allan Stevenson. 4 vols. Amsterdam: Paper Publications Society (Labarre Foundation), 1968.

Bufalino, Gesualdo. *Il Guerrin Meschino. Frammento di un'opra dei pupi* (Guerrino Meschino. Fragment of a puppet show). Milan: Bompiani, 1993.

Bussani, Illidio. *Il Romanzo cavalleresco in Luigi Pulci* (Chivalric romance in Luigi Pulci). Turin: Bocca, 1933.

Butler, W. F. *The Lombard Communes.* New York: Scribner's, 1906.

Cabani, Maria Cristina. *Le Forme del cantare epico-cavalleresco* (The forms of the chivalric epic poem in octaves). Lucca: Pacini Fazzi, 1988.

Campbell, Tony. "Portolan Charts from the Late Thirteenth Century to 1500." In *The History of Cartography,* ed. J. B. Harley and David Woodward, 1: 371–463. Chicago: University of Chicago Press, 1987.

"El Cantare di Fierabraccia e Uliuieri: Italienische Bearbeitung der Chanson de Geste Fierabras" (The poem of Fierabraccia and Oliver: Italian reworking of the epic poem Fierabras). Ed. E[dmund] Stengel. *Ausgaben und Abhandlungen aus dem Gebiete der Romanischen Philologie* 2. Marburg: Elwert'sche, 1881.

Cantari d'Aspramonte inediti (Magl. VII 682) (The unedited verse epic Aspramont . . .). Ed. Andrea Fassò. Collezione di opere inedite o rare 137. Bologna: Commissione per i Testi di lingua, 1981.

Cantari cavallereschi dei secoli XV e XVI (The chivalric poems in octaves of the fifteenth and sixteenth centuries). Ed. Giorgio Barini. Collezione di opere inedite o rare [89]. Bologna: Romagnoli, 1905.

I Cantari di Rinaldo da Monte Albano (The octaves on Rinaldo of Mount Alban). Ed. Elio Melli. Collezione di opere inedite or rare 133. Bologna: Commissione per i Testi di lingua, 1973.

Caretti, Lanfranco. "Critica e filologia: Andrea da Barberino e Giangiorgio Trissino" (Criticism and philology: Andrea da Barberino and Giangiorgio Trissino). Review of *L'Aspramonte,* ed. Boni. *Il Nuovo Corriere* (Florence), Sept. 10, 1951, 3.

Castellani, Arrigo. *La Prosa italiana delle origini: Testi toscani di carattere pratico* (Early Italian prose: Nonliterary Tuscan documents). 2 vols. Bologna: Pàtron, 1981.

Catalano, Michele. "La Data di morte di Andrea da Barberino" (The death date of Andrea da Barberino). *Archivum Romanicum* 23 (1939): 84–87.

Catalogue des livres de la Bibliothèque de feu M. le Duc de la Valliere . . . (Catalog of the books of the library of the late Monsieur . . .). 6 vols. Paris: Nyon, 1784.

Catalogue of the Choicer Portion of the Magnificent Library, formed by M. Guglielmo Libri. . . . London: Sotheby, 1859.

Catalogue of the Library at Chatsworth [Duke of Devonshire]. 4 vols. London: Chiswick, 1879.

Cecchi, Emilio, and Natalino Sapegno. *Storia della letteratura italiana: Il Trecento*

(History of Italian literature: The fourteenth century). 2: 632–36. Milan: Garzanti, 1965.

Cervantes, Miguel de. *"Don Quixote de la Mancha": Facsímil de la primera impresión.* Facsimile of the first edition [by Juan de la Cuesta, Madrid, 1605]. Alfaguara, Hispanic Society of America. Palma de Mallorca: Papeles de son armadans, 1968.

La Chanson d'Aspremont: *Chanson de geste du XII*^{e} *siècle. Texte du manuscrit de Wollaton Hall* (The Song of Aspremont: Twelfth-century epic poem after the reading of the Wollaton Hall manuscript). Ed. Louis Maurice Brandin. 2 vols. Les classiques français du Moyen Age. 2d ed., rev. Paris: Champion, 1923–24.

La Chanson de Roland (The Song of Roland). Ed. Cesare Segre. Documenti di filologia 16. Milan: Ricciardi, 1971.

Charroi de Nîmes: Il carriaggio di Nimes. Canzone di gesta del XII secolo (The war train of Nîmes: Twelfth-century epic poem). Ed. Giuseppe E. Sansone. Storia e civiltà 7. Bari: Dedalo, 1969.

Chevalier, Ulysse. "Barberino." In *Répertoire des sources historiques du Moyen Age: Bio-bibliographie,* 1: col. 428. Paris: Picard, 1905.

Ciarambino, Gerardo C. A. *Carlomagno, Gano e Orlando in alcuni romanzi italiani del XIV e XV secolo* (Charlemagne, Ganelon and Roland in some Italian romances of the fourteenth and fifteenth centuries). Collezione di cultura 10. Pisa: Giardini, 1976.

Cocai, Merlin [Girolamo Folengo]. *Il Baldo* (Baldus). Trans. Giuseppe Tonna. 2 vols. Milan: Feltrinelli, 1958.

Codici e incunaboli miniati della Biblioteca Civica di Bergamo (Manuscripts and illuminated incunables at the Civic Library in Bergamo). Bergamo: Credito Bergamasco, 1989.

Colby-Hall, Alice M. "La géographie rhodanienne des *Nerbonesi:* Réalisme artificiel ou signe d'authenticité?" (The Rhone area geography in Nerbonesi: Artificial realism or hallmark of authenticity). In *Essor et fortune de la Chanson de geste dans l'Europe e l'Orient latin: Actes du IX*^{e} *Congres International de la Société Rencesvals pour l'etude des épopées romanes. Padoue-Venise, 29 août–4 septembre 1982,* 2: 655–62. Modena: Mucchi, 1984.

——. "In Search of the Lost Epics of the Lower Rhône Valley." In *Romance Epic,* ed. Keller, 115–27.

Concordanza della Commedia *di Dante Alighieri* (Concordance to Dante's Comedy). Ed. Luciano Lovera, with Rosanna Bettarini and Anna Mazzarello. 3 vols. L'officina dei Classici 2. I millenni. Turin: Einaudi, 1975.

Concordanza del Decameron (Concordance to the Decameron). Ed. Alfredo Barbina. 2 vols. Florence: Giunti-Barbèra, 1969.

Contini, Gianfranco. "La Canzone della *Mort Charlemagne*" (The epic song on the death of Charlemagne). In *Mélanges de Linguistique romane et de Philologie médiévale offerts à M. Maurice Delbouille,* 2: 105–26. Gembloux: Duculot, 1964.

Cordié, Carlo. "Ancora *Razza* (con riferimenti a Teofilo Folengo . . .)" (The word "razza" again [with reference to Teofilo Folengo . . .]). *Medioevo romanzo* 5 (1978): 281–88.

Croce, Benedetto. *La Spagna nella vita italiana durante la Rinascenza* (Spain in Italian life during the Renaissance). 2d ed., rev. Scritti di storia letteraria e politica 8. Bari: Laterza, 1922.

Croce, Marcella. "Manifestations of the Chivalric Traditions in Sicily/Aspetti della tradizione cavalleresca in Sicilia." Ph.D. diss., University of Wisconsin–Madison, 1988.

D'Ancona, Alessandro. "*Il Tesoro* di Brunetto Latini versificato" (The verse reworking of Brunetto Latini's Treasure). *Atti della R. Accademia dei Lincei*. Classe di Scienze morali, storiche e filologiche, Year 285, 4th ser. 4 (1888): 111–274.

D'Ancona, Alessandro, and Orazio Bacci. *Manuale della letteratura italiana* (Manual of Italian literature). 6th ed. 6 vols. Florence: Barbèra, 1897–1904.

Dante Alighieri. *La Divina Commedia* (The Divine Comedy). Ed. C. H. Grandgent, rev. by Charles S. Singleton. Cambridge, Mass.: Harvard University Press, 1972.

D'Aragona, Tullia. *Il Meschino altramente detto il Guerino Opera, nella quale si veggono & intendono le parti principali di tutto il mondo* . . . (Meschino otherwise called Guerrino, work in which one sees and learns about the principal parts of the entire world . . .). Venice: Sessa, 1560.

De Bartholomaeis, Vincenzo. "*La Discesa di Ugo d'Alvernia all'Inferno* secondo il frammento di Giovanni Maria Barbieri" (Ugo of Alvernia's descent into Hell according to the Giovanni Maria Barbieri fragment). *Memorie della R. Accademia di Bologna,* Classe di Scienze morali, Sezione di Scienze storico-filologiche e Sezione di Scienze giuridiche, 2d ser., 10 for 1925–26 (1929): 1–54.

De Marco, Barbara. "The Sounds of Change: Arabic Linguistic Influences in Sicily." In *Synchronic and Diachronic Approaches to Linguistic Variation and Change,* ed. Thomas J. Walsh, 94–101. Georgetown University Round Table on Languages and Linguistics 1988. Washington, D.C.: Georgetown University Press, 1989.

De Seta, Cesare. *Storia della città di Napoli dalle origini al Settecento* (History of the city of Naples from its origins to the eighteenth century). Rome: Laterza, 1973.

Della Mora, Giovanni. *Milone d'Anglante: Morfologia e storia di un personaggio dell'epopea carolingia* (Milone of Anglante: Morphology and history of a Carolingian cycle epic hero). Strumenti di Ricerca 33. Rome: Bulzoni, 1981.

Delcorno Branca, Daniela. "Fortuna e trasformazioni del *Buovo d'Antona*" (The fortunes and transformations of Buovo of Antona). In *Testi,* ed. Holtus, Krauss, and Wunderli, 285–306.

Dionisotti, Carlo. "Appunti su antichi testi" (Notes on early texts). *Italia medioevale e umanistica* 7 (1964): 77–131.

———. "Appunti su cantari e romanzi" (Notes on epic poems and romances). *Italia medioevale e umanistica* 32 (1989): 227–61.

———. "*Entrée d'Espagne, Spagna, Rotta di Roncisvalle*" (The Entry into Spain, Spain, and the Rout at Roncisvalle). In *Studi in onore di Angelo Monteverdi,* ed. G. G. Marcuzzo, 207–41. Modena: STEM, 1959.

———. "Fortuna e sfortuna del Boiardo nel Cinquecento" (The critical fortunes of Boiardo in the sixteenth century). In *Il Boiardo e la critica contemporanea: Atti del convegno di studi su Matteo Maria Boiardo, Scandiano-Reggio Emilia 25–27 aprile 1969*, ed. Giuseppe Anceschi, 221–41. Biblioteca dell'*Archivum Romanicum*, ser. 1: Storia-Letteratura-Paleografia 107. Florence: Olschki, 1970.

La Discesa di Ugo d'Alvernia allo Inferno secondo il codice franco-italiano della Nazionale di Torino (Ugo of Alvernia's descent into Hell according to the Franco-Italian codex at the National Library, Turin). Ed. Rodolfo Renier. Scelta di curiosità letterarie inedite o rare dal secolo XIII al XIX 194. 1883. Bologna: Commissione per i Testi di lingua, 1968.

Dizionario della lingua italiana (Dictionary of the Italian language), ed. Giacomo Devoto and Gian Carlo Oli. Florence: Le Monnier, 1971.

Dizionario enciclopedico della letteratura italiana (Encyclopedic dictionary of Italian literature). Giuseppe Petronio, dir. 5 vols. Bari: Laterza, Unedi, 1966–68.

Dizionario etimologico italiano (Italian etymological dictionary). Ed. Carlo Battisti and Giovanni Alessio. 5 vols. Florence: Barbèra, 1957.

Dizionario storico della letteratura italiana (Historical dictionary of Italian literature). Ed. Umberto Renda and Piero Operti. 4th ed. Rev. by Vittorio Turri. Turin: Paravia, 1959.

Enciclopedia Dantesca (Dante encyclopedia). 6 vols. Rome: Istituto della Enciclopedia Italiana, 1970–76.

L'Entrée d'Espagne: Chanson de geste franco-italienne publiée d'après le manuscrit unique de Venise (The Entry into Spain: Franco-Italian epic poem published according to the reading of the unique manuscript located in Venice). Ed. Antoine Thomas. 2 vols. Société des Anciens Textes français [61]. Paris: Firmin-Didot, 1913.

Fabio, Franco. *La Materia cavalleresca prima dell'Ariosto* (Chivalric material before Ariosto). Naples: Scientifica, 1972.

Fassò, Andrea. "Cortesia, mito ed epopea" (Courtliness, myth and epic). In *Omaggio a Gianfranco Folena*, 1: 87–107. Padua: Programma, 1993.

Li Fatti de Spagna: *Testo settentrionale trecentesco già detto "Viaggio di Carlo Magno in Ispagna"* (The Deeds of Spain: Fourteenth-century text in northern dialect formerly called "The Voyage of Charlemagne to Spain"). Ed. Ruggero M. Ruggieri. Istituto di Filologia Romanza della Università di Roma, Studi e testi 1. Modena: Società Tipografica Modenese, 1951.

Ferri, Giustino L. Review of *Guerrin Meschino*, by Domenico Tumiati. *Nuova Antologia*, 5th ser., 164.1 (1913): 451–56.

Flora, Francesco. *Storia della letteratura italiana* (History of Italian literature), vol. 1. 3d ed. 3 vols. [Milan]: Mondadori, 1945.

Flutre, Fernand. *Table des noms propres avec toutes leurs variantes, figurant dans les romans du Moyen Age écrits en français . . .* (Table of proper names with all their variants, which appear in French medieval romances . . .). Poitiers: C.E.S.C.M., 1962.

Foffano, Francesco. *Il Poema cavalleresco* (The chivalric poem). Storia dei Generi letterari italiani 58. Milan: Villardi, 1904.

Forni Marmocchi, Aurelia. "Reminiscenze dei *Reali di Francia* nella *Spagna in prosa*"

(Echoes of The Royal House of France in the prose Spain). *Atti dell'Accademia delle Scienze dell'Istituto di Bologna,* Classe di Scienze morali, Year 74, *Rendiconti* 68 (1979–80): 165–83.

———. "Il Romanzo cavalleresco anonimo conservato nella seconda parte del ms. Add. 10808 del British Museum" (The anonymous chivalric romance preserved in the second part of . . .). *Atti dell'Accademia delle Scienze dell'Istituto di Bologna,* Classe di Scienze morali, *Memorie* 71 (1976–77): 5–70.

Franceschetti, Antonio. "On the Saracens in Early Italian Chivalric Literature." In *Romance Epic,* ed. Keller, 203–11.

———. "L'*Orlando Innamorato* e la tradizione dell'*Aspremont*" (Roland in Love and the Aspremont tradition). *GSLI* 147 (1970): 518–33.

Françon, Marcel. "Guerin Mesquin chez le Pretre Jean" (Guerrino Meschino in Prester John's kingdom). *Bulletin de la Société de mythologie française* 87 (1972): 104–14.

———. "*Guerino Meschino,* Morgain-la-Fée, et Tannhäuser." *Romance Notes* 16 (1975): 457–59.

Frati, Ludovico. "Tradizioni storiche del purgatorio di San Patrizio" (Historical traditions of St. Patrick's purgatory). *GSLI* 17 (1891): 46–79.

Freud, Sigmund. *Totem and Taboo.* Trans. James Strachey. New York: Norton, 1950.

Friedman, John Block. *The Monstrous Races in Medieval Art and Thought.* Cambridge, Mass.: Harvard University Press, 1981.

Gamba, Bartolommeo. *Li Reali di Francia nei quali si contiene la generazione degli imperatori, re, principi, baroni e paladini, con la bellissima istoria di Buovo d'Antona* (The Royal House of France in which is contained the lineage of emperors, kings, princes, barons and paladins, with the wonderful story of Buovo of Antona). ,Venice: Alvisopoli, 1821.

Gaspary, Adolfo. *Storia della letteratura italiana* (History of Italian literature). Trans. Vittorio Rossi. 2d ed., rev. 2 vols. Turin: Loescher, 1900–1901.

Gautier, Léon. *Les épopées françaises: Étude sur les origines et l'histoire de la littérature nationale* (French epics: Study on the origins and history of the national literature). 2d ed., rev. 5 vols. Paris: Société Générale de Librairie Catholique, 1878–97.

Ghiselli, Alfredo. Review of L'*Aspramonte,* ed. Boni. *Lettere italiane* 4 (1952): 206–10.

Girone il Cortese: Romanzo cavalleresco di Rustico o Rusticiano da Pisa volgarizzamento inedito del buon secolo (Chivalric romance by Rustico or Rusticiano of Pisa, unedited fourteenth-century vernacular reworking). Ed. Francesco Tassi. Florence: Società Tipografica, 1855.

Golubovich, Girolamo. *Biblioteca Bio-bibliografica della Terra Santa e dell'Oriente francescano* (Bio-bibliographical library of the Holy Land and the Franciscan East). 5 vols. Florence: Quaracchi, 1906–27.

Gorni, Guglielmo. "Metodi vecchi e nuovi nell'attribuzione di testi volgari italiani" (Old and new methods in the attribution of vernacular Italian texts). In *L'attribuzione,* ed. Besomi and Caruso, 183–209.

Graesse, Jean George Théodore. *Trésor de livres rares et précieux* (Treasury of rare and precious books). 7 vols. Dresde: Kuntze, 1859–69.

Graf, A[rturo]. "Di un poema inedito di Carlo Martello e di Ugo conte d'Alvernia" (An unedited poem about Charles the Hammer and Ugo, count of Alvernia). *Giornale di filologia romana* 1 (1878): 92–110.

———. *Miti, leggende e superstizioni del medio evo* (Myths, legends and superstitions of the Middle Ages). 2 vols. Turin: Loescher, 1892–93.

Grande dizionario della lingua italiana (The complete dictionary of the Italian language). Ed. Salvatore Battaglia. 17 vols. to date. Turin: UTET, 1961–.

Grazzini, Antonfrancesco. *Le Rime burlesche edite e inedite di Antonfrancesco Grazzini detto Il Lasca* (Edited and unedited burlesque rhymes by Antonfrancesco Grazzini called "The Roach"). Ed. Carlo Verzone. Raccolta di opere inedite o rare di ogni secolo della letteratura italiana. Florence: Sansoni, 1882.

Grendler, Paul F. "Chivalric Romances in the Italian Renaissance." In *Studies in Medieval and Renaissance History*, ed. J. A. S. Evans and R. W. Unger, 10:59–102. New York: AMS, 1988.

Grisward, Joël H. *Archéologie de l'épopée médiévale: Structures trifonctionnelles et mythes indo-européens dans le cycle des Narbonnais* (Archeology of the medieval epic: Trifunctional structures and Indo-European myths in the Narbonnais cycle). Bibliothèque Historique. Preface by Georges Dumézil. Paris: Payot, 1981.

Harris, Neil. "Il Guerino o l'Ancroia a scelta in una silografia quattrocentesca" (Interchangeability of Guerrino and Ancroia in a fifteenth-century wood-engraving). *La Bibliofilía* 91 (1989): 95–100.

Hawickhorst, Heinrich. "Über die Geographie bei Andrea de' Magnabotti" (On Andrea de' Magnabotti's geography). *Romanische Forschungen* 13 (1902): 689–784.

Heijkant, Marie-José. "L'emploi des formules d'introduction et de transition stéréotypées dans le *Tristano Riccardiano*" (The use of stereotypical introductory and transitional formulae in the Riccardian Tristan). In *Courtly Literature: Culture and Context. Selected Papers from the Fifth Triennial Congress of the International Courtly Literature Society, Dalfsen, The Netherlands, 9–16 August 1986*, ed. Keith Busby and Erik Kooper, 271–82. Utrecht Publications in General and Comparative Literature 25. Amsterdam: Benjamins, 1990.

Henry, Albert. "*Berta da li gran pié* et la *Berte* d'Adenet" (Big-footed Bertha and Adenet's Bertha). *Cultura neolatina* 21 (1961): 135–40.

Hind, Arthur M. *Catalogue of Early Italian Engravings Preserved in the Department of Prints and Drawings in the British Museum*. 3 vols. London: Trustees [of the British Museum], 1910.

Holtus, Günter, Henning Krauss, and Peter Wunderli, eds. *Testi, cotesti e contesti del franco-italiano: Atti del 1º simposio franco-italiano (Bad Homburg, 13–16 aprile 1987) In memoriam Alberto Limentani* (Texts, analogues, and contexts of Franco-Italian: Acts of the first Franco-Italian symposium . . .). Tübingen: Niemeyer, 1989.

Horrent, Jacques. "Les versions françaises et étrangères des *Enfances de Charlemagne*" (French and foreign versions of the Boyhood of Charlemagne). Académie Royale de Belgique, *Mémoires de la Classe des Lettres,* Collection in 8°, 2d ser., 64.1. Brussels: Palais des Académies, 1979.

Inventario Ceruti dei manoscritti della Biblioteca Ambrosiana (Ceruti's inventory of manuscripts at the Ambrosian Library). 5 vols. Trezzano: Etimar, 1973–79.

Karttunen, Klaus. *India in Early Greek Literature.* Studia Orientalia 65. Helsinki: Finnish Oriental Society, 1989.

Kay, Sarah. "The Nature of Rhetoric in the *Chanson de Geste.*" *Zeitschrift für romanische Philologie* 94 (1978): 305–20.

Keller, Hans-Erich, ed. *Romance Epic: Essays on a Medieval Literary Genre.* Studies in Medieval Culture 24. Kalamazoo, Mich.: Medieval Institute, 1987.

Kinter, William L., and Joseph R. Keller. *The Sibyl: Prophetess of Antiquity and Medieval Fay.* Philadelphia: Dorance, 1967.

Knudson, Charles A. "Le thème de la princesse sarrasine dans *La Prise d'Orange*" (The theme of the Saracen princess in The Capture of Orange). *Romance Philology* 22 (1968–69): 449–62.

Krauss, Henning. *Epica feudale e pubblico borghese: Per la storia poetica di Carlomagno in Italia* (Feudal epic and bourgeois audience: Toward a poetical history of Charlemagne in Italy). Ed. Andrea Fassò. Trans. F. Brugnolo, A. Fassò, and M. Mancini. Padua: Liviana, 1980.

Langlois, Ernest. *Table des noms propres de toute nature compris dans les chansons de geste imprimées* (Table of all proper nouns included in printed epic poems). Paris: Bouillon, 1904.

Latini, Bruno. *Il Tesoro . . . volgarizzato da Bono Giamboni* (The Treasure . . . retold in the vernacular by Bono Giamboni). Ed. P. Chabaille. 4 vols. Collezione di opere inedite o rare dei primi tre secoli della lingua. R. Commissione pe' Testi di lingua. Bologna: Romagnoli, 1877–83.

Lefay-Toury, Marie Noëlle. *La tentation du suicide dans le roman français du XIIe siècle* (The temptation of suicide in twelfth-century French romance). Collection: Essais sur le Moyen-Age 4. Paris: Champion, 1979.

Levi, E[zio]. "I Cantari leggendari del popolo italiano nei secoli XIV e XV" (Legendary epic poems of the Italian people in the fourteenth and fifteenth centuries). *GSLI,* suppl. 16 (1914): 1–171.

Ludovisi, Ididio. *L'Ugo d'Alvernia secondo il codice franco-veneto della Biblioteca vescovile di Padova* (Ugo of Alvernia according to the Franco-Venetian codex at the Bishop's Library, Padua). Aquila: Mele, 1895.

Luzio, Alessandro, and Rodolfo Renier. "Delle relazioni di Isabella d'Este Gonzaga con Ludovico e Beatrice Sforza" (Some correspondence . . .). *Archivio storico lombardo,* 2d ser., 7, Year 17 (1890): 74–119.

MacArthur, Douglas. "Les versions du *Libro di Fioravante*" (The versions of the Book of Fioravante). *Filologia romanza* 7.1–2 (1960): 121–28.

Maracchi Biagiarelli, Berta. "L'*Armadiaccio* di Padre Stradino" (The Book Cabinet of Father Stradino). *La Bibliofilìa* 84 (1982): 51–57.

Marchetti, Italiano. "Sulla 'Gionta' al Ciriffo Calvaneo" (On the 'addition' to Ciriffo Calvaneo). *Rinascimento* 5.1 (1954): 81–103.

Marinelli, Peter V. *Ariosto and Boiardo: The Origins of* Orlando Furioso. Columbia: University of Missouri Press, 1987.

Martelli, Mario. "Schede sulla cultura di Machiavelli" (Notes on Machiavelli's culture). *Interpres* 6 (1985–86): 283–330.

Martelli, Mario, and Rossella Bessi. *Guida alla filologia italiana* (Guide to Italian philology). Florence: Sansoni, 1984.

Marti, Mario, et al. *Problemi e testimonianze della civiltà letteraria italiana* (Problems and testimony of Italian literary civilization). 6 vols. Florence: Le Monnier, 1982.

Mattioli, Laura. *Luigi Pulci e il* Ciriffo Calvaneo (Luigi Pulci and the Ciriffo Calvaneo). Padua: Sanavio, 1900.

Maugis d'Aigremont. Ed. Ferdinand Castets. *Revue des langues romanes* 36 (1892): 5–416.

Melli, Elio. "A proposito dei *Cantari di Rinaldo da Monte Albano*" (Regarding the Rinaldo of Mount Alban in octaves). *Studi e problemi di critica testuale* 8 (1974): 73–81.

——. "I *Cantari di Rinaldo* e l'epica francese" (The verse Rinaldo and French epic). *Atti dell'Accademia delle Scienze dell'Istituto di Bologna,* Classe di Scienze morali, Year 64, *Rendiconti* 58 (1969–70): 102–56.

——. "Estratti di un perduto codice del *Rinaldo da Montalbano* in un manoscritto autografo di Lionardo Salviati" (Extracts of a lost codex of Rinaldo . . .). *Convivium,* n.s., 29 (1961): 326–34.

——. "Intorno al testo dei *Cantari di Rinaldo:* Ridiscussioni di un editore" (On the text of the verse Rinaldo: More thoughts by an editor). *Studi e problemi di critica testuale* 11 (1975): 13–25.

——. "Nella selva dei *Rinaldi:* Poemetti su Rinaldo da Mont'Albano in antiche edizioni a stampa" (In the dark wood of the Rinaldo textual tradition: Short epic poems on Rinaldo of Mount Alban in early print editions). *Studi e problemi di critica testuale* 16 (1978): 193–215.

——. "Rapporti fra le versioni rimate del *Renaut de Montauban* e il *Rinaldo* in versi del manoscritto Palatino 364" (Relationships between the verse versions of Renaut de Montauban and the verse Rinaldo of Palatine MS 364). *GSLI* 141 (1964): 369–89.

——. "Riecheggiamenti danteschi in un cantare toscano del secolo XIV." *Filologia romanza* 5 (1958): 82–87.

Melzi, Gaetano. *Bibliografia dei romanzi e poemi cavallereschi italiani* (Bibliography of Italian romances and chivalric epic poems). 2d ed. [Rev. ed. Paolo Antonio Tosi.] Milan: Tosi, 1838.

Meredith-Jones, C. "The Conventional Saracen of the Songs of Geste." *Speculum* 17 (1942): 201–25.

Meregazzi, Luisa M. "L'*Ugo d'Alvernia:* Poema franco italiano" (Ugo of Alvernia: A Franco-Italian epic poem). *Studi romanzi* 27 (1937): 5–87.

Michelant, H[enri]. "Titoli dei Capitoli della Storia Reali di Francia" (Chapter headings for the story Royal House of France). *Jahrbuch für romanische und englische Literatur* 11 (1870): 189–209, 298–312; 12 (1871): 60–72, 217–32, 396–406.

Ministero della Pubblica Istruzione. *Indici e cataloghi, IV: I codici palatini della R. Biblioteca Nazionale Centrale di Firenze* (Indexes and catalogs, IV: The Palatine codices of the BNCF). Ed. Luigi Gentile. 2 vols. Rome: I principali librai, 1890.

Modigliani, Ettore. "Una nuova redazione italiana in prosa del *Romans d'Aspremont*" (A new Italian prose reworking of the Romance of Aspremont). *Rassegna critica della Letteratura italiana* 3 (1898): 97–101.

Möhren, Frankwalt. "Huon d'Auvergne/Ugo d'Alvernia: Objet de la lexicographie française ou italienne?" (Huon of Auvergne or Ugo of Alvernia: object for study by French or Italian lexicography). *Medioevo romanzo* 4 (1977): 312–23.

Moisan, André. *Répertoire des noms propres de personnes et de lieux cités dans les chansons de geste françaises et les oeuvres étrangères dérivés* (Repertoire of proper names of characters and places cited in French epic poems and in foreign works derived from them). 2 vols. Publications romanes et françaises 173. Geneva: Droz, 1986.

Momigliano, Attilio. "I Reali di Francia" (The Royal House of France). *Corriere della Sera,* Mar. 31, 1948. Rpt. in *Ultimi studi,* 103–6. Studi critici 2. Florence: Nuova Italia, 1954.

Morosi, Andrea. "Breve storia della *Storia di Rinaldo*" (Brief history of the Story of Rinaldo). *Interpres* 1 (1978): 285–93.

———. "La Leggenda di Rinaldo da Montalbano nel Quattrocento italiano" (The legend of Rinaldo of Mount Alban in fifteenth-century Italy). 2 vols. Tesi di Laurea, Università degli Studi di Firenze, Facoltà di Lettere e Filosofia, 1977–78.

Müntz, Eugene. *Les collections des Médicis au XVe siècle: le musée—la bibliothèque—le mobilier* (Fifteenth-century Medici collections: Museum—library—furnishings). Paris: Librarie de l'art, 1888.

Les Narbonnais*: Chanson de geste publiée pour la première fois* (The Narbonnais: Epic poem published for the first time). Ed. Hermann Suchier. 2 vols. Société des Anciens Textes français. Paris: Didot, 1898.

The National Union Catalog 1973–77. 135 vols. Totowa, N.J.: Rowman, 1978.

Neri, Ferdinando. "Le Tradizioni italiane della Sibilla" (The Italian traditions of the Sibyl). *Studi medievali* 4 (1912–13): 213–30.

———. "La Voce 'lai' nei testi italiani" (The word "lai" in Italian texts). *Studi danteschi* 21 (1937): 182–83.

Il Novellino: Libro di novelle e di bel parlar gentile (The Novellino: Book of short stories and of fine, courteous speech). Intro. by Giorgio Manganelli. Biblioteca Universale Rizzoli. 3d ed. Milan: Rizzoli, 1989.

Nyrop, Kristoffer. *Storia dell'epopea francese nel Medio Evo* (History of French epic in the Middle Ages). Trans. Egidio Gorra. Turin: Loescher, 1888.

"*Orlando:* Die Vorlage zu Pulci's *Morgante*" (Orlando: The model for Pulci's

Morgante). Ed. Johannes Hübscher. *Ausgaben und Abhandlungen aus dem Gebiete der Romanischen Philologie* 60. Marburg: Elwert'sche, 1886.

Orvieto, Paolo. *Pulci medievale* (Medieval Pulci). Rome: Salerno, 1978.

Osella, Giacomo. "Andrea da Barberino nel giudizio degli stranieri" (Andrea da Barberino in the critical judgment of foreigners). *Convivium* 14 (1942): 120–25.

———. "Il Guerrin Meschino." *Pallante* 10, fasc. 9–10 (1932): 11–173.

———. "L'Inferno del *Guerrino*" (Hell in Guerrino). In *Congresso (VII) Nazionale delle Tradizioni Popolari. Chieti, 1957. Atti,* 466–72. Florence: Olschki, 1959.

———. "Su Andrea da Barberino" (On Andrea da Barberino). *Convivium* 12 (1940): 363–80.

Palumbo, Lorenzo. "Andrea da Barberino." *Gymnasium* (Turin), Apr. 15, 1953, 343–44.

Paolucci, Luigi. *La Sibilla appenninica* (The Apennine Sibyl). Biblioteca di *Lares* 25. Florence: Olschki, 1967.

Paris, Gaston. "Anseïs de Carthage et la *Seconda Spagna*" (Anseïs of Carthage and the Second War in Spain). *Rassegna bibliografica della letteratura italiana* 1 (1893): 174–83. Rpt. in *Mélanges de Littérature Française du Moyen Age,* ed. Mario Roques, 169–82. Paris: Champion, 1912.

———. *Histoire poétique de Charlemagne* (Poetical history of Charlemagne). 1865. Rev. ed. by G. Paris and Paul Meyer. Paris: Bouillon, 1905.

———. Review of *Ricerche intorno ai* Reali di Francia (Research on The Royal House of France), by Pio Rajna. *Romania* 2 (1873): 351–66.

Paris e Vienna: *Romanzo cavalleresco* (Paris and Vienna: Chivalric romance). Ed. Anna Maria Babbi. Medioevo veneto. Venice: Marsilio, 1991.

Pasqualino, Antonio. "Dama Rovenza dal Martello e la leggenda di Rinaldo da Montalbano" (Dame Rovenza of the hammer and the legend of Rinaldo of Mount Alban). In *I Cantari: Struttura e tradizione. Atti del Convegno Internazionale di Montreal: 19–20 marzo 1981,* ed. M. Picone and M. Bendinelli Predelli, 177–98. Biblioteca dell'*Archivum Romanicum,* ser. 1: Storia-Letteratura-Paleografia 186. Florence: Olschki, 1984.

———. "Narrative Structures of the *Reali di Francia.*" In *Strutture e generi delle letterature etniche: Atti del simposio internazionale, Palermo, 5–10 aprile 1970,* 71–100. Palermo: Flaccovio, 1978.

———. "Per un'analisi morfologica della letteratura cavalleresca: *I Reali di Francia*" (Toward a morphological analysis of chivalric literature: The Royal House of France). *Uomo e cultura* 3.5–6 (1970): 76–194.

———. *Le Vie del cavaliere dall'epica medievale alla cultura popolare* (The knight's passage from medieval epic to popular culture). Studi Bompiani. Milan: Bompiani, 1992.

Patch, Howard Rollin. *The Other World, According to Descriptions in Medieval Literature.* Smith College Studies in Modern Languages, n.s. 1. Cambridge, Mass.: Harvard University Press, 1950.

Peters, Rudolf. *Über die Geographie im* Guerrino Meschino *des Andrea de' Magnabotti* (On the geography in . . .). Halle (Saale): n.p., 1906.

Petrarca, Francesco. Rime *e* Trionfi (Verses and Triumphs). Ed. Mario Apollonio and Lina Ferro. Brescia: La Scuola, 1972.

Pinto, Olga. *Storia della Biblioteca corsiniana e della Biblioteca dell'Accademia dei Lincei* (History of the Corsinian Library and of the Library of Lincei Academy). Collana di monografie delle biblioteche d'Italia 3. Florence: Olschki, 1956.

Pischedda, Giovanni. *Il Personaggio romanzesco nell'Italia medioevale* (The romance character in medieval Italy). Miscellanea selecta 4. Aquila: Japadre, 1968.

Pitrè, Giuseppe. "Le Tradizioni cavalleresche popolari in Sicilia" (Popular chivalric traditions in Sicily). *Romania* 13 (1884): 315–98.

Pompeati, Arturo. *Storia della letteratura italiana* (History of Italian literature). 4 vols. Turin: UTET, 1953–62.

Ponte, Giovanni. Review of *I reali di Francia* (The Royal House of France), intro. by Aurelio Roncaglia. *Rassegna della letteratura italiana,* 7th ser., 1, Year 74 (1970): 462–63.

Ptolemaeus, Clavdius. Cosmographia: *Tavole della geografia di Tolomeo* (Cosmography: Ptolemy's geographical tables). Intro. by Lelio Pagani. Bergamo: Stella Polare/ Lucchetti, 1990.

Pulci, Luigi. *Morgante.* Ed. Franca Ageno. La Letteratura italiana, Storia e testi 17. Milan: Ricciardi, 1955.

Quaglio, Antonio Enzo. "Parole del Boccaccio" (Boccaccio's words). *Lingua nostra* 21 (1960): 41–47.

Rajna, Pio. *Le Fonti dell'*Orlando Furioso: *Ricerche e studi* (The sources of Orlando Furioso: Research and studies). 2d ed., rev. Florence: Sansoni, 1900.

———. "L'onomastica italiana e l'epopea carolingia" (Italian naming and Carolingian epic). *Romania* 18 (1889): 1–69.

———. "Una Riduzione quattrocentesca in ottava rima del primo libro dei *Reali di Francia*" (A fifteenth-century abbreviated version in octaves of The Royal House of France, Book I). In *Bausteine zur romanischen Philologie: Festgabe für Adolfo Mussafia,* 227–54. Halle (Saale): Niemeyer, 1905.

———. "I 'Rinaldi' o cantastorie di Napoli" (The "Rinaldi" or Neapolitan singers of tales). *Nuova Antologia,* 2d ser. 12 (of the collection 42) (1878): 557–79.

———. "Rinaldo da Montalbano" (Rinaldo of Mount Alban). *Il Propugnatore* 3, pt. 1 (1870): 213–41; pt. 4 (1870): 58–127.

———. "La Rotta di Roncisvalle nella letteratura cavalleresca italiana" (The Rout at Roncisvalle in Italian chivalric literature). *Il Propugnatore* 4, pt. 1 (1871): 52–78.

———. "Sibilla" (Sibyl). In his *Origini dell'epopea francese,* 179–98. Florence: Sansoni, 1884.

———. "Uggeri il danese nella letteratura romanzesca degl' Italiani" (Ogier the Dane in Italian romance literature). *Romania* 2 (1873): 153–69; 3 (1874): 31–77.

Ranke, Leopold von. "Zur Geschichte der italienischen Poesie" (History of Italian poetry). *Abhandlungen der Königl,* Akademie der Wissenschaften zu Berlin, 1835 (published 1837). Rpt. in *Abhandlungen und Versuche,* 157–75. New ed. Leipzig: Dunder, 1888.

Razzoli, Giulio. *Per le fonti dell'*Orlando Innamorato *di Matteo Maria Boiardo, Parte*

I: I primi trenta canti del poema (For the sources of Roland in Love by Matteo Maria Boiardo, Part I: The first thirty cantos of the poem). Milan: Albrighi, 1901.

Reinhard, Adolf Franz. *Die Quellen der* Nerbonesi (The sources of Nerbonesi). Altenburg: Bonde, 1900.

Renier, Rodolfo. "Guerin Meschino." *Fanfulla della Domenica* (Rome), July 9, 1912, 1–2.

Révah, I. S. "L'*Auto* de la Sibylle Cassandre de Gil Vicente" (The one-act religious play The Sibyl Cassandra by Gil Vicente). *Hispanic Review* 27 (1959): 167–93.

Review of *Die Quellen der* Narbonesi [*sic*] (The sources of Narbonesi), by Adolf Franz Reinhard. *GSLI* 37 (1901): 442.

Romanzi dei Reali di Francia (The romances of the Royal House of France). Ed. Adelaide Mattaini. Milan: Rizzoli, 1957.

Romanzo cavalleresco inedito (British Library Add. MS 10808) (Unedited chivalric romance . . .). Ed. Aurelia Forni Marmocchi. Biblioteca di Filologia Romanza della Facoltà di Lettere e Filosofia dell'Università di Bologna 6. Bologna: Pàtron, 1989.

Roncaglia, Silvia. "*I Reali de Francia* di Andrea da Barberino tra romanzo e fiaba" (The Royal House of France . . . between romance and folk tale). Tesi di Laurea. Università degli Studi di Bologna, Facoltà di Magistero, 1993–94.

Rossi, Vittorio. *Storia della letteratura italiana: Il Quattrocento* (History of Italian literature: The fifteenth century). Milan: Vallardi, 1938.

Ruggieri, Ruggero M. Review of *Der* Anseïs de Cartage *und die* Seconda Spagna (Anseïs of Carthage and the Second War in Spain), by Helmut Brettschneider. *Archivum Romanicum* 22 (1938): 137–39.

———. Review of *L'Aspramonte*, ed. Boni. *Cultura neolatina* 13.1 (1953): 241–42.

Russo, Luigi. *Compendio storico della letteratura italiana* (Historical compendium of Italian literature). 2d ed. Messina: D'Anna, 1967.

———. "La Letteratura cavalleresca italiana dal *Tristano* ai *Reali di Francia*" (Italian chivalric literature from Tristan to The Royal House of France). *Belfagor* 6 (1951): 40–59. Rpt. in *Storia della letteratura italiana: La civiltà europea*, 1: 469–90. Florence: Sansoni, 1956.

Rutebeuf. *Oeuvres complètes* (Complete works). Ed. Edmond Faral and Julia Bastin. 2 vols. Fondation Singer-Polignac. Paris: Picard, 1977.

Sapori, Armando. *The Italian Merchant in the Middle Ages*. Trans. Patricia Ann Kennen. New York: Norton, 1970.

Schmidt, Barbara. "Ein Vergleich zwischen der Chanson de Geste von *Aiol et Mirabel* und der italienischen Prosabearbeitung: *La Storia di Ajolfo del Barbicone*" (A comparison between the epic Aiol and Mirabel and the Italian prose reworking: The Story of Aiolfo del Barbicone). Diss., Humboldt-Universität, Berlin, 1949.

La Seconda Spagna e l'Acquisto di Ponente ai tempi di Carlomagno: Testi di lingua inediti del sec. XIII tratti da un MS. dell'Ambrosiana (The Second War in Spain and the Conquest of the West at the time of Charlemagne: Unedited thirteenth-century vernacular texts from an Ambrosian manuscript). Ed. Antonio Ceruti. Scelta di curiosità letterarie inedite o rare dal secolo XII al XIX 118. Commissione per i Testi di lingua. Bologna: Romagnoli, 1871; Bologna: Forni, 1968.

Setton, Kenneth M., ed. *A History of the Crusades.* 6 vols. Madison: University of Wisconsin Press, 1969.

La Spagna: *Poema cavalleresco del secolo XIV* (Spain: Fourteenth-century chivalric epic). Ed. Michele Catalano. 3 vols. Collezione di opere inedite o rare 111–13. Bologna: Commissione per i Testi di lingua, 1939–40.

Spiegel, Gabrielle M. "Genealogy: Form and Function in Medieval Historical Narrative." *History and Theory* 1 (1983): 43–53.

Spongano, Raffaele. "Scheda per *I Reali di Francia*" (Notes for The Royal House of France). *Studi e problemi di critica testuale* 34 (1987): 325–26.

Statius. *Thebaid I–IV. Silvae.* Trans. J. H. Mozley. Loeb Classical Library, 1955.

———. *Thebaid V–XII. Achilleid.* Trans. J. H. Mozley. Loeb Classical Library, 1957.

Storia di Rinaldino da Montalbano: *Romanzo cavalleresco in prosa* (Story of Rinaldino of Mount Alban: Chivalric romance in prose). Ed. Carlo Minutoli. Collezione di opere inedite o rare dei primi tre secoli della lingua. Bologna: Romagnoli, 1865.

Stussi, Alfredo. *Nuovo avviamento agli studi di filologia italiana* (New introduction to the study of Italian philology). Strumenti: Linguistica e critica letteraria. Bologna: Mulino, 1988.

Tanturli, Giuliano. "I Benci copisti: Vicende della cultura fiorentina volgare fra Antonio Pucci e il Ficino" (The Benci copyists. Vicissitudes of Florentine vernacular culture between Antonio Pucci and Ficino). *Studi di filologia italiana* 36 (1978): 197–313.

La Tavola ritonda o l'Istoria di Tristano: *Testo di lingua* (The Round Table or The Story of Tristan: Vernacular text). Ed. Filippo Luigi Polidori. Collezione di opere inedite o rare dei primi tre secoli della lingua. 2 vols. Bologna: Romagnoli, 1864–66.

Thomas, Henry. *Short-Title Catalogues of Spanish, Spanish-American and Portuguese Books printed before 1601 in the British Museum.* London: Trustees of the British Museum, 1966. Rpt. of vols. for 1921, 1940, 1944.

Tomalin, Margaret. *The Fortunes of the Warrior Heroine in Italian Literature: An Index of Emancipation.* Ravenna: Longo, 1982.

The Travels of Sir John Mandeville and *The Voyage of Johannes de Plano Carpini; The Journal of Friar William de Rubruquis; The Journal of Friar Odoric* from Hakluyt's *Navigations, Voyages and Discoveries.* New York: Dover, 1964.

Il Tristano riccardiano (The Riccardian Tristan). Ed. E[rnesto] G[iacomo] Parodi. Collezione di opere inedite o rare dei primi tre secoli della lingua. R. Commissione pe' Testi di lingua. Bologna: Romagnoli, 1896.

Trolli, Domizia. "Il Lessico dei *Ricordi* di Giovanni di Pagolo Morelli" (The lexicon of . . . Morelli's book of remembrances). *Studi di grammatica italiana* 5 (1976): 67–175.

———. "La Lingua di Giovanni Morelli" (Giovanni Morelli's language). *Studi di grammatica italiana* 2 (1972): 51–153.

Tumiati, Domenico. Guerrin Meschino: *Dramma cavalleresco* (. . . Chivalric drama). 2d ed. 1912; Milan: Treves, 1928.

Tyssens, Madeleine. "Poèmes franco-italiens et *Storie Nerbonesi:* Recherches sur les sources d'Andrea da Barberino" (Franco-Italian epics and the Nerbonesi stories: Research on the sources of Andrea da Barberino). In *Testi,* ed. Holtus, Krauss, and Wunderli, 307–24.

Tyssens, Madeleine, and Claude Thiry, eds. *Charlemagne et l'Épopée romane: Actes du VIIe Congrès International de la Société Rencesvals. Liège, 28 août–4 septembre 1976* (Charlemagne and the romance epic: Acts of the seventh International Congress of the Rencesvals Society . . .). 2 vols. Paris: Belles lettres, 1978.

Varanini, Giorgio. "Andrea da Barberino." In *Dizionario critico della letteratura italiana,* 1: 65–67. 2d ed.

Vesconte, Pietro. *Carte nautiche* (Nautical charts). Intro. by Lelio Pagani. Bergamo: Grafica Gutenberg, 1977.

Villani, Giovanni. *Cronica: Con le continuazioni di Matteo e Filippo* (Chronicle: With continuations by Matthew and Phillip). Ed. Giovanni Aquilecchia. Nuova Universale Einaudi 159. Torino: Einaudi, 1979.

Villani, Matteo. *Cronica* (Chronicle). Ed. Giuseppe Porta. 2 vols. Biblioteca di Scrittori italiani. [Parma:] Fondazione P. Bembo, 1995.

Vitale, Maurizio. Review of l'*Aspramonte,* ed. Boni. *Nuova Antologia* 456 (1952): 457–59.

Vitale-Brovarone, Alessandro. "De la Chanson de *Huon d'Auvergne* à la *Storia di Ugone d'Avernia* d'Andrea da Barberino: Techniques et méthodes de la traduction et de l'élaboration" (From the Song of Huon of Auvergne to the Story of Ugone of Avernia by Andrea da Barberino: Techniques and methods of translation and amplification). In *Charlemagne,* ed. Tyssens and Thiry, 2: 393–403.

Vitullo, Juliann. "Contained Conflict: Wild Men and Warrior Women in the Early Italian Epic." *Annali d'italianistica* 12 (1994): 39–59.

———. "The Medieval Epic Romance and a New Urban Order." Ph.d. diss., Indiana University, 1991.

———. "Orality, Literacy, and the Romance Epic in Italy: The Case of Andrea da Barberino's *Ugo d'Alvernia.*" *Italianist* 13 (1993): 29–46.

Vocabolario degli Accademici della Crusca (Dictionary of the Crusca Academy). 5th ed. 11 vols. Florence: Galileiana, 1863–1923.

Weeks, Raymond. "Études sur *Aliscans*" (Studies on Aliscans). *Romania* 30 (1901): 184–97; 34 (1905): 237–77; 38 (1909): 1–43.

———. "Origin of the *Covenant Vivien.*" *University of Missouri Studies* 1.2 (1902): 81–144.

———. "The Primitive *Prise d'Orange.*" *PMLA* 16.3 (n.s. 9.3) (1901): 361–74.

Werner, Adolfo. "L'*Aspramonte* di Andrea de' Mangabotti e i suoi rapporti co' *Reali di Francia*" (Andrea de' Mangabotti's Aspramont and its relationship to The Royal House of France). *GSLI* 32 (1898): 132–38.

Wilkins, Ernest Hatch. *A History of Italian Literature.* Cambridge, Mass.: Harvard University Press, 1954.

Wormald, Francis, and Phyllis M. Giles. *A Descriptive Catalogue of the Additional*

Illuminated MSS in the Fitzwilliam Museum Acquired between 1895 and 1979 (Excluding the McClean Collection). 2 vols. Cambridge: Cambridge University Press, 1982.

Zagaria, R[iccardo]. Review of "Il Guerrino Meschino," by Osella. *Aevum* 6 (1932): 685–86.

Zonghi, Aurelio, Augusto Zonghi, and A. F. Gasparinetti. *Zonghi's Watermarks.* Ed. E. J. Labarre. Monumenta chartae papyraceae historiam illustrantia, or Collection of Works and Documents Illustrating the History of Paper 3. Hilversum, Holland: Paper Publications Society, 1953.

Index of Lexemes

(a)(b)bavagliare, 90, 148n.71
a (di) buon'ora, 56, 57, 84, 140–41n.38
adretegiare. See indrieteggiare
a(f)fibbiarsi, 74; (part.) 138n.34. See also fibbia
affossare, 60, 84, 142n.60
Affumato, 35
albergare, 56
(al)lattare, 56, 57, 84, 141n.39
alloggiamento, 56–57, 84, 140n.34
alloggiar(si), 40, 56, 84, 138n.26, 140n.33
alloppiare, 90, 148n.72
alloppio, 90
andare a vicitare, 58, 86, 141n.47
antiguardo, 57
asprissimo, 56, 84, 140n.29
attender(si) a medicare, 63, 64, 85, 144n.84
atti d'amore, 86

bacchetta, 110
balestrata, 56, 57, 86, 141nn.41, 43
bandire la croce adosso, 109–10, 149n.21
bassa condizione, 90
bastia, 87, 146nn.49, 50
battaglia giudicata, 87, 147n.54
baviera dell'elmo, 87
bella criatura, 108–9, 149n.18

bella diceria, 40, 58, 85, 138n.30
ben(e) fare, 58, 86, 141n.44
biada, 112
bigordare, 60, 84
bigordo, 60
biordar(si), 84
bontà di, 61, 84, 142n.63
bottiniere, 87
bussine, 61, 62, 143n.73

camaglio dell'elmo, 61, 85, 109, 142n.65
capitano generale, 40, 85, 138n.32
capitolare, 88, 147nn.58, 59
capitolo, 40, 88, 108, 138n.28
carissimo, 25, 30, 56, 57, 84, 141n.40
carriaggio, 61, 62, 85, 143n.74
certificare, 23, 88
cioè: glosses with, 27–28, 55, 88–89, 136n.39
col(l)azione (col(l)ezione), 40, 56, 57, 84, 138n.27
collottola, 87, 146n.48
correggia al collo, 109, 149n.20
cosa, come la c-stava, 41, 138nn.38, 39, 146n.45

deretano (diretano, dretano), 56, 57, 58, 84, 141nn.41, 43
detto, come di sopra è, 58–59, 71, 86, 141–42n.50, 146n.45

dibatter(si), 56, 84, 140n.30
disfare infino (insino) a' fondamenti, 41, 85, 138n.36
disutile (disutole), 41, 62, 138n.35

(e)dificio ('difizio), 81–82, 146n.40

fanti a piè, 61, 62, 84
fare (dare) la credenza, 88
fare piazza, 58, 86, 141n.48
fatto, come il f-sta(va), 58, 86, 141n. 46, 146n.45
faville, 82, 146n.41
fibbia, 41, 74. See also *affibbiarsi*
figliare, 149n.27, 113
forcella (forciella, forcilla) del petto, 61, 85, 142n.66

garbino (gherbino), 91
generale capitano. See *capitano generale*
gente a piè, 84. See also *fanti a piè*
ghiaia, 60, 142n.57
giogo, 79
gioielli (dell'elmo), 40, 56, 57, 84, 85, 138n.33, 140n.37
giungere forza a forza (ira a ira), 55, 86, 140n.27
giusta mia possa, 58, 86, 141n.45, 146n.44
gola. See *gorga*
gorga, appendu(ti) per la: and var., 60–61, 86, 142n.62
gorgerino (gorzerino, gorgera), 61, 142–43n.68
grossa, 109, 149n.19
guadagnato, -a, 38
guanto sanguinoso, 61, 86, 142n.67

imbavagliare. See *abbavagliare*
indietreggiare (indrieteggiare), 63–64, 85, 143n.81
infingardo, 90

interpido (interpito), 88, 147n.63
intrinsico, 90, 148n.73
intronare, 61, 63, 85, 143n.78
investigato dal dimonio, 89
isso fatto, 108, 149n.16

lai(s), 89
lamentarsi della fortuna, 59, 86, 142n.52
lancia arrestata, l-in (a) resta, 63, 85, 143n.75
lega francesca (galesca), 89
liccia, 87, 146nn.49, 50
licenziare, 56, 57, 141nn.41, 43
limosinieri, 108
loppio. See *alloppio*

mam(m)aluc(co), 60, 84, 142n.58
maninconoso, 56, 84, 140n.31
mescolarsi, 63, 85, 143n.79
metter(si) in punto, 40, 63, 85, 138n.31, 143n.77
mortale nimico, 58, 86, 141n.49
moschea, 78, 145n.36; cf. 9, 145n.35

neo, 89; (rel). *niello*, 147n.65
nettare, 37
nimicare, 87, 147nn.55, 56
nimico mortale. See *mortale nimico*
(e) nota che, 59, 86, 142n.54, 146n.45
notificare, 40, 56, 57, 85, 138n.29

palle di metallo, 87
panziera, 87, 146n.47
paterino, 90
petrone, 56, 84, 140n.32
pondo della battaglia, 62, 86, 143n.70
ponte levatoio, 87
porcinaglia, 108
prospero vento, 61, 86, 142n.64

rabbonacciare, 91
rast(r)ello, 87, 146–47nn.52, 53

religiosi, 53, 86

ricapitolare. See capitolare

(ri)fare testa. See testa

riediguardo (retriguardo): and var., 56, 57, 140n.35

sagri libri, 108

salvo condotto, 88, 147n.61

schianciare, 63, 84; (var.) schiancire, 64; a schiencio, 84

segnarsi il viso, 22, 89–90, 148n.69

segn(i)o della croce, 90, 148n.70

sì o no, 41–42, 80

sinestrare, 61, 63, 64, 85, 144n.83

sotto brevità, 59, 142n.55

spallaccio (spallacciuolo), 61–62, 85

steccato, 62, 85, 143n.71

stretti e serrati, 62, 143n.72

tagliare a pezzi, 41, 55, 86, 138n.37, 140n.28

testa, (ri)fare, 63, 85, 143n.80

toccarsi il dente, 88, 147n.57

togliarsi dinanzi, 75

torna la storia, 28, 42, 55, 86, 136n.40, 140n.25

uditore, 6, 59

vantaggio, 55, 140n.26

velli, 113

veritiere, 89, 147n.66

verrettone, 63, 85, 109, 143n.76

vettuvaglia, 149n.28

zibibbo, 78, 145n.37

Index of Manuscripts

Bergamo, Biblioteca Civica "Angelo Mai"
  MA 297 (formerly Alfa 3.16), 126
Florence, Accademia della Crusca
  64, 126
Florence, Archivio di Stato
  Catasto 19, 5, (ch. 1) 133n.2
    339, 5, (ch. 1) 133n.3
  **Diplomatico Normale 1376 10
    nov. S. Maria Nuova,** (ch. 1)
    133n.5
  Guardaroba Mediceo 28, 144n.3,
    145n.22
Florence, Biblioteca Medicea-
  Laurenziana
  Ashb. 530, 126
    537, 126
  Gaddi rel. 40, 9
    50, 5, 111, 127, (ch. 1) 133n.14
  Med. Pal. 78, 1
    82, 11, 93
    CI, 3, 11, 34–35
    CI, 4, 8, 66, 68, 69, 78, 81, 84–86,
      89, 127, 144n.17
  Pluteus XLII, 37, 33, 66, 67–68, 69,
    127; textual examples from, 70,
    71, 72, 76, 77, 80, 81, 82, 83, 88,
    91, 92
    XLIII, 9, 126
    XLIII, 18, 33, 48, 126, 134nn.18, 30
    XLIV, 30, 11

LXI, 34, 126, 134n.20
LXI, 40, 66, 68, 69, 127, 144n.18;
  textual examples from, 71, 72,
  74, 75, 77, 78, 79–80, 81, 82, 83,
  88, 89, 91
LXII, 27, 126, 134n.20
LXXXIX, inf. 64, 66, 68, 127,
  144n.16
Redi 177, 32, 126, 134n.30
Florence, Biblioteca Moreniana
  Moreniano Frullani 12, 34, 125
Florence, Biblioteca Nazionale Centrale
  II.I.14, 7, 32, 44, 125
  II.I.15, 7, 32, 43, 45, 48, 64, 67, 69,
    125, 126; textual passages from,
    46, 47, 48, 49, 50, 52, 53, 54, 55,
    56, 57, 63, 64. *See also* Andrea,
    Works: Storia del re Ansuigi
  II.I.16, 126
  II.I.47, 11
  II.II.54, 126
  II.II.56, 34, 125
  II.II.58, 54, 126, (ch. 1) 133n.14
  II.II.59, 33, 69, 126, 134n.30
  II.IV.35, 126
  II.IV.679, 7, 126, 134n.30
  II.VII.3, 126, 134nn.18, 30
  Conv. Sopp. C. 1, 720, 6, 111, 127,
    (ch. 1) 133n.14
  Magl. Cl. XXIV, 146bis, 10, 126,
    (ch. 1) 133n.1

Magl. Cl. XXXV, 169, 54
Magl. Strozzi XXI, 135, 20
Nuovi Acquisti 509, 10
Pal. 578, 11, 93, 121
Pal. 583, 34, 125
Pal. 677, 34, 125
Panciat. 34, 126, (ch. 1) 133n.14
Panciat. 35, 126, 134n.18
Panciat. 158, 15. *See also Diario*
Poligrafo Gargani, packets 601–
    602, 137n.10
Florence, Biblioteca Riccardiana
    Ricc. 1812, 126, 134n.20
        1904, 33, 66, 67, 68, 69, 78, 127,
            144n.16, 144–45n.19; textual
            examples from, 73, 86
        1909, 126
        1912, 126, 134n.20
        1921, 32, 126
        2183, 20, 136n.13
        2197, 64, 68
        2226, 20, 79, 111, 127, (ch. 1)
            133n.14
        2244, 134n.20
        2266, 7, 33, 127
        2267, 127
        2308, 7, 34
        2309, 7, 34, 125
        2327, 126
        2410, 7, 34, 125
        2432, 33, 127
        2481, 126, 134n.30
        2933, 126, 134nn.18, 30
London, British Library
    Add. 10808, 1, 21, 35, 39
    Add. 22821, 11
Milan, Biblioteca Ambrosiana
    C 35 Sup., 11, 32, 43
Naples, Biblioteca Nazionale
    XIX–25, 13

XX-91, 13
Oxford, Bodleian Library
    Canon. ital. 27, 7, 9, 10, 15, 17, 18,
        20, 33, 60, 61, 83, 86, 88, 90, 111,
        126; textual examples from, 76, 77,
        78, 79, 82. *See also* Appendix B **129,**
        125
    Douce 121, 67
Paris, Bibliothèque Nationale
    Ital. 98, 33, 111, 127
        491, 7, 33, 111, 127
Parma, Biblioteca Palatina
    Pal. 30, 127
        32, 32, 126, (ch. 1) 133n.14,
            134n.30
        35, 126
Philadelphia, University of Pennsylvania
    Ms. Codex 16, 127
Private collections
    Former **Dyson Perrins 71,** 127
    Former **Phillipps 929,** 10, 125
    Former **Phillipps 6554,** 127
Rome, Biblioteca Angelica
    78, 125
    2263, 7, 34, 125
    2313, 125
Rome, Biblioteca Corsiniana
    Rossi 62, 125
Rome, Biblioteca Nazionale Centrale
    Fondo V. Emanuele 231, 126
        232, 125
Vatican City, Biblioteca Apostolica
    Vaticana
    Barb. lat. 3988, 127
    Barb. lat. 4101, 32, 126, 134n.30
    Chig. G.VI.162, 127
Venice, Biblioteca Marciana
    Ital. cl. 11, XXXVIII, 7, 125, 134n.30

General Index

L'Acerba, 67

Achilleid, 9, 35

Achiron. *See* Chiron

L'Acquisto del Ponente, 11, 32, 50, 91, 121

Aeneas (It. Enea), 24. *See also Fatti d'Enea*

Aeneid, 9, 24, 92

Ageno, Franca, 11, 67

Agolante, 45, 71, 72, 94

Aiol, 7

Aiolfo, 21, 35

Aiolfino, 50

Albani library, 31, 137n.4; lost ms. from, 31–33, 34, 43, 44, 45, 46, 48, 54, 125, 137n.3

Albertazzi, Adolfo, 45, 66

Alda (Fr. *Aude*), 20, 26–27, 72, 81

Alexander Romance, 9, 19

Alexander the Great, 17–18

Almonte, 21, 71, 72, 94

Aluigi. *See* Louis

Amadigi di Gaula (B. Tasso), 13

Amone, 72, 73

Andrea da Barberino, Maestro: attributions to, 3–4, 7, 43, 44–45, 64, 65, 66–67, 86, 92, 93–94, 107–8; autocitation, 70–71, 145n.26; character description of, physical, 77–78, 86, 108–9, 112, 114; — psychological, 22–23, 30; compositional

techniques of, 2, 6, 10, 15, 69, 99–100; enumeration in, 16, 28–29; genealogy in, 20–21, 30, 35–36, 47, 49–52, 65, 72–73; geography in, 2, 9, 16–19, 20, 30, 69, 76–77, 98, 113–14, 117, 118–19, 135n.9; influence on later authors, 2, 4, 10–12; language in, 2, 3, 15, 21, 24–26, 29; lexicon in, 30, 39–40, 85–86 (*see also* Andrea, Works: *Storia del re Ansuigi*; Lexical Index; *Storie di Rinaldo*); life of, 2, 3, 5–6, 8, 10; ordering of works of, 31, 44, 46–47, 49, 54, 59, 62, 67, 71, 75–76, 92; poemetto by, 8, 24, 36; public performance by, 6, 8, 10; rhetorical devices in, 24–26, 27, 30; structure in, 3, 6, 28–29, 31; style in, 2, 3, 14–30, 52–54, 57, 59, 60, 61, 64, 69, 92; verisimilitude in, 14–17, 19, 21, 22, 27, 30, 36, 40, 41, 52, 60, 61, 62, 63, 85, 87, 88, 95, 96, 104, 122; verse in, 8, 24, 70, 103

—sources: biblical, 8, 54; classical, 9, 23, 30, 35–36, 52; chivalric, 2, 8–9, 17, 20–22, 31, 46, 50, 53, 56; Dantesque, 8, 63; French, 2, 8–9, 31, 57, 60, 64, 65, 67, 70, 76, 89, 110 (*see also Anseïs*); historiographic, 2, 9, 14–15, 59, 60, 62, 70, 87, 88; liturgical, 9, 24; nonchivalric, 2, 9

—works: *L'Aspramonte*, 6, 7, 10, 11, 12,

13, 17, 31, 32, 33, 34, 40, 41, 44, 47, 50, 51, 76; *Guerrino il Meschino,* 3, 7, 9, 10, 11, 15, 17–20, 24, 32, 33, 34, 41, 69, 75, 98; cultural importance of, 13; magazines inspired by, 13; print tradition in, 3, 7, 10, 12, 13, 122; theatrical versions of, 13; translations of, 12; transmission of, 7, 13; versification in, 12–13 (*see also Libro di Rambaldo; Storie di Rinaldo*); *Prima Spagna, La,* 4, 6, 31–42, 65, 85, 103; *Reali di Francia, I,* 3, 6, 9, 10, 11, 12, 13, 15, 17, 19, 22, 28, 32, 34, 35, 36, 37, 38, 41, 44, 50, 56, 59, 65, 95, 96, 99; genealogical list in, 51, 65–66, 73; *Storia del re Ansuigi, La,* 4, 6, 31, 32, 36, 43–64, 65, 67; lexicon of, 53, 55–64; extant ms. of, 43, 44–46, 48, 51, 52, 64; and relation to *Aiolfo,* 54; — to *Aspramonte,* 43–45, 54; — to *Nerbonesi,* 43–49, 50, 52, 53, 54; — to *Prima Spagna,* 44, 45–46, 47, 51, 64; — to *Reali,* 44, 53, 54; *Storia di Aiolfo del Barbicone, La,* 7, 10, 11, 17, 41, 60, 73, 91, 96; *Storia di Ugone d'Alvernia, La,* 7, 8, 10, 11, 15, 23–24, 32, 33; *Storie Nerbonesi, Le,* 6, 9, 10, 11, 16, 25, 31–32, 33, 34, 36, 37, 40, 41, 65, 66, 95 (*see also* Andrea, Works: *Storia del re Ansuigi*). *See also Storie di Rinaldo da Montalbano, Le*

animals, 52, 102; centaur, 23–24; dog-man, 12; dragons (serpents), 12, 20; griffon, 113; horse, 76, 113, 114, 116; lions, 20; manticore, 20. *See also* bestiary, similes

Anseïs de Carthage, 43, 44, 45, 46, 47, 49, 52, 72

Ansuigi, 36, 46–47, 49, 50–51

Ariosto, Ludovico, 1, 10, 12, 28, 61, 87, 88, 91

armor and arms, 40, 41, 61–62, 76, 82, 84, 86–87, 106, 109, 114, 116, 146n.46. *See also* Lexical Index: *baviera, bigordo, camaglio, fibbia, gorgerino, lancia, panziera, spallaccio, verrettone*

Arthur (legendary king), 13, 51

Arts of Rhetoric, 24–25, 40

Aspramonte (fourteenth-century prose), 26

Astolfo, 72, 73

Auto de la sibila Casandra, 12

B., citadino fiorentino, 94, 95–97, 100, 101, 102, 103, 122. *See also Libro di Rambaldo*

Baldus (Folengo), 12

battle descriptions, 15, 16, 19, 21–22, 41, 55, 62, 63, 64, 85, 102–3, 119. *See also* armor and arms; narrative motifs: battle formation

Bertolini, Virginio, 93, 94, 97, 100

bestiary, 2, 20. *See also* animals; similes

Boccaccio, Giovanni, influence on Andrea: motivic, 27, 35, 37, 82; linguistic, 57, 58, 60, 61, 64, 88, 89; stylistic, 22, 24. *See also Decameron, Il; Filocolo; Teseida*

Boiardo, Matteo Maria, 1, 10, 11, 65

Boni, Marco, 11, 31, 64, 75, 94

Bosolino, 10, 50

Branca, Vittore, 8

Brettschneider, Helmut, 43, 45

Burchiello, Il, 61

Cabani, Maria, 27, 59

cantare: genre, 2, 10, 11, 15, 24, 64, 69; formulae in, 27, 28, 55, 59, 70, 97; lexicon of, 56, 57, 61, 91; motifs in, 54, 62, 77; performance of, 6, 8; similes in, 55, 91–92. *See also cantastorie; cantatore*

Cantari cavallereschi, 61

Cantari d'Aspramonte, 17, 39, 56, 58, 62, 75, 88

Cantari di Rinaldo: lexicon of, 39, 56, 58, 60, 62, 75, 81, 87, 88, 89, 90, 92

cantastorie, 8, 13, 28, 58, 61, 65

cantatore, 2, 6, 27

Canzoniere, Il. See Petrarch

Carlo magno: literary figure, 13, 22, 25, 26, 28, 32, 34, 38, 43, 45, 46–47, 48–49, 50, 51, 69, 71, 73, 76, 85, 95, 98, 109

Carolingian cycle, 2, 15, 24, 26, 31, 36, 39, 54, 56, 59, 63, 69, 91, 92

Castracane, Castruccio, 12

Castets, Ferdinand, 11

Catalano, Michele, 11, 34, 43, 45

Cervantes, Miguel de, 13

Chanson d'Aspremonte, 17, 72, 76

Chanson de Roland, La, 57

chansons de geste, 1, 2, 6, 8, 14, 20, 22. *See also* Carolingian cycle

Charlemagne, legendary. *See* Carlo magno

Chrétien de Troyes, 8

Chiron, 35–36

Ciarambino, Gerardo, 88

Cimatore, Bartolomeo di Francesco (copyist), 33, 48

Ciriffo Calvaneo, Il, 6, 11, 78

Clarice, 21

Cligès, 8

colophons, 10, 33, 34, 68, 69, 121

Combattimento tra Orlando e Ferraù, 39, 103

Compagni, Dino, 87, 109

Conte de la Charette (prose), 9

copyists, 6, 10, 53. *See also* Cimatore, Bartolomeo; Giordani, Giordano

Corónica del noble cavallero Guarino Mezquino, La, 135n.54

Cosmographia (Ptolemy), 9, 79, 97

courtly elements, 26–27, 29, 30, 108

Cristoforo Fiorentino ("L'Altissimo"), 11

Croce, Benedetto, 45

Cronaca Parigina, La ("Franconestorum"), 9, 15

Cronica (G. and M. Villani), 9, 15, 87

Ctesias, 76

Cuchermoys, J. de. *See* Rochemeure, Jean de

Danese, Il, 67

Dante, 1, 2, 8; commentaries on, 89; false attributions to, 34; lexicon of, 56, 57, 58, 61, 64, 88, 90, 92. *See also Divina Commedia, La*

D'Aragona, Tullia, 12–13

dating: of compositions, 67–69; of manuscripts, 32–33, 43, 68–69

Decameron, Il, lexicon of, 40, 41, 56, 57, 58, 60, 61, 87, 89, 90

Del Prete, Leone, 7

Diario fiorentino (anon., BNCF, Panciat. 158), 15, 40, 41, 60, 61, 62, 63, 88

Dionisotti, Carlo, 1, 67

Dittamondo, Il, 67

Divina Commedia, La, 35, 40, 56, 57, 89, 90, 133n.3

Dodonello di Mombello, 66, 73

Doon de Maience, 2

dwarfs, 73

Earthly Paradise, 12

L'Entrée d'Espagne, 6, 34, 50–51, 72

Eripes di Brettagna: father of Ansuigi, 36, 51–52

Estense court at Ferrara, 2, 12, 65

Fatti d'Enea, I, 9

Fatti de Spagna, Li, 34

Fatti di Cesare, I, 9, 61

Fazio degli Uberti, 60

Filocolo, 9, 60
Fioravante, 21, 22, 34, 39, 52, 89; lexicon
    of, 28, 38, 56, 60, 90, 92
Fiore, Il, 64, 90
Fiore di virtù, Il, 60
Firenzuola, Agnolo, 90
Flora, Francesco, 60
Folco di Candia, 65
Folieri: doctor of Amerigo of Nerbona,
    70
folklore: Italian, 3, 13, 65
Forni Marmocchi, Aurelia, 38, 67
Fortunato, Il, 11
Franceschetti, Antonio, 11
Francesco da Barberino, 60
Franco-Italian literature, 2, 8, 21, 50, 67,
    70, 73
Freud, Sigmund, 23

Galiziella, 100
Gano, 34–35, 46, 72, 73, 74
Gautier, Léon, 44
Gentile, Luigi, 93
Gherardo da Vienna, 26
Ghirardo da Fratta, 71, 72–73, 90
Giambullari, Bernardo, 6
giants, 52, 102
Giordani, Giordano di Michele (copy-
    ist), 33, 69
Giovanni delle Bande Nere, 68
Giovanni Fiorentino, Ser, 90
Girone il Cortese, 7
Gorni, Guglielmo, 93
Grandes chroniques de France, Les, 70
Grendler, Paul, 14
Gualtieri, 22–23
Guarino Mezquino. See Andrea, Works:
    Guerrino, translations
Guerin mesquin. See Andrea, Works:
    Guerrino, translations
Guido da Pisa, 9
Guido di Bagotte, 17

Guido di Borgogna, 49
Guidone Selvaggio, 66, 73, 145n.29
Guidone, son of Ansuigi, 49–50,
    139n.12
heresy. *See* Lexical Index: *paterino*
Hernández Alemán, Alonso, 12
Heroides, 9, 52
Historiae Philippicae (Justinus), 9
historiography, Renaissance, 14
Homer, 102
Huon d'Auvergne, 2. *See also* Andrea,
    Works: *Storia di Ugone d'Alvernia, La*

Incoronazione del re Aloysi, La, 11
Inferno. See Divina Commedia, La
interlace formulae, 137n.41. *See also*
    Lexical Index: *torna la storia; cantare,*
    formulae in
Ives di Brach, 49
Iorans. *See* Joans
Iseres: son of Mazzarigi, 72; unnamed
    daughter of, 45, 50
Isidore, Saint, 20
Isola, I. G., 7, 47, 50, 67
Isoré, Ysoré. *See* Iseres
Italia liberata da' Goti (G. Trissino), 12

Jacopo di Tieri: father of Andrea, 5
Joans: son of Ansuigi, 49, 50

Lai de Lanval, 9
Latini, Brunetto, 1, 20
lectiones difficiliores, 110, 111, 112, 120,
    122
lectiones singulares, 115
Libro del Meschino di Durazzo, Il, 7, 34.
    See Andrea, Works: *Guerrino*
Libro di novelle e di bel parlar gentile, Il
    (Novellino), 9
Libro di Rambaldo da Risa, Il, 4, 7, 11,
    93–122; author of, 94, 122 (*see also*
    B., Citadino fiorentino); dating of, 94,

111, 120–22; ecdotic analysis in, 111–21; geography in, 95–99, 113–14, 117, 118–19; lexicon of, 91, 108–11; manuscript of, 93, 121; proper names in, 94–95; and relation to *Aspramonte*, 93, 94, 96, 103, 108, 122; — to *Guerrino*, 7, 11, 93, 94, 96, 97, 98, 99, 100, 101, 103, 105–8, 111, 122; — to *Ugone*, 93, 94, 96, 99, 100, 101, 103, 108, 122; structure of, 100–102, 111, 121–22; style of, 102–4, 122; trivialization in, 111–14, 118. *See also* Bertolini, Virginio; Appendix C
lost manuscripts: Melzi *Aspramonte*, 125. *See also* Albani library
Louis (king) (It. *Aluigi, Luigi*), 22, 25, 47, 66
Ludovisi, Ididio, 8
Luigi. *See* Louis

Machiavelli, Niccolò, 12
maestro: professional title, 6
Michele, Maestro, 8, 70
Mainetto, 32, 44, 53
Mandeville, Sir John, 9, 19, 76, 118
Marie de France, 8–9
marionette theater, 3, 13
Marsilio, 35, 45–46, 48, 52, 94, 98, 102
Matter of Britain, 26
Matter of France, 26. *See also* Carolingian cycle
Matter of Rome, 9
Mazzarigi, 72
Medici (family), 2, 62, 68
Megasthenes, 102
Melli, Elio, 67
Meschino altramente detto il Guerino, Il (D'Aragona), 12–13
Meschino di Durazzo, Il. See Andrea, Works: *Guerrino*
Michelangelo Cristoforo da Volterra, 11, 93

Michelant, Henri, 31, 44
Milon d'Anglant (Mellone d'Angrante), 20, 73
Minutoli, Carlo, 11, 66
Modigliani, Ettore, 21
Morandino di Riviera: son of Morando, 50
Morando (Fr. Morant de Rivier), 50, 139n.15
Morelli, Giovanni, 88
Morgante, Il, 11, 60, 67–68, 78, 91, 122
Morosi, Andrea, 67, 68, 71
Muslims: ethno-religious group, 78, 106

Namieri, 23
Namo di Baviera, 72
narrative motifs: amorous scenes, 26–27, 45, 53, 102 (*see also* Lexical Index: *atti d'amore*); baptism, 54, 81, 107; battle formation, 63, 81; body guard, 38, 81; burial methods, 29, 36–37, 76, 80; celebrations, 29, 101–2; curative bath, 38–39, 80, 145n.38; dress, 53–54; embassies, 28, 53, 102; enchantment of Orlando, 74–75; exotic races, 19–20, 52, 76–77, 102, 106, 112, 117–18; fortifications, 87; Fortune, 29, 59, 116 (*see also* Lexical Index: *lamentarsi della fortuna*); hawking, 82, 108; heraldry, 36; highwaymen, 74; idols, 74; interpreters, 104 (*see also* Lexical Index: *interpido*); laments, 27, 59; old age, 48–49; pavilion, 45–46; processions, 15, 53, 139n.22; royal birthmark (*see* Lexical Index: *neo*); sickness, 82; sparks off armor (*see* Lexical Index: *faville*); spoils of war, 37–38, 52, 80, 87, 139n.18; suicide, 23, 83, 146n.43; texts of letters, 52, 102, 139n.20; vow of chastity, 81, 145n.39; weddings, 29, 102. *See also cantare*, motifs in

Neri, Ferdinando, 12
Noches de Invierno, 12
Nyrop, Kristoffer, 45

Olivieri (Fr. *Olivier*), 1, 20, 73
oral transmission, 8, 9
Orlandino (Folengo), 12
L'Orlando (anon.), 1, 28, 39, 64, 90, 97
Orlando (Dolce), 12
Orlando: character, 1, 26–27, 34, 36, 38, 51, 65, 72, 73, 75, 82, 103
Orlando furioso (Ariosto), 6, 12, 78
Orlando innamorato (Boiardo), 6, 11
Osella, Giacomo, 8, 94, 100, 103
Otherworld, 8, 103. *See also* Earthly Paradise, sibyls
ottava rima, 1, 3, 6, 11, 13, 15, 28, 122. *See also cantare*
Ovid, 2, 9
ownership of mss., 9, 52, 68–69, 137n.9

Palmerino (Dolce), 12
Paradiso. See Divina Commedia
Paris e Vienna, 59, 60
Paris, Gaston, 44, 45, 67
Petrarchan language, 56, 58, 64, 70, 133n.4
popes, 73, 95
Povero Aveduto, Il, 11
Prester John (legendary figure), 19; *Letter of —,* 9, 12, 19
Prise de Pampelune, La, 6, 34
Ptolemy. *See Cosmographia*
Pulci, Luca, 6, 11
Pulci, Luigi, 6, 10, 11, 58, 61, 67, 70, 87, 122
Purgatorio. See Divina Commedia, La

Quadriregio, Il, 67

Rajna, Pio, 9, 12, 14, 31, 43, 45, 66–67, 69, 70, 71, 93

Rambaldo. See Libro di Rambaldo
Ramondo di Navarra ("il Pro"), 49, 53
Ranke, Leopold von, 31, 32, 33, 43, 44, 45
Razzoli, Giulio, 11
rinaldi. See cantastorie
rinaldini (literary genre), 65, 69
Rinaldino da Montalbano, 11, 66
Rinaldo (character), 21, 65, 72–73
Rinaldone: bastard of Rinaldo, 66
Rochemeure, Jean de, 12
romance genre, 1, 8, 12–13, 69
Rotta di Roncisvalle, La, 1, 39, 56
Ruggieri, Ruggero, 44

Sacchetti, Franco, 60, 62
saints, 75
Salamone di Brettagna, 35–36, 51, 52, 72
Salviati, Lionardo, 63–64, 68
Saracens: literary construction, 16, 25, 37, 54, 60, 66, 72, 73–74, 77–78, 80, 99, 102, 106–107, 112, 114, 135n.5
saut du même au même, 116
Seconda Spagna (ed. Ceruti), 11, 32, 43, 44, 52, 91, 121; attributed to Andrea, 44–45
Sercambi, Giovanni, 87, 88
Sette salmi penitenziali, 24, 34
Sibilla (Sartorio), 13
sibyls, 12, 105
similes: anvil, 91; boar, 92; bull, 92; chicken, 55; classical, 23, 92; Dantesque, 92; dragon, 91; elephant, 91; lion, 91; tower, 92; wolf (*lupo*), 91; vegetable, 91
Spagna, La (verse, ed. Catalano), 10–11, 34, 37, 39, 46, 55, 62, 72, 87, 91
Spagna (prose), (Med. Pal. CI, 3), 34–35, 81
Spagna magliabechiana (BNCF II.I.47), 11

Spain: epic cycle of wars in, 31–32, 34, 43, 45–46, 47, 50–51, 72, 75
Spanish literature, 12–13
Statius, 9, 24, 35, 37
Storia del conte Ugo d'Avernia, La (verse), 11
Storia della guerra di Troia, 64
Storia di Elia d'Orlino, La, 8. *See also* Andrea, Works: *Storia di Aiolfo*
Storie di Rinaldo da Montalbano, Le: 3, 4, 7, 8, 11, 33, 63, 65–92; characters in, 72–73; genealogy in, 72–73; geography in, 78–80; lexicon of, 63–64, 74, 75, 78, 79, 81–82, 84–92; manuscripts exemplars, 63–64, 66, 67–69; narrative motifs in, 73–76, 80–83
—relation to Andrea's works: to *Aiolfo*, 73, 77, 79, 81, 83; to *Ansuigi*, 72, 80, 81, 82; to *Aspramonte*, 71–72, 73, 74, 75, 78, 82–83; to *Guerrino*, 69, 75, 76, 77, 78–80, 82, 83; to *Nerbonesi*, 70, 74, 78, 82–83; to *Prima Spagna*, 72, 80; to *Reali*, 67, 69, 70, 73, 78, 82, 83; to *Ugone*, 69, 70, 77, 81, 82
Storie fiorentine (Malispini), 41
"Stradino" (Giovanni Mazzuoli), 68–69, 93
Strozzi, Tito Vespasiano, 12
Suchier, Hermann, 9

Tassi, Francesco, 7
Tavola Ritonda, La, 6, 9, 39, 69, 83; lexicon of, 57–58, 60, 90
Terigi, Teris: bastard of Ansuigi, 50
terza rima, 8
Teseida, 9, 24, 27, 35, 37, 61, 62
Thebaid, 9, 37
Tito Vespasiano ovver Gerusalemme desolata (G. B. Lalli), 13

Tomalin, Margaret, 67
travel accounts: medieval, 19, 79, 88, 118. *See also* Mandeville, Sir John
Tristano riccardiano, Il, 38–39, 54, 58, 60
trivialization process. *See Libro di Rambaldo*
Troiano, 34, 71, 72
Tumiati, Domenico, 13
Turpin, 14, 15

Uberto, duke of San Marino, 70
Ugolino, 50
Ugone: character in *Ansuigi*, 50–51
Ulivieri. *See* Olivieri
Urmano di Parigi, 14, 70

Vandelli, Giuseppe, 28
Varchi, Benedetto, 61
Vendetta di Gesù Cristo, 54
Vergil, 83
Vespasiano da Bisticci, 40
Vicente, Gil, 12
Vincenzio isterliano, Giovanni (poet), 8, 70
Villani, Giovanni: lexicon of, 15, 60, 88, 90
Villani, Matteo: lexicon of, 15, 40, 41, 58, 61, 62, 87, 88, 91
Vitale, Maurizio, 21, 59
Vocabolario degli Accademici della Crusca, 63, 78

watermarks, 13, 33, 68, 121, 144–45nn.16–19
Werner, Adolfo, 94
William of Orange (It. Guglielmo d'Oringa): character, 2, 22, 23, 25, 38, 39, 48; cycle, 6

Gloria Allaire is visiting assistant professor of Italian at Ohio University, Athens. She is editor of the forthcoming *Il Tristano panciatichiano: Text and Translation.*